PUBLIC OPINION AND THE STEEL STRIKE

A Da Capo Press Reprint Series

CIVIL LIBERTIES IN AMERICAN HISTORY

GENERAL EDITOR: LEONARD W. LEVY

Brandeis University

INTERCHURCH WORLD MOVEMENT

PUBLIC OPINION AND THE STEEL STRIKE

SUPPLEMENTARY REPORTS OF THE INVESTIGATORS
TO
THE COMMISSION OF INQUIRY,
THE INTERCHURCH WORLD MOVEMENT

DA CAPO PRESS • NEW YORK • 1970

A Da Capo Press Reprint Edition

This Da Capo Press edition of *Public Opinion and the Steel Strike* is an unabridged republication of the first edition published in New York in 1921. It is reprinted from a copy of the original edition owned by the Oberlin College Library.

Library of Congress Catalog Card Number 77-119052

SBN 306-71938-X

Published by Da Capo Press
A Division of Plenum Publishing Corporation
227 West 17th Street, New York, N. Y. 10011

Manufactured in the United States of America

PUBLIC OPINION AND THE STEEL STRIKE

SUPPLEMENTARY REPORTS OF THE INVESTIGATORS

TO

THE COMMISSION OF INQUIRY,
THE INTERCHURCH WORLD MOVEMENT

BISHOP FRANCIS J. McCONNELL
Chairman

DANIEL A. POLING
Vice-Chairman

GEORGE W. COLEMAN   NICHOLAS VAN DER PYL
ALVA W. TAYLOR   JOHN McDOWELL
MRS. FRED BENNETT

Advisory { BISHOP WILLIAM MELVIN BELL
{ BISHOP CHARLES D. WILLIAMS

HEBER BLANKENHORN
Secretary to the Commission

With the technical assistance of
THE BUREAU OF INDUSTRIAL RESEARCH, NEW YORK

NEW YORK
HARCOURT, BRACE AND COMPANY
1921

PRINTED IN THE U S. A. BY
THE QUINN & BODEN COMPANY
RAHWAY, N. J.

FOREWORD

THE Report on the Steel Strike of 1919, made by the Commission of Inquiry, Interchurch World Movement, announced that a second volume would contain supplementary reports. The first volume was the work of the Commission, made after extensive field investigation by the members of the Commission, assisted by the staff of technical investigators.

The Commission's members were chosen from representative denominations as follows: Mrs. Fred Smith Bennett (Presbyterian); George W. Coleman (Baptist); Alva W. Taylor (Disciples); John McDowell (Presbyterian); Nicholas Van der Pyl (Congregationalist); Francis J. McConnell (Methodist); Daniel A. Poling (United Evangelical); Advisory:[1] Bishop William Melvin Bell (United Brethren); Bishop Charles D. Williams (Protestant Episcopal).

The inquiry was undertaken by the authority of the Executive Committee of the Interchurch World Movement at the request of the Movement's Industrial Relations Department, Dr. Fred B. Fisher,[2] director, and it was ordered that the report when completed be submitted to the Executive Committee of the Movement.

The field investigation lasted from the second week in October, 1919 (the strike having begun September 22) to the first of February, 1920 (the strike having ended January 8, 1920) and included an informal approach looking to mediation, November 28 to December 5. In January, February and March the Commission from its own records and the

---

[1] The advisory members did not take part in the field investigation but signed the report after full examination of it and the evidence on which it was based.

[2] Now Bishop Fisher (Methodist) of India.

iii

investigators' reports, formulated the Report on the Steel Strike, which was unanimously adopted by the Commission at a two-day session, March 29-30, 1920, and the Executive Committee of the Interchurch Movement so notified.

The Executive Committee received the report on May 10, 1920, and considered it in conference with the members of the Commission. The complete document was referred to the following sub-committee of the Executive Committee:[1] Dr. Hubert C. Herring (Congregationalist), Bishop James Cannon, Jr. (Methodist South), Mr. Warren S. Stone (Congregationalist). Their report, made June 25, was unanimous for adoption.

At its session of June 28, the Steel Report was adopted unanimously by the Executive Committee, all members having been informed of the calendar for the day. A copy of the Report was transmitted to President Wilson on July 27 and the text given to the press on July 28, 1920.

This second volume is the work of the investigators, first submitted to the Commission during the investigation, then re-submitted for revision to the members of the Commission from December, 1920, to May, 1921, and ordered printed as accepted with the introductory notes of the secretary as editor. Primary responsibility for the present reports rests with the signing investigators; the Commission holds itself responsible for the use made of these reports in preparing the Steel Report.

The Commission was particularly fortunate in its Secretary, Heber Blankenhorn, member of the Bureau of Industrial Research, formerly Captain, U. S. A., attached to the General Staff at Washington; then at General Headquarters of the A. E. F. in France; later attached to the Peace Commission. He had charge of the field investigation and the investigators.

[1] Two additional appointees were unable to serve.

The field investigators whose reports were accepted by the Commission are:

George Soule, editor and writer on industrial research for many publications; author of War Department Report on Industrial Service Section of Ordnance Dept.; co-author with J. M. Budish of " The New Unionism."

David J. Saposs, research assistant to Prof. John R. Commons; co-author with Commons and Associates of " History of Labor in the United States; " special investigator, U. S. Commission on Industrial Relations; expert, Bureau of Statistics, New York State Department of Labor; Industrial investigator, Carnegie Corporation Americanization Study.

Marion D. Savage, formerly instructor at Wellesley College; assistant at Denison House, Boston; resident in charge at Spring St. Neighborhood House of Presbyterian Church, New York City; specialist in economics.

Robert Littell, industrial student, formerly with American Mission to Allied Maritime Transport Council (London), American Relief Commission (Paris) and Supreme Economic Council.

M. K. Wisehart, member of staff of N. Y. *Evening Sun* as special investigator and Washington correspondent; European correspondent for *Leslie's Weekly;* author of report on New York political conditions for League of Women Voters.

Bureau of Applied Economics, Washington, D. C.

Over half of the supplementary reports are in this volume but some have been condensed in text. They must not be considered merely as supporting documents to the Steel Report but are separate fuller studies of special phases within the scope of the general investigation. As in the case of the first volume the supplementary reports were made with the technical assistance of the Bureau of Industrial Research. To members of the Bureau the Commission is further indebted for seeing this volume through the press.

A central idea runs through this selection of reports; it is suggested by the title—*Public Opinion and the Strike.* In every labor controversy there is more or less talk about the

"weight of public opinion." This volume affords some of
the data to be reckoned with in deciding what public opinion
is in reference to a strike,—the opinion reflected by the
press, opinion as checked or controlled or molded by the relations of industrial companies to the organs of civil government in industrial communities, the opinion of groups of
workers, opinion as influenced by reports of spies, opinion as
to the conceptions or misconceptions of foreign-speaking communities. From this point of view it seems to us that the
material of this volume has value altogether apart from its
specific relation to the steel strike.

To all of those who have thought of the Interchurch Report as radical we would like to say that every condition in
the steel industry which the Report criticized is remediable,
—and remediable without the inauguration of anything even
resembling social revolution. There is no improvement
which we suggest which the leaders of the steel industry
cannot themselves put into effect.

The industry's leaders recognize this. Following our report and the Cabot Fund investigations the Steel Corporation
announced (March 7, 1921) that two evils, the seven-day
week and the long turn at the change of shifts, " have been
entirely eliminated " and that an announcement concerning
the twelve-hour day could be expected " in thirty days or
a little more." On April 18 the chairman of the Steel Corporation announced to the stockholders: " The officers of the
Corporation, the presidents of subsidiary companies and a
majority of others in positions of responsibility are in favor
of abolishing the twelve-hour day, and for this reason and
because of the public sentiment referred to, it is our endeavor and expectation to decrease the working hours—we
hope in the comparatively near future. We have been disappointed by our inability heretofore to accomplish our purpose in this regard."

The most important matter of all,—the policy of control of the labor force,—is quite capable of reform by motion of the management.

FRANCIS J. McCONNELL,
Chairman.

DANIEL A. POLING,
Vice-Chairman.

CONTENTS

I

REPORT ON UNDER-COVER MEN

A Study of Industrial Espionage in the Steel Strike, and After

By Robert Littell

CONTENTS

Foreword

Widespread systems of espionage are an integral part of the anti-union policy of great industrial corporations. So reads one of the conclusions reached by the Commission of Inquiry in its Report on the Steel Strike. "Spying is the least noble side of the war waged for the 'open shop' in steel."

What, precisely, are the characteristics of modern industrial espionage? Does the system in any way affect public opinion? This study, apparently the first detailed examination conducted during a strike, came to be made under the following circumstances.

Mr. Littell, while aiding the Commission in its investigation of charges of violence and radicalism among the strikers, requested evidence on these matters from an "independent" steel concern, the ———— Company [1] at Monessen, Pa., near

---

[1] Deleted names here and elsewhere in this report are in the original documents in the possession of the Commission.

Pittsburgh. The general manager and the superintendent of the concern professed to have plenty of such evidence and, pushing a button, ordered, " Bring in the labor file." The file, the repository of this concern's labor intelligence and the basis of its labor policy, freely offered into the investigator's hands, turned out to contain some 600 reports by under-cover men (spies) together with black-lists, letters to and from other strike-bound steel companies in Monessen and to the Federal government, and contracts with "labor detective agencies." The steel company heads freely discussed the file's contents with the somewhat surprised investigator, told him to take it along and copy what he desired and later introduced him to the officers of one of the detective agencies which furnished the spies.

The investigator therefore was assigned to the study of espionage, not because it was sensational but because steel companies regarded it as customary.

The Monessen file was analyzed, the investigation was extended to other towns in the Pittsburgh region and then to the Chicago-Gary district; ramifications leading to Ohio, Washington and New York were followed and data collected including original documents from the spy-strike-breaking companies, interviews with the managers of two spy firms, affidavits and court documents.

These are not "revelations"; these are the facts thinly hid in steel towns. Steel workmen in scores of towns know the spying exists but are too accustomed to it to try hard to find who the spies are.

Collating these data with others in its possession the Commission in its Report on the Steel Strike (pp. 18; 22-9; 120: 209; 211-35) published its findings:—that the existence of widespread well financed privately incorporated spy concerns constitutes an integral part of industrial corporations' policy of " not dealing with labor unions; " that their " operatives," inside the plants or inside the unions or outside both, during that strike spied, secretly denounced, engineered raids and arrests, and incited to riot. " It was a customary inevitable part of the anti-union alternative." The labor detectives " bled both sides; and the Federal Government files contained their patriotic reports." The Commission examined the relations between espionage and the suppression of civil liberties and Federal governmental action; noted how even bishops were dogged by spies. Finally the Commission recommended, because " activities of labor detectives do not seem to serve the best interests of the country," that the government investigate them and their cooperation with the Department of Justice, with a view to Federal regulation or abolition.

War, periodically overt, generally chronic, was what the Commission found in the steel industry. The Commission considered this finding particularly indicated by the widespread espionage. The finding concerned not theories about the class-struggle, but facts about the actual maintenance of the " open shop."

After the Interchurch inquiry, and using Mr. Littell's study as a starter, Sidney Howard, with the assistance of Robert Dunn, conducted in 1920 a rather startling research into the extent of the spy business. The investigation was carried on under the auspices of Dr. Richard Cabot of Boston, professor of Social Ethics at Harvard, with the fund for industrial research left by Charles Cabot who as a stockholder of the United States Steel Corporation had once brought about an investigation of the Corporation by stockholders. Mr. Howard's report [1] finds the spy-business national in scope and lucrative; that one of the managers declared there was " more money in industry than there ever was in crime," that one of the agencies was paid an annual retainer of $125,000 by a single client (until the client, a well known clothing

[1] Published, under the title " The Labor Spy," by the *New Republic*.

manufacturer, discontinued it for the more satisfactory procedure of an agreement with a labor union) ; that one of the agencies paid an income tax for 1918 of $258,000. His inquiry includes the big companies, the Sherman Service, Corporations Auxiliary, Mooney and Boland, Thiel, Berghoff and Waddell, Burns, Pinkerton, Baldwin-Felts and " R. J. Coach & Co. Engineers Commercial, Industrial and Financial." Each of these companies has offices in scores of cities, frequently under disguised names. Their network covers the country. Conditions have not changed except for the worse, the report finds, since ten years ago when the U. S. Commission on Industrial Relations recommended Federal action against " the so-called detective agencies," with observations such as the following : [1]

According to the statement of Berghoff Bros. & Waddell, who style themselves " labor adjusters," and who do a business of strike breaking and strike policing, there are countless men who follow this business at all times. They say they can put 10,000 armed men into the field inside of 72 hours. The fact that these men may have a criminal record is no deterrent to their being employed, and no check can be made on the men sent out by these companies on hurry calls.

It is impossible then to criticize the present report on under-cover men in the steel strike as " an exceptional instance " ; instead it is a typical spadeful out of the subsoil of " business enterprise." Industrial espionage is confined to America ; what espionage there is in Europe is a government monopoly ; no other civilized country tolerates large-scale, privately-owned labor-spying.

Modern systems of under-cover men are of two sorts ; espionage run directly by big corporations as an integral private part of the management, always at work ; and " labor detective " agencies, advertising their business, and called in by

[1] U. S. Industrial Relations Commission Final Report, Vol. I, p. 57.

manufacturers during "labor trouble." The first kind is not studied here in detail; this study goes into the second kind which, naturally, more steadily serves smaller companies and is called in by big corporations only to help out their own systems. But many of the operatives of the professional agencies have worked in the corporations' systems and the activities of both kinds are of one stripe. Moreover, the national conditions making possible, or "necessary," the business of all these operatives are principally due to the no-conference industrial relations' policies of the great corporations. The Steel Report sets forth the consequences of spy-systems; this study only tries to determine who and what the under-cover man is.

The concerns analyzed are a higher type than the old fashioned "pinks." The modern concerns show more brains. They realize that up-to-date war relies heavily on propaganda. Their "operatives" or "representatives" (spies) are trained propagandists and are so offered for hire. For the propaganda the new concerns take their ideas—or at least their patter—from modern employment managers, from civic federations, from the spokesmen of the "open shop." Their preachments contain texts on optimistic "getting together" and "getting on" and "thrift" and self-made "success." The modern spy works like workmen, talks like workmen, whispers depressing rumors, stirs up racial spite, and argues "failure" to strikers; even in his daily-mailed spy-reports he advises, not so much "sluggers" as "influence" by municipal authorities to close up public meeting places.

Why, when taxed with such practices, do great business men still go on hiring detectives as new "labor troubles" arise? "They must have espionage"; they believe that. They see no alternative. "Does any one doubt the wisdom, justice and necessity of a spy system on the part of the U. S.

Steel Corporation in sheer self defense?" So reads an apology for the United States Steel Corporation by a New England minister, which was circulated by the Corporation after the Interchurch inquiry, as a pamphlet, prefaced with a commendatory letter by Mr. E. H. Gary.

The questioning sweeps wider. Must our social organization, our civilization, be shot through with spies? The last pages of this study and the final records of the Interchurch's steel investigation show the spy practice reaching out into social entities as far removed from manufacture as is the church. The record shows a spy ransacking church offices in New York; other spy reports utilized to jeopardize the whole purpose of a vast cooperative Christian enterprise; spying cloaked under the wing of a public body, the National Civic Federation, and a "report" sent by the Civic Federation's Chairman to the offices of the Steel Corporation there to be weighed with others on the desk of Mr. Gary.

Can we live without spies? The question is raised by the facts; hence the importance of this study.

—H. B.

UNDER-COVER MEN IN THE STEEL STRIKE

I—*Examples of Under-Cover Reports*

THE quickest start into a study of the characteristics of modern industrial espionage is through reading a score of samples of the reports of the under-cover men. The examples here are all from the "labor file" of the ———— Co.,[1] a steel manufacturing company in Monessen, Pa. The reports are signed in code, for example "Z-16." The men represented by the codes were employees chiefly of two agencies, The Corporations Auxiliary Co. and the Railway and Industrial Protective Association. The agencies, hired under contract by the ———— Co. for the steel strike emergency, supplied "Z-16" and the rest of the under-cover men.

Some 600 under-cover reports were in the file, together with copies of contracts with the agencies, blacklists, lists of "agitators," secret denunciations, official letters to and from other steel companies in Monessen, and letters to the Department of Justice at Washington. The principal companies in the steel industry in Monessen that exchanged under-cover information were the Carnegie Steel Co., American Sheet and Tin Co., Pittsburgh Steel Co., Pittsburgh Steel Products Co., Page Steel and Wire Co., and Monessen Foundry and Machine Co. The first two are subsidiaries of the United States Steel Corporation, the rest "independents." One of the latter furnished the "labor file."

Two things should be borne in mind. First, this under-cover file—and all the documents in this study—were not obtained by under-cover methods. They were freely handed

[1] Deleted names are in the copies or photostats of the original documents, now in the files of the Commission of Inquiry.

out to an investigator who presented his written credentials, explained his aims and asked, not for spy stuff, but for proofs of "violence" or "radicalism" among the strikers. Copies of the file were made with the permission of the steel company and its name is withheld here only because at a later interview the management suggested the omission. During the strike the spying was something the management did not feel ashamed of nor really hide.

Second, the present study does not include the blacklists, etc., in the file (which are analyzed in the Steel Report, pp. 221-35). Under-cover men's reports may blacklist a worker or land him in jail but this study concerns itself chiefly with what the under-cover system is, not so much with what it results in. This is a description of how the dynamite is made, not how it wrecks.

The later data, the interviews with the managers of the Corporations Auxiliary Co. and other concerns, the inspections of their offices and copies of court records are valuable only as they interpret the under-cover reports. The ceaselessly circulated, anonymously mailed under-cover reports *are* the espionage system and hence are first presented, that the reader may judge them for himself.

Of the under-cover men, " Z-16 " and " X-199 " were hired from the Corporations Auxiliary (which will be dealt with at length later). " No. 203," a Pole, was hired from the Railway and Industrial Protective Association. " No. 103 " was also a Corporations Auxiliary man; the original of " No. 150 " or " Op (operative) 150 " was unknown but probably came from some smaller " detective agency." His letters were sent directly to the ———— Steel Company's office without being first rewritten in the detective concern's home office; this accounts partly for their more evident illiteracy.

The attention given to anonymous communications is brought out by the following, which should be compared with the "dirty scrap of paper" traced in the Steel Report (pp. 222-25). This denunciation was mailed to the ——— Co.'s president in New York, went back to Monessen for investigation and several spies reported on it. Only guesses can be made as to the denunciator, perhaps some spiteful neighbor who will later claim reward. The under-cover reports show what the spies found—nothing.

Monessen, Pa.

Mr. ———, president of ——— Co.
    Woolworth Bldg.,
        New York City, N. Y.
Dear Sir:
    There is a widow lady by name Anie Witewitch at 107 Forest Str. Monessen, Pa. living by kindless support of ——— Co., Monessen, Pa. Her Husband Hawrile Witowitch From his careleslee fault was killed un the Mills of said Company about a year ago.
    On the first place this lady is not American citizen but an instigator and Bolshevik part foreigner.
    She not takes care of her children nor home, but leaves the house uncleaned and children unwashed, uncombed, hungry, craying day after day and herself run around neighbor women carrying tales, gossips, slanders and lies from one to the other making them angry, mad at each other make them quareling and suit, she is a regular instigator. . . .
    Herself never do any kind of work but hires an other women to clean her house and wash her clothes and bragging herself that she received thousands of dollars from above mentioned Company and Societies for her husband, so—she do not have to be worry about the work—she said and less for her home or children.
    She is regular instigator and agitator she agitates people for strike and then instigates them against capitalism and against Law against Burgess proclamation and now against loyal American citizens and special police carrying in her pockets pepper and salt seeking for chance to throw it to their eyes a. s. f.
    This is not all yet nor any intrigue; if you do not believe in these, go on and investigate from neighbors or watch closely after her movements and actions and you will find the true.
W. G. Y./E. w.

Monessen, Pa.   Oct. 22, 1919.
Report of No. 203.
at 9:20 A. M. I arrived in Pittsburgh got in touch with Mr.
K————, by whom I was instructed to proceed to Monessen,
Pa. and communicate with Mr. ————, on my arrival in
Monessen I communicated with Mr. ———— by telephone and
was instructed by him to come to his residence at 6:30 P. M. Mr.
———— gave me instructions to investigate a woman by the
name of *Mrs. Witowich of 107 Forest St.* to find out whether she
is aggitating among the employes that are out on strike at the
present time, and to find out what her feelings are towards the
company, he also instructed me to be on the alert for men who
are holding others back from going to work. Dureing the day
and evening I talked to 8 Slavish men, and they frankly stated
that they are ready to go back to work at once, and that they are
holding back for no other reason than that they would be called
scabs and have a bad name among their fellow employes after the
strike would be over and they further stated that young single
men are the ones that are holding out the most.
     I discontinued at 9 P. M.
                         Respectfully
                             submitted
                                         No. 203.

                                                   Oct. 23, 1919.
Report of No. 203.
     Dureing the morning I talked to several Polish and Slavish
men around town, and several told me that last Sunday the American men employed in the Tin Plate mills held a secret meeting
out in the country of which the foreigners had no slightest idea
and they do not know what the Americans discussed at this meeting but they do know that since the secret meeting Americans
have started to return to work, so the foreigners are under the
impression that the American men received what they wanted,
and that the company thought the foreigners would follow the
Americans to work.
     Later I talked to a clerk in the store of the Ruthenian co-op-
erative association 205-11 shoemaker Ave. he stated that about 3
hundred families get their groceries at this store on credit and
almost half of these custimers owe bills ranging from $25.00 to

$80.00 and which they cannot pay, and he stated that he has heard about 100 of these customers say that this is their last week of strike, they must return to work next week.

In the afternoon I entered into conversation with Mrs. *Wytewish of 107 Forest St.* she stated that her husband was a strong union man and to his memory she is strong for the union too, any time she can persuade any of them to join the union she will do so and thru her efforts about 20 men have joined the union since the strike the union is a great organization and every man and woman that works for a living should be a member, she further stated that she has no hard feelings towards the company at whose plant her husband was killed. she is receiving $42.62 each month and her and her children must thank the company for this money, but there is one man she despises and that is a man by the name of ————. The reason she hates him is when she wanted to get some money from the company to pay off the building loan on her home this man ———— told the company not to give it to her, and she was refused the money and she told me about some one smashing the windows in ———— home, and that ———— accused her of knowing who did it but she does not know, and if she did know, she would not tell him.

Dureing the evening I talked to about 20 Slavish and Polish men and they all think that there will be nothing to this strike and that the sooner they go back to work the more money will be left in their pockets. I discontinued at 9:20 P. M.

Respectfully

submitted No. 203.

How a widespread detective organization acts as a catch-all for the " benefit " of industry and the sort of thing it catches is illustrated in the following from " No. 103," of Corporations Auxiliary, who was in Braddock apparently by accident.

New York Office, 580 Hudson Terminal
Chicago Office, 1051 Peoples Gas Bldg.
Cleveland Office, 1836 Euclid Ave.
Pittsburgh Office, Wabash Bldg.
St. Louis Office, Chemical Bldg.
Cincinnati Office, Union Trust Bldg.
Detroit Office, Book Bldg.

THE CORPORATIONS AUXILIARY COMPANY
Wabash Bldg., Pittsburgh, Pa.

J. H. Smith, Pres. & Treas.
John Weber, Secy.
D. G. Ross, Gen. Mgr.
H. C. Breton, Res. Mgr.

November 7th, 1919.

————, Gen'l Supt.,
———— Company,
Monessen, Pa.

Dear Mr. ————:

I am enclosing a copy of a report of one of our operatives working out of our Detroit office, who was on a visit to his people at Braddock and which would be of some interest to you.

I will kindly ask that if you make use of any of this information that you take the necessary precaution not to disclose the identity of the operative.

Yours very truly,
THE CORPORATIONS AUXILIARY COMPANY,
By S. Dewson,
Resident Manager.

B-W:P-11.

Braddock, Pa., October 30, 1919.

Dear ————:

While going through some of the poolrooms I asked why the Slavish people do not work instead of being out on the strike. One of the Slavs said,

" We would go back but our priest says we will win by staying and sticking together. We believe in him same as we believe in his religious duties."

Going in the next corner on the street I talked to some of the American people. I got some information that was rather surprising. I learned that this Slavish priest, Kaorynski[1] is a pro-German, very radical and talks Bolshevism to his parish saying always, " You put up the works they belong to you. Don't let anything stop you from getting what belongs to you. If you stay

---

[1] *Note.*—The reference of course is to the Slovak priest, Father Kazinci, who testified before the Senate Committee and whose stand on the strike issues brought him into national prominence.

out you win and I know you will. I am sure, positive, if you don't win this strike I'll blow my head off, but you have to stick."

Rev. Kaorynski said, "The man who goes to fight Germany ought to be hanged." (This was in time of war.)

Further inquiry reveals that Rev. Kaorynski has had some kind of a "fall out" with Chas. Denkey, Supt. of Braddock works of the Carnegie Steel Co., over some kind of land where he couldn't build a school or house sometime ago, owing to U. S. Steel Corp. not giving him the land or something of that sort.

Other inquiries: Rev. Kaorynski is a pro-German, radical and agitator, preaching Bolshevism and to take the mills over and let the workmen run it, instead of being slaves of capitalism. Kaorynski also controls the parish at Donora, Rankin, Homestead and Braddock.

Have also information about Burgess Callahan of Braddock Borough. Callahan goes to a club at 848 Talbot Ave. and drinks whiskey (which sells freely in this club) with the foreigners and tells them to "stick" instead of doing his duty like the Duquesne and McKeesport Burgesses. They charge $15.00 initiation fees at this club. Policeman Andy Kotnik has been and is also drinking at this club in his uniform many times. Michael Mechalik, also a policeman, drinks in this club as well as burgess Callahan, whiskey being sold across the bar in this club.

The foreigners seeing the Braddock authorities are with them against "scabbing" say, "The leaders (union) must be right if the Burgess and policemen don't say anything, but stick with us."

Mikolay Madry, who works at the W. E. Mfg. Co. is also an Anarchist and Bolshevist, and M. Pelo. . . .

I left these fellows and went to 10th St. and Cherry Way (on my way home) I saw all the windows in one house broken. I asked a lady next door,

"What's the idea?"

"Nothing," she replied, "just simply the boys next door are not striking in order to support their widowed mother. My God, its a perfect shame and outrage."

I bid my family goodbye and left for Detroit on the twelve o'clock noon train.

Respectfully,

No. 103.

B-W :P-11
11-7-19.

Spies in the union organization were evidenced by the presence in the file of minutes of union meetings. The spy was either in an official position or had access to official documents.

THE CORPORATIONS AUXILIARY COMPANY.
Wabash Building, Pittsburgh, Pa.

Oct. 6th, 1919.

J. H. Smith, Pres. & Treas.
John Weber, Secy.
D. G. Ross, Gen. Mgr.
S. S. Dewson, Res. Mgr.

Regular Monthly Meeting of
District No. 6 I. A. of M.
and
Executive Board Meeting
in
Pittsburgh, Pa.
Sunday, October 5, 1919.

Meeting called to order at 2:50 P. M. with President Fullerton in the chair and sixteen delegates present.

It was reported that Secretary J. B. Gent would be absent at some organization meetings at Braddock, so the chair appointed A. M. R. Lawrence to act as Secretary, pro tem.

The reading of the minutes of the previous meeting were dispensed with as the Secretary's books were not present, and there will not be any minutes of that meeting.

Business Agent Kelly reported that he had spent a great deal of the past month in attendance at meetings of different lodges in the district, and at conferences of the National Organizing Committee. He also visited various plants of the steel industry and refuted statements of the employer's that any gains had been made by them in the strike. He called particular attention to the Jones & Laughlin Steel Co. plant on Second Ave. He stated that where that plant used to make shipments of 120 to 130 cars of material per day, they had only averaged about 30 cars per day since the strike began. He claimed, from his observation, that if the men will hold out for another week, the strike will be won. He reported that there were quite a number of organizers of the different crafts now in the field, and that they were doing considerable proselyting among the workers. He also reported the unionizing of a considerable number of machinists in some of the plants on the South Side. Kelly stated that only a few of the plants were doing any work of value; that the most of them had a few men employed in making considerable noise in the plants, and that considerable smoke was issuing from the stacks, in order to create the impression that the industry was being carried along in an uncrippled condition; and stated that all newspaper reports that certain plants were operating with a majority of the men working was pure propaganda to hoodwink the unwary, and induce the men to return under the impression that the men had lost. He presented a bill of $275 for salary and expenses for the month of September which was ordered paid.

A bill of $176.00 for the band used in the Labor Day parade and one of $130.00 for the uniform dress worn by the machinists in that parade, were read.

Knowing that there were practically no funds, it was advocated that these bills would have to wait until some future date. Kelly reported that there had been collected enough money on the Year Book, to cover the indebtedness, and suggested that the bills might be paid out of that money, said fund to be re-imbursed from the per capita assessment to be levied on the locals to defray the Labor Day expenses.

Some discussion was had on this point, some holding that it would not be right to divert that money, another held that the band bill in particular was one of wages, and he held that it should be paid at once, if possible to do so, claiming that no one desired to wait for wages earned. It was moved by Wilkin, seconded by Ross, that these bills be paid out of the Year Book monies, and that said fund be reimbursed as soon as the assessment on the locals had been collected. Carried without further argument.

Your very truly,

THE CORPORATIONS AUXILIARY COMPANY,

By ————,

Superintendent.

U-S :P-12.

The great bulk of the Monessen "labor file," however, was made up of the daily reports such as the following literal transcriptions from reports of operatives No. 150, "Z-16," and "X-199."

———— Co., Friday
Op. 150

Monnessen, Oct. 10
Pa.

Things were very quiet on the street today and I did not see any disorly groups. I went over to the meeting held at the Itlain Hall on 8th St. Charloroi and there was about 1500 men the greater number was foreng as there was 3 womans on the Platform. Feeney arrived at 3:05 P. M. and he at once said that he had binn informed that there was a Rat in the Hall but had binn put out and if there was any more to put them out Some one Said that there was a colord man and all begane to look around for the Colored man and there was some Excitment for a few minutes and as there was a few colord men Feeney called out to the men to be carefull as they might get the wrong man. He Started to speak and he told the men the Way that the State Police were beating men and Women over the with there clubs and at Donner the State Police had arested a woman and took her and a 3 month old child to the Station and that he went down there as soon as posable with a Lawyer to see if he could get her out and the Burgess said he would let her out on $10.00 fine and Feeney said that he Paid the fine out of his own pocket he went on and told of how at Warren Ohio that the Tumbell Steel Co. had Signed the Union Scale and that Co. Employed 5,200 and he told of Some Steel plants that had closed there plants but they would open up and would Sign the Union agreements he Spoke of a meeting to be Held in the Labor Temple, Pitts. tonight and he would be there he also gave the men to understand that the Brother Hood of R. R. Trainmen were Ready to go out Just as soon as they got orders to The next speaker was a party by the name of Patterson and he told of how the first time that he atended a meeting of the Steel Workers there was not over 150 in the Hall and he was glad to see such a large number. he told of Judge Garey and what he thought of him and that Judge

Garey wanted to make himself a bigger man than the U. S. Government and that the State police was only tools of the Steel trust and they were aresting peacefull and Lawabiding men and women. but the men must stand together and the fight was won he told the men that they must look out for men that would betray them and other workers must realize their duty to the Steel strikers for the steel strike is more than a ordinary strike in the first place a strike in the basic industry of the Nation and 2nd place a strike of unskilled who have not been corrupted by Craft Union and this strike thrusts direct to capitolism there is over 300,000 men on strike and he said that in 1912 there 25000 workers out on a strike in Lawrence Mass. and made the Capitaless tremble and what might come of this strike of so many steel workers but the strikers are not frightened but are firm and they are gaining Every day he told he men not to take any notice to the Papers as it was all a Lie and what few men went back to work are not doing anything but Just making a Noise around the Mills The next speaker was a man by the name of Jonsky and he spoke in Polish and the speaker to follow was forengers the meeting was over at 4:55.

———

——— Co., Thursday
Op. 150

Monnessen, Oct. 14.
Pa.

Things were a little quiet on the St. today but the men are going from one Point to another and they are very uneasy this morning at 9:45 A. M. I was Passing 5th and Donner St. and I seen 3 young men talking and I heard one of them say burning houses. I steped at once and stood along side of them as if Reading the paper and it was a young Italian who was trying to get the other two men to go back to work. he said that he had binn at work for 8 days and had no trouble of any kind I got to talking with him after these men had gone and I asked him if there was any forengers going back to work at the Pitts. Steel Co. and he said that there was New Men going to work every day. the woman folks are getting very uneasy and going around you can here them tell there husband to go to work and some of the Grocerys are cuting out the credit System and some one will have to go to work. this afternoon I seen men going in and out the Club Room up in Whild Cat Holler this is a Austriana Club. this club can keep open as they will not be bothered by the police as they dont go down that far.

Z-16 Reports for
Wednesday, October 15th, 1919.

In accordance with instructions previously received I left Pittsburgh via P. & L. E. railroad and arrived in Monessen.

After getting located I walked towards the plant of the ———— Co., and there met three Poles who were discussing the strike situation. I listened to their conversation and ascertained that two of them were in favor of the strike, while the third man in the group was opposed to it, saying that he feared the company would close down the plant entirely for six months or so. The other two men argued the point with him and maintained that it could not be done, because the coal miners would walk out the first of November, and this would help the steel workers to win. their cause.

I managed to participate in their conversation, and stated that in my opinion there was no chance of the miners closing down the mines and declaring a nation wide strike, substantiating my arguments on the fact that the R. R. employees had also said they would do so, and when the time for action came they failed to strike in support of the steel workers, and I arrived at the conclusion that the miners would do the same as the R. R. Men.

In further conversation with these chaps I inquired how the plants were operating and they conceded that some of the men were working, and still more would return to work tomorrow.

Later in the day while visiting one of the saloons I overheard one of the patrons saying that at tomorrow's meeting the union would pay every man who was out on strike $7.00 a week strike benefits, if he was a single man, while every married man would receive $14.00 per week. I managed to get in conversation with this man to argue the point and assured him his conception was a mistaken one, if for no other reason than that the Amalgamated Association had only about $55,000 in its treasure when the strike started and they are without funds at present.

Generally speaking everything is quiet, and the general belief here is that the coal miners will help the steel strikers.

Today was pay day and as the men had money they did not seem to care whether they went back to work or not. My personal opinion is that most of the men if they knew that a greater number of men were returning to work, they would feel more inclined to do likewise, and the whole plant would be in full operation, as many of the men are nearly broke and really dont seem to know what to do.

Early tomorrow morning I shall again visit the vicinity of the plant and also try to secure room and lodging among the foreign element.

Nothing further of particular interest developed today, this being my first day in the town. I trust however, to become acquainted very rapidly with the different elements and factions here and believe I shall be able to influence a good many men. to return to work.

Z-16.

P-17: U-S
10-16-19.

Z-16 Reports for
Thursday, October 23rd, 1919.

Continuing on this matter today, conditions here seem to be entirely unchanged. The only thing I hear is that some of the bosses from the local mills are going about town urging people to return to work. The consequence is that some of the Foreign element go to their relatives and acquaintances and tell them that the Company is getting cold feet and is now running after them, begging them to come back to work.

Here is a story I heard today at the Post Office: A middle aged man came in the Post Office, met a couple of his friends and they engaged in conversation among themselves. One of them asked the other:

" When are you going back to work? "

" I am going to wait until the rest return. Of course I could go to work—the boss even told me to come and he would give me a good job and urged me not to listen to any of the others, but I refused," answered the man inquired of.

When I mention this bit of conversation I overheard, I do so simply to show more conclusively the frame of mind these people are in, and how they receive such urgings on the part of the bosses. Instead of having a salutary effect I fear very much it is creating a bad impression and will have a tendancy of confirming statements given out by the strike leaders at headquarters as to the progress being made and rather deter men from returning to work rather than influence them to do so.

On the other hand taking my tip from what I hear, I did all in my power to help the bosses convince the men they ought to go back to work and told all those whom I got in contact with that if the boss asks them to go to work they ought to go ahead and that I wished some of the bosses would ask me to come to work, expressing the opinion that it is far better to do so when the boss asks one than to go around begging for work and not be able to get a job.

One of the fellows I was in conversation with today I argued this point with to considerable extent but I fear I was not entirely successful in convincing him of the soundness of my arguments. In the course of our conversation he told me that the Company has plenty of orders on hand to deliver, meaning to convey by the idea that it is only a question of a short time until the company is forced to give in and grant all demands of the strikers in order to be able to make these deliveries, for which they have contracted.

"And what would you do suppose the plant remained closed and shut down for the next six months?" I then asked him pointedly.

"Oh, I don't care," was all he would say.

This is a fair illustration of the type of people one has to deal with here who seem either unwilling or unable to reason intelligently. The majority of these foreigners have saved up quite a little bit of money and feel they are independent for the present. They believe everything the strike leaders tell them and it is exceedingly difficult to convince them of the fallacy of the present move.

I learned today that tomorrow, Friday, October 24th, another meeting of the Union will be held in Charleroi, which I shall make it a point to attend again. I am looking forward to a rather interesting and exciting time because the majority of the workers are becoming very impatient as to the outcome of the present situation.

Furthermore, I feel convinced that next Monday morning a greater number of men will return to work, although of course quite a few will be influenced to remain out waiting to see what November 1st will bring forth on which day the coal miners are to strike and this feature is being held out to them by the leaders in order to stick together.

Z-16.

U-S:P-25
10-24-19.

Z-16 Reports for
Wednesday, October 29th, 1919.

Continuing on this matter today, speaking in general, there is good order being maintained around the plant of the ——— Company, with the sole exception of the morning hours when some of the former employees who used to work here may be seen around the street corners. They will congregate in the vicinity of the plant if for no other reason than to see who and how many men are reporting for work.

This morning one of the men who congregated there make a remark that he would like to see the strike come to an end so he could return to work.

"I would like to go to work myself, and if a bunch of you fellows made up your minds to go in I think we all could go ahead and not waste any more time," I replied and suggested.

However, this chap seemed to be afraid and said:

"I won't take a chance."

"Chance, I am completely broke and I can't go out and steal to make a living," I told him.

"That's right, but don't you think your life is worth more to you than anything else," he answered and inquired in return.

I then told him what the organizers said at the last meeting I attended, to the effect that no single man who came to headquarters should apply for help and assistance from the Union and added significantly,—

"Therefore, if I am not as good as anybody else, what is the use of being on strike."

"Well, you see it is this way, the married people are more in need than we are," remarked one of the married men in the group.

"No, I don't think so because as a rule a married couple have more money saved than either you or I because they can live more economical keeping house, etc., besides they can keep boarders, or have a son or daughter, or perhaps even both, who are working and earning money, so the father of a household doesn't miss a day, but if either you or I have a little extra money we would go ahead and spend it," I explained.

They could not answer these arguments but simply remarked they would wait and see what transpired.

During the remainder of the day everything remained quiet and orderly and nothing further of particular importance transpired worth while recording here.

Z-16.

U-S: P-38
10-31-19.

X-199 Reports for
Friday, October 31, 1919.

Continuing on this matter today there were quite a few men this morning hanging around on the streets near the wire works.

This morning about 1:45 A. M. there was an explosion on the hill. A clipping descriptive of same is hereto attached.

There is a possibility of there being some bombs in the strikers possession as a woman told me that she had received information that there were quite a few bombs in the strikers possession.

The miners will possibly hold their meetings with the steel strikers. The next meeting will be held Sunday afternoon at 3:00 P. M.

X-199.

E-H: P-27.
11-3-19.

X-199 Reports for
Friday, November 14th, 1919.

Continuing on this matter today I reported for work at the plant at 7:40 A. M., commenced working at 8:00 A. M., worked steadily until noon, had the customary thirty minutes for lunch, and discontinued for the day at 5:30 P. M.

I worked in the rod mill pushing out. We had several stops in the morning and afternoon on account of the lack of steam in the boilerhouse, and a couple of times the steel wasn't hot enough so we had to take it out, and therefore delay the operations.

The office clerks are shoveling coal, and they seem to be working very fine.

I might state the men are doubled on some of the jobs.

During the noon period I talked with the Italian from the fence department and asked him if they are running any better and he told me they have started another machine I also heard they are going to start the open hearth on Monday as they have enough men to start one furnace.

After 4:00 P. M. I went to work on the balling machine on the scrap wire, but there were no bosses around, and I only received credit for working eight hours, when I really worked nine and one half.

The men are gradually coming in every day.

X-199.

P-17: E-H.

11-17-19.

II—*Analysis of Under-Cover Reports*

The foregoing samples typify all the material in the 600 under-cover reports. Read in bulk, they lead to several conclusions. These are strengthened by an analysis of the reports in detail, from the various points of view of the instructions given the operatives, their methods of operation, their minds and opinions, and the many sides of a great strike as seen and reported by them.

Little appears in these reports to show the control the detective agency exercises over its operatives, and the workings of the relation between them. In one way or another they are hired, " trained " and planted in the field, where they remain unknown to each other and often to the manufacturing company for whose benefit the reports are made.

It is interesting to trace the first steps of the operative in a new field, and hear him explain the technique by which he insinuates himself into the confidence of the workers. This is how " X-199," a Slavish operative hired from the Corporations Auxiliary Company of Pittsburgh, described the process.

In accordance with instructions received from my Superintendent at the Pittsburgh home office of our Company this morning I left Pittsburgh over the P. & L. E. Railroad and on arrival in Monessen endeavored to get located first.

I experienced considerable difficulty in securing living quarters, but finally succeeded in obtaining a room with Mrs. MacKinzie, No. 160 First Street.

My landlady's husband and her father are both working in the tube mill and by nursing their acquaintance I shall, undoubtedly, gain much valuable information which might not ordinarily come to the casual stranger in town. It also will place me in a rather

24

advantageous position inasmuch as it would put me in touch with local conditions and situations that arise and make me acquainted among the working element.

"Z-16" has the same plan:

I shall . . . try to secure room and lodging among the foreign element. . . .

"Z-16" and "X-199," both agents of the Corporations Auxiliary, and fairly well trained, rapidly make friends and circulate among their acquaintances. But "150," an operative of unknown source who speaks only English, is continually wandering up and down, following men or eavesdropping. And "203," a Polish operative, does not have the wide range of experience that fall to "Z-16" or "X-199." He is nearly always between pool room and barroom, or talking to miscellaneous and unknown men.

During the day and evening I visited several pool rooms, stores and other places where the strikers lounge around. . . . During the morning I loafed around the Ruthenian Hall.

Found 19 Polish, Russian and Slavish men. . . . I talked to several married men of mixed nationalities. ("203")

One of the chief duties of the operative is to attend and report strikers' meetings.

I will try to get into the hall for the meeting tomorrow. I intend to try to get by with the story that I formerly belonged to the union, but that I was hard up last summer and could not keep my dues up. ("X-199")

After luncheon I prepared to go to Charleroi to attend the meeting, and on the way I met the two fellows I had talked to in the morning with whom I arranged to attend the meeting with, and we had no difficulty in gaining admission to the hall. ("Z-16")

Though occasionally operatives "uncover themselves" as a rule they are clever enough to remain undetected. But their presence among the ranks of the strikers is well known, to the strike leaders at any rate. "X-199" in reporting a meeting, notes, apparently with some glee that a Slavish speaker

addressing the audience . . . in his native tongue . . . stated that he was making use of his native tongue so that the detectives present at the meeting would not understand what he was saying.

And again

In a meeting when one of the organizers asked those men who were for remaining on strike to raise their hands, and as naturally no one could disobey and they all raised their hands.

"X-199" adds that

then Feeney said he knew that there were numerous detectives in the crowd, putting down every word he said, and so he did not expect all the men to stay out that had raised their hands.

Though the operatives, "Z-16" and "X-199" can in general be said to report meetings, listen to workmen and persuade them to go back to work, there are certain things they are so continually on the watch for that it is evident they had specific instructions in regard to them. In particular they must report the number of men *at work* at the various plants, the number seen going to work, the sentiment of those still on strike, the names of "agitators," and particularly union leaders who use any phrases or expressions which might make them indictable under various existing laws restricting the freedom of speech. Besides these finer shades of criminality, cases of ordinary violence should be reported, illegal sale of liquor, gambling, disorderly houses. There is no attempt, according to any of the operatives' reports, to get evidence against any but strikers and strike leaders. The orders to them are obviously dictated by the employers under pressure of a widespread strike: "Get something on the strikers and their organizers."

The reports contain many vague quotations of " radical " remarks:

At a meeting yesterday a Slav was talking and he was telling the people how fine the Bolsheviki were.

Without summarizing the remarks that led to his opinion of a meeting " X-199 " characterizes it as of an anti-government nature, condemning the administration, which was ruled by " capitalism, of which Gary was the head."

The accounts of meetings abound in statements that leaders made speeches of an " incendiary " and " near-red " character. But as far as jail sentences go, the operatives do not seem to have succeeded in their instructions.

" 203," hired from the Railway and Industrial Protective Association, was sent definitely on the track of certain individuals. He talked to a parcel carrier who was suspected of having broken windows in a company official's house, but reports: " I could not get him to say that he was in the vicinity of the store or Mr. W's house."

" 150 " was sent on the trail of a foreign widow who had been anonymously denounced to the Company but has to admit

I talked to her (Mrs. Witowich) for over one half hour and I could not get anything out of her and she did not say anything out of the way.

" 150," the only American among the operatives, a monolinguist, and of all the least endowed with brains, specializes in loose careless denunciation.

I was around 11th and 12th Sts. for a while this afternoon and I seen this Charlie Caronze, who speaks at the meeting in the first pool room from 12th St., and he was doing a lot of talking

to some men in there. He was talking in the Italian language.
This pool room is a very bad hang-out and there is gambling of all
kinds in there. ("150")

He went again next day, but "did not see any money up."
"203" and "150" are detective agents simply negative
in their work. The men from the Corporations Auxiliary
are of a slightly higher order. But in the main their reports
are simply those of detectives. Their duties are, first to find
out how the strike is going, who the leaders are and what they
are saying; second, to destroy the effect of the strike meetings and leaders by counter-propaganda. In other words they
are detectives and strike-breakers both in one. Their reports
are full of what could be given no other name than espionage.
For instance, of a woman who said that her husband was on
strike, and that if the strike failed, the workers "would
be three times bigger slaves than before," "X-199" remarks: "I endeavored to learn this lady's name, but was
unsuccessful, but she lives at 11 S—— Ave., and not very
far from the P—— Mill."

As a rule "Z-16" mixes with the strikers, ready to pounce
on loose optimistic talk of winning the strike, and to argue
with the supporters of the Union. "Z-16" states his purpose (substantiated by a letter from the Corporations Auxiliary to the company that employs him), as follows:

I trust, however, to become acquainted very rapidly with the
different elements and factions here and believe I shall be able
to influence a good many men to return to work.

Talking with men who are blaming the Union in some
way, "Z-16"—

agreed with them very thoroughly and told them that all a union
wants is for them to pay in their dues with money they had to
work so hard for to earn, and then tell them to go to some place.
A woman in the post office asked a fellow today to go with her

and cash a Liberty Bond as her money was all gone and the children in the house wanted shoes. I got next to her and told her she should not sell her Liberty Bond, but she explained she really needed money and was obliged to do so. She explained that none of her boarders were working, yet she still keeps them, but I advised her to tell those fellows to go to work or else throw them out, but she wouldn't do that to any one, saying—"I had those boys before and I will keep them now."

I took occasion to take all four of these men to a cafe, bought them a drink and we left in time to see the men leaving the plant after stopping work for the day. When my companions saw the men file past coming from work they became very envious and jealous and one of the group was prompt to say:

"I don't care what happens, I am going to work tomorrow."

"If you do I'll do so myself for I am in pretty poor shape financially and have a family of my own to support," I stated.

Yesterday while I was talking to a few of the men I told them regarding my observations, and then I said:

"If you don't believe it go down the street and be convinced."

I, myself, was out early this morning and saw a couple of the fellows I was talking with yesterday. When they saw so many men going to work they didn't have very much to say except this,—

"Those fellows are nothing but regular bums."

"I think you are wrong—a fellow who works and is willing to work cannot be called a Hobo, only those men who are loafing like we are doing can properly be termed bums," I replied.

One of the fellows I was then talking with smiled and remarked:

"I have been loafing for the past six weeks, yet I am no bum, I got money."

"Yes, but your money won't last very long," was my answer, adding—

"As soon as you spend your last dollar you also will be a bum, while you wouldn't have to do that if you were able to work and save your money."

"You would make a good preacher," was the remark of the fellows.

"Oh, no, I am not a preacher—one has got to work and I for one want to work to be independent," I replied.

" X-199 " also follows the same tactics, as when he told a woman whose husband was afraid to go back to work: " Why, the strike is entirely lost."

Again while speaking to a striker who thought the railroad men would also go on strike, and that this would end the steel strike very soon, " X-199 " argues:

> I tried to convince him that the railroad men could not go out on strike as the Government controlled it, and further impressed on him that if the coal miners went back, which they are thinking about, the steel strike would be lost.
>
> " The steel workers were only depending on the coal miners, but if they go back to work, and won't sympathize with the steel men, then the steel workers will not even have a chance," I told him.

" Z-16 " seems to have full confidence in his ability to make a considerable impression among the wavering ranks of the strikers:

> The meeting tomorrow afternoon at Charleroi undoubtedly will have considerable effect on the attitude of the men and I shall carefully watch and take opportunity to seize upon every opening that may be given me to continue propagating along these lines and today I really feel as if we shall see a serious break in the ranks of the strikers here very shortly now.

He records his achievements:

> I remained with these two fellows (casual companions) for the better part of the day, and I understand they will go back to work tomorrow morning.

And later says he " thinks he had induced about 100 men or more to return to work."

Though " Z-16 " may exaggerate the numerical extent of his success, there is little doubt that the 500 " skilled operatives " the Corporations Auxiliary asserts having had at work on the Steel Strike in the latter part of November had some effect in inducing men to return to work. As " agitators " they competed with union organizers, and in many a situation like that at Monessen, where there were perhaps as many vacillating as determined men the result of the persuasion of these under-cover men played a part. Only guesses can be made as to what happened in other towns where the " operative " may have held office in the Union organization itself. [1]

The four operatives here recorded spent most of their time circulating among the strikers. But at length the ———— Company decided it wanted to have a man inside its plant, which was suffering severely from the strike, not more than 10% of its men being at work. Accordingly " X-199 " reported for work, and the following accounts of his activities there, as a spy or " conciliator," with the duty of reporting loafing or inefficient foremen, and even minor grievances, are worth quoting:

Continuing on this matter today I reported for work at 6:30 A. M., commenced working at 7:00 A. M., had the customary period for lunch and discontinued for the day at 5:30 P. M.

I did not have much trouble in securing a position. I waited for Mr. Watkins for about a half an hour, and he inquired where I worked before, and after an examination sent me to work with foreman Harry, in the wire fence department. I worked with a fellow by the name of John, and our foreman would come and help us occasionally.

I did not have much of an opportunity to get about the shop, as I was kept busy.

At lunch time I talked with a pipe-fitter, and I inquired how many men worked in his department, and if I could get on.

During working hours I was talking to my foreman all the time, and during one of our conversations I informed him I did not care for the Bolshevists, and he said the government would run them out of the country.

The men are coming back, slowly, this morning there were four

[1] See disclosures at Akron, O. (Chapter IV.)

men hired while I was in the office, and there are about 80 or 90 men working.

There were about 50 pickets scattered around the streets and they watched us when we came out of the plant.

I noticed one man this evening discontinue working at twenty minutes to five and get ready to go home, and I think this should be stopped, as he is wasting fifty minutes when he does this.

We are now working nine and one half hours, but we are going to commence working ten, and get paid for eleven hours.

Nothing further of importance came to my attention that would be worthy of incorporating in this report. ("X-199." Nov. 10, 1919.)

Continuing on this matter today I reported for work this morning at 7:49 A. M., started my operation at 8:00 A. M., and discontinued for the day at 4:30 P. M., taking lunch from noon until 12:30 P. M. . . .

We had about forty minutes for lunch, and coffee was tendered free of charge. Mr. Watkins personally gave me a cup.

During the luncheon period I went around the yard and engaged in conversation with some negroes, and the steam-fitter, my conversation concerned chiefly the union in an effort to find out just how their sentiments were. The steam-fitter told me he had never joined the union and that he had remained out of work for three weeks. The negroes seemed absolutely conservative and very well satisfied with conditions. . . . There are no pickets standing around the streets. As yet I have never heard any man outspoken in such a manner that would lead me to believe that they are of radical tendencies or Bolshevist sympathizers.

I am gradually becoming acquainted with the men, and more familiar with my work, and should gradually be able to exert a conservative influence over those whose tendencies seem to be of a radical feature, however this will depend generally upon my ability to get into their confidence and to associate with them after working hours. ("X-199." Nov. 15, 1919.)

Continuing on this matter today, I reported for work at the plant at 7:35 A. M., had the customary period for lunch, and discontinued for the day at 5:30 P. M. . . .

" X-199 " is of all the operatives the readiest to give credit to the other side:

> The meeting was conducted in an orderly manner. . . . The American speaker gave a very good address. . . .
> The streets, as usual, are overcrowded with strikers, and frankly speaking, they have an abundance of self-confidence, and assert that they will win, even if it takes the winter through or longer.

" 150 " is the readiest to accept hearsay: "I understand. . . . There was some men stopped this morning on their way to work. . . . I was told there was 17 foreigners. . . . I understood they all looked as if they were drinking."

" 150 " (an American) spells " was," " wuz " frequently. " 203 " is less illiterate. The reports of these two were examined in their own handwriting, while those of " X-199 " and " Z-16 " were typewritten,—and, it is evident, edited in the home office, for the fine flourishes with which " X-199 " starts his first reports slowly lapse to an average of very plain English, with an occasional tell-tale passage such as this:

> Speaker Brown gave a lecture on successful strike, resembling names of Seymore, Stedtman and Eugene V. Debs, the political prisoners: " Man that don't produce owns everthing."

The operatives know nothing of the labor movement in general, though they are laboring men themselves.

The operatives disagree both among themselves and day by day in their own reports as to the strength of the strike feeling. " 203 " is usually " informed by some Polish men that at least half their number will return to work by the first of next month." Occasionally he strikes a group of men who " all tell me they are out to win this strike if it takes a year." In general he feels it safe to say:

> During the evening I talked to several men around town, some stated that if the strike lasts six months they will stick to the end

and others stated that if this strike is not over in a week or so it will never be won, and they might as well return to work. . . . I talked to several married men of mixed nationalities. They stated that they are allowed more food per week now than three weeks ago, and they can stay on strike for a year with the food they receive.

" X-199 " finds the foreigners " sure and confident that they will win this strike." " The men in this section seem to be very determined and declare this is going to be a ' fight to death.' In talking with them one is impressed that they feel positively certain they will win out."

Additional operatives' reports contain the following:

. . . They all say that they do not think this strike will be won, and they are just waiting for some 20 or 50 men breaking away to work and they will all follow them. (" 203 ")

My personal opinion is that most of the men, if they knew that a greater number of men were returning to work, they would feel more inclined to do likewise, and the whole plant would be in full operation, as many of the men are nearly broke and really don't seem to know what to do. (" Z-16 ")

Gauging the sentiment among the men, I feel convinced the great majority of them by now are too lazy to go to work. A few of them told me that they had stuck and held out so long it wouldn't pay them now to give in at this time. (" Z-16 ")

. . . A decisive defeat at this time for the miners would almost automatically nullify the steel strike. Their usual line of reason is that the miners, by curtailing production, will eventually close down the steel plants. Scab labor at present employed by the steel interests will be thrown out of employment, and these factors, the steel strikers assert, are of prime importance to their cause. Quite a few of the men, with whom I have been mingling, speculated upon the possibilities of a TRIPLE ALLIANCE; that is, the railroaders are to ally themselves with the steel workers and the miners. (" X-199 ")

If Palmer pushes that injunction and John Lewis calls the strike off, the coal miners will not go back to work, neither will the steel

workers, and they are going to stick together and fight it out to
the last. (" Z-16 ")

It was the belief of the operatives that it was the union
meetings which most of all held the strikers in line. All the
meetings recorded in these reports were held at Charleroi,
across the Monongahela River from Monessen. Meetings
were prohibited in Monessen, and strikers by hundreds walked
over to the meetings in all weather.

The great trouble seems to be that too many meetings are being
held which enables the leaders, agitators and organizers to keep
up the good spirits of the men. (" Z-16 ")

The meeting adjourned at 5 :30 P. M. The meeting was very
enthusiastic and all men shouted and whistled and said they will
stick together until they win. . . . I talked to several men and
they were all sure that the strike will be won next week and not
one will return to work until it is won. (" 203 ")

The meeting lasted until late in the evening. It left the men
with contradicting emotions.

*It is very difficult for me to understand why the local authorities
permit these regular meetings to be held in Charleroi on every
Tuesday, Friday and Sunday afternoon of each week. When the
men attend a meeting like this and hear such imflammatory
speeches their body and soul is with the strike organization. They
are incensed and inflamed. Today following the meeting the excitement of the moment has worn off. More mature deliberation
is taking place and they are actually regaining their senses. The
day following the meeting they are only luke-warm. On the second day following the meeting all interest in the strike will be
lost. The men will be heard discussing their intention of returning to work. They will say:*
" Look at those negroes working in the plant. Why can't we
work, too. Why are we being kept out, etc."
But the trouble is, on the third day a new meeting takes place.
For lack of nothing better to do the men will attend. They are

again becoming inflamed and the whole process starts all over again.

Undoubtedly it occurs to me that our clients have considerable influence with the local authorities. No meetings are being held in Monessen territory, nor in any of the other nearby mill centers, and I cannot see why these meetings could not be suppressed in Charleroi also. It, undoubtedly, would be a boon for all steel interests in this particular section. ("Z-16")

"Undoubtedly it occurs to me that our clients have considerable influence with the local authorities." There is the nub of the free speech discussion.

Rumors of violence, stories of bombs, plot scares pervade the atmosphere of the strike. The under-cover reports' inferences do not add much to the sum of reliable information:

Among the stories told me shortly after my arrival in town are, a report that two negroes were shot yesterday morning and that another man was shot through the eye on a street car. Another report was to the effect that a bomb had been placed under the house of a man who had returned to work. ("X-199")

This morning, about 1:45 A. M., there was an explosion on the hill. A clipping description of same is hereto attached.

There is a possibility of there being some bombs in the strikers possession, as a woman told me that she had received information that there were quite a few bombs in the strikers possession.

I think it would be highly advisable to arrange to have all Croatians stopped from buying firearms, black jacks and other weapons, as I overheard a conversation in which one of them said that he would arm himself and get even with some of the negroes. I followed this man around to the post office and the pool room, but did not see him buy any firearms, and eventually he went to the depot and boarded a Pittsburgh bound train.

At first I had a good notion to follow this chap into town, but considering the matter I came to the conclusion that there are a good many loud-mouthed fellows who delight in praising themselves in front of their friends, but the loudest talkers are the most harmless. ("Z-16")

John Myers explained in Slavish, the general conditions throughout the country, urging the strikers against committing violence or inciting trouble of any nature, and to persuade all " scabs " to give up their jobs. He said the fact that the " scab " labor hindered the outcome of the strike, was one important thing they had to contend with, and he assured those present, that steps would be taken to remove this difficulty. (" X-199 ")

There were no disorders and the labor leaders told the men to keep quiet and to avoid making a disturbance. (" Z-16 ")

As far as the American organizers are concerned, they do not tell the strikers to fight or call men " scabs," but they urge them to use arguments and tell the men that the strike is already won and that the steel trust has not a " Chinaman's chance " to beat them.

On the other hand, the foreign leaders tell the men in their own tongues to get the men who are scabbing and beat " H—— out of them." (" X-199 ")

Former employes will congregate in the vicinity of the plant if for no other reason than to see who and how many men are reporting for work. (" Z-16 ")

As I happened to walk towards the plant of the Monessen Machine & Foundry Company, I learned that five of the pickets were arrested for stopping men going to work. These were core makers and molders. (" Z-16 ")

I noticed some of the men walking to work, and still others riding in the street cars, and I further noticed little groups of men standing on the corner, but everything was peaceful and quiet. (" X-199 ")

A number of the men told me that the company was giving free board to all scabs, was furnishing them with guns and treated them to whiskey three times a day. (" X-199 ")

I might advance the information. I think prohibition has a good deal to do about this strike, for every time I enter a saloon I hear some one saying:—

"To H—— about working if we cannot get a drink once in awhile. Water is no good; it only makes one sick. Let Mr. Carnegie drink water, but we won't."
I told them that the whiskey might come back when the strike is over. (" Z-16 ")

There are human touches in the bleak monotony of the reports, so human as to create, for a moment, an impression of general reliability. General unreliability, however, is overwhelmingly the characteristic of the reports as a whole. The most credulous of manufacturers reading the reports must have had doubts as to whether he was getting his money's worth. The most sincere of manufacturers, misled into substituting espionage for some sane method of industrial relations with his workmen, would ransack these reports quite in vain for any real revelation of why his workmen struck. In one report " X-199 " faithfully records a grievance so common and so loudly proclaimed by the strikers that there was no casual visitor to a small steel town who had not heard it. And yet it is the only example of a grievance, a real grievance, such as all the groups talking on street corners were boiling over with, that any of the operatives thinks worth while recording. Perhaps it was because, being a " Hunkie " himself, " X-199 " felt it more keenly than any of the questions of hours or wages which did not concern him:

The principal topic of conversation and of complaint among the men is, that now they are being called Foreigners, Hunkies, Wops, Pollocks, etc., but that during the war they had all been considered 100 per cent. Americans, when they worked long hours, subscribed to Liberty Bonds, Red Cross, Y. M. C. A., Salvation Army Relief, Jewish Relief and all such war contributions, when they responded to every call and every demand that was made on them, and even went overseas to fight for freedom and democracy. They resent now being called Foreigners and to be deprived of the privilege of free speech, the right of assembly, etc. (" X-199 ")

III—*The Corporations Auxiliary Co.*

In the interview during which these documents were lent to the investigator they were frankly discussed as under-cover reports on what was going on among the workers. Almost as little real concealment of purpose characterized the statements obtained in the next step in the investigation.

To find out how wide were the ramifications of this system, what sorts of companies employed this method of espionage, and what ideas or skill guided the Corporations Auxiliary, the general superintendent of the ———— Company of Monessen was asked for a letter to their office. He readily agreed, and dictated a letter to " Mr. S. S. Dewson, Resident Manager, the Corporations Auxiliary Co."

The offices of the Corporations Auxiliary are in the Wabash Building, Pittsburgh. The floor directory announces that they occupy room 636. This room, on the door of which the Company's name appears in full, is used only by stenographers, who direct the visitor to room 647. This is marked " private." Another door to the same set of offices bears the name " Consolidated Manufacturing Co." Neither of these last two doors has any sign to show that these are offices of the Corporations Auxiliary Co.

Mr. S. S. Dewson (others in the office always refer to him by the code name " D.W.") is a small, dark, thin-faced man, always polite, usually very communicative, and seldom inquisitive. A series of some half dozen interviews with him brought out a great deal of information concerning the scope and policy of the Corporations Auxiliary Company, of which the following are the most relevant:

The Corporations Auxiliary has offices in New York, Chicago, Cleveland, Pittsburgh, St. Louis, Cincinnati, Detroit and Buffalo. It employs about 2000 men, scattered throughout various industries. About 500 were employed in connection with the steel industry, and that end of the business was, on December 21, three months after the beginning of the strike, still growing and expected to expand even more. As yet the United States Steel Corporation had had no dealings, but " were expected to shortly," despite the fact that " they had their own system." Coal operators began to make a few contracts toward the end of December, but up to then had done no business with them.

The 500 operatives or under-cover men in the steel mills were divided into squads. They did not report directly to the local steel managers for whom they operated, but to the home office, to a sort of " squad leader," who had about 15 men under him. He gave advice, handed in their reports, if necessary went to see them in the towns where they were at work. As a rule the under-cover men seldom go to the home office, and do not know who else may be working with them side by side in the same town.

The operatives, since their work was largely among foreigners, were to a great extent foreigners themselves. They were better educated and more intelligent, so Mr. Dewson said, than the average foreigner. But a regular period of training was required of them, training founded on " economic truth," for as Mr. Dewson said, " You've got to have knowledge of economics in industry—that's why the steel men come to us and take our advice; they only know steel, we know the labor end of it because we have been studying that 25 years."

As an example of the principles of " economic truth " taught to the operatives Mr. Dewson produced a pamphlet called " Constructive Propaganda." Examination of the contents develops the " economic truth " on which the Corporations Auxiliary Co. founds its claim to be able to provide the employers with information and advice. These " operatives " are taught to be propagandists since propaganda is " one of the greatest forces " to " preserve peace and harmony in industry, to prevent and avoid troubles, strikes, disputes and help everybody get a square deal."

One way is to help you by suggestions, ideas, lines of argument, and so on, to spread the gospel of good cheer, harmony, contentment, confidence and satisfaction among the men with whom you work. In other words, assist you to become propagandists of progress and well-being for the sake of the company, the men and yourself. . . .

They read lessons in the " Philosophy of Success," in " Foresight," in " Character Building." They are told to have " confidence " and are expected to encourage a similar state of mind in the men among whom they work, for—

. . . What reason have workmen to mistrust and suspect the company?
Why is it that things which are done for the workmen's benefit are looked on with suspicion by the men?
The company needs your work and realizes that it must have your confidence if you are to be a good workman and it does its best to treat its men right and do what it can for them.
Why not have confidence in this and give the concern a chance to make good the same as the concern is giving you a chance. . . .

They are taught " Why high wages are not what they seem " and provided with arguments to use against workmen who want more pay:

. . . Just now neither labor nor capital is getting ahead. Markets are not so good as they were a short time ago and production costs are up. The trouble is that the manufacturer and his employe have not discovered that they are in precisely the same boat.

Both have failed to realize that an increase in wages without better and cheaper methods of producing goods always brings higher prices—and that higher prices will always eat up higher wages. Whether you work with your head or your hands your future depends on how much you can produce, and distribute, and save.

If you are perfectly sure that you can produce more, and distribute more, and save more by quarreling with your employer, by all means do so. But who believes that quarreling pays?

If you can produce more and distribute more and save more by taking a genuine interest in your job, by cooperating to the best of your ability, then cooperation is the key to prosperity. You can never hope to better yourself by cutting down production or by restricting output. . . .

And here men who work " under-cover," who get the names of men active in the Union, who do what could be given no other name than that of espionage, read that " side by shoulder, capital and labor learned that each had much of good before unnoticed. They found honesty with each other brought trust between them. . . ."

A pamphlet "To Foreigners who are ' going back ' " in which threats are sugar-coated with advice apparently solely for the foreigner's own good, has this to say:

Don't go, friend, if you want to come back here. . . . If you go you will face two bad things: First: THIS COUNTRY PROPOSES NOT TO LET YOU COME BACK. . . . Congress is working on this new immigration law now . . . it will keep out foreigners. . . . Second: . . . Do you think your country will let you out once you are within her borders? Don't fool yourself. . . .

. . . Better stick, friend . . . to the sure thing here.

Europe is still plunged in an abyss of dark uncertainty; over here, all is certain.

Europe is a smoldering ruin. Over here all is fair.

Most of the men who want to go over are Slavs, Hungarians and Italians. If you are one of them, take this tip: DON'T GO IF YOU WANT TO COME BACK!

All this, it must be remembered, is under the title of "Constructive Propaganda." As Mr. Dewson said: "You know how it is, the radical is the one who talks all the time, while the conservative keeps quiet, so of course, it is the radical that gets listened to. . . . Our men talk to the men and calm them down."

Mr. Dewson's own economic beliefs threw light on the general purpose of his company:

"I won't say there aren't in the steel industry a good many things that shouldn't be improved, but as to wages, they are better than in any other industry—with this exception, that the highly skilled men are getting too much money in proportion to what the common laborer receives.

"In my opinion the steel manufacturers are fighting the public's fight. They could easily have given in and raised their prices, but they fought for the public. Judge Gary is absolutely right. . . . The strike will cost the companies an awful lot of money, but they will see it through to the end for the principle of the thing.

"The steel strike has done a lot of good after all. It has made employers realize that there are many conditions in industry that must be improved."

His summary of the general purpose and policy of the Corporations Auxiliary Company is along much the same lines. "This is not a detective agency; we are not against the workers, nor are we spying against them. We are not like the Sherman Service Co., Pinkerton, etc. Other firms rake together a bunch of wharf rats. We of course don't supply information the way they do, and we supply advice as well as information." The function of the operatives, as expressed by him is to harmonize relations between worker and employer. In relation to the worker they are a "calming influence"; they spread propaganda "of the right sort," founded on economic truth, they help him see his work in its proper relation to the company and the community.

Mr. Dewson explained the duty of the operative to enter whatever union movement there may be.

" Our aim is to work into labor and control it with sensible ideas founded on economic fact. . . ." " The Unions work to improve conditions, we point out defects to the employer, to secure better wages for the men; we frequently even gain increases for the workers through our suggestions, because we know the situation. . . . What the unions accomplish by radicalism we accomplish by peaceful means. . . . Our aim is to work into labor and control it with sensible ideas founded on economic fact. We expect eventually to control the unions, which have fallen into radical hands in the last few years. We work to control labor to lead it in the right direction, away from radicalism."

The following supposedly imaginary example quoted from Mr. Dewson takes an added interest from the fact that at the time of the interviews with him he was twice called to Wheeling " to give advice and help in the situation there," and that at this very time the strike broke badly in Wheeling. Organizers of the National Committee were refused entrance to a meeting of local strikers who then voted to return to work.

" Now, for instance, this is how we work. We might do this in Wheeling for example. We might have 40 to 50 men there in different trades, working in from all angles. We could expect 10 or 15 of them to reach positions of influence in local unions. Five or more would become union officials. We might expect in that way to have men as international officers or even members of the State Federation of Labor."

He declared that " the Corporations Auxiliary had men who were officers of international unions "; that " a member of the steel strike national committee was their man." Of their influence in the heart of labor's ranks he asserted as an example, concrete, not " imaginary " this time:

" Take Akron, Ohio, for example; we control the situation there. There is no trouble in Akron. When the A. F. of L. organizer comes to Akron he reports to our man." [1]

Even veiled in the high language of " good relations " between capital and labor, these statements are a plain admission of a network of secret agents, hired by the employers, to spy on labor and filter into its organization, there to stall and neutralize its efforts.

[1] See addendum to next chapter, " Under-Cover Men Inside the Unions."—H. B.

IV—*Under-Cover Men Inside the Unions*

How do under-cover men work inside the unions, especially as union officers? Do their tactics bear out in the slightest degree the assertions of "a beneficent curbing influence" made by the managers of detective agencies?

There are a number of documents in existence revealing precisely what the spy-inside-the-union does, chiefly in the shape of confessions made by operatives after leaving the employ of the agencies. No such detailed confession of operations inside a union during the steel strike was obtained in this investigation. Instead herewith are given excerpts from a long affidavit by an operative, reciting his activities inside the machinists' union. The period was before the steel strike. The original affidavit is in the possession of the machinists' union in Chicago. It needs neither analysis nor comment to make plain the real purposes of under-cover men, why they are put inside the unions and how great is the gulf between their practice and their employers' expressions of principles.

The affidavit is cited to center attention on the practices revealed, not on the persons named. Hence in these excerpts the affiant is designated by his code number while employed, "S-32," other persons are labeled "AA," "BB," etc., and the labor detective agency for present purposes is termed the "XX-Co."

In March, 1916, "S-32" answered an advertisement in the papers for a machinist who "must be able to do a day's work for efficiency service," and found himself finally in the offices of the XX-Company in Chicago, where he was questioned at length. He admitted he was a member of a labor organization. He was told that his job would be " efficiency work," meaning to notice and report waste of material by the men, report what men were wasteful and also what " good fellows were in the shop so that they can be promoted." " S-32 " was told to try to obtain work in the Stromberg Motor Service Company, where such a man was wanted. But he would have to try to get a position in the regular way, by application. And actually he was not hired until his third attempt.

He started to work as a repair man, and every day wrote a report for the XX-Co. Though he thought his reports were very good, as he had " reported every detail so far as waste was concerned or where improvement could be made," such as " putting safety guards on open emery wheels," yet they did not satisfy the XX-Co. manager who wrote:

" ' S-32,' you don't understand your work yet. What we want to know is all about the men in the factory. If they belong to any labor organization. If they talk unionism. If they are stirring up trouble. . . . Never mind how they are throwing away screws, tools and nuts . . . we are not interested . . . that is up to the Superintendent."

To show him where he could improve his usefulness, he was given a set of Rules for Operatives, some of which he quotes from memory:

Try at all times to find out who is a member of a labor organization.
Report same at once in your daily report.
Be a good mixer.
Try to find out how the fellows feel, if they are dissatisfied or if they are satisfied with their jobs.
Try to find out if they urge the fellows to join the organization.
Be always on your guard.
In the organization (labor union) where you are a member, try to get as popular as you possibly can.

Try to hold as many and high offices as you can.

Try always to keep in close touch with other officers of your organization, in particular with the business agents.

" S-32 " obeyed the rules well, for not long after he was elected President of Machinists' Lodge No. 337, Delegate to the Chicago Federation of Labor, and a member of the organization committee.

At the same time there were changes in the XX-Co. offices and a manager known inside the office as P. O. appeared on the scene, with orders to " liven things up " and secure more business: in other words, to get more contracts for placing operatives with various manufacturers.

From the Joint Organization Committee (of the machinists) reports had come that organization had started at the Michle Printing Press Company. P. O. sent for " S-32 " and said to him: " Now you must start a firebrand in that shop; you must do everything possible to stir up the men; make hot speeches in the organization committee so we will be able to get a job in that firm." Not long after " S-32 " was told to " lay low," as a contract for service in the Michle Printing Press Company had been secured and they " could not afford to do any more organizing there."

From then, January, 1917, on, " S-32 " says, " Life was all excitement because P. O. was able to make it exciting " and instructed him to " stir up some report on the Western Electric Co. Tell us the Business Agents are ready to organize the workers there, because I want a contract there. Stir up some trouble at the Bude Motor Works . . . in the Stewart Speedometer Co., because we want a contract there."

" How is trouble stirred up ? " " S-32 " asks, and explains the process at length:

In the first place a man will appear in the organization committee (of the machinists' union) and say that conditions in such and such a plant are rotten, that such and such a plant should be organized. The Business Agents will be asked to have pluggers to be distributed in such factories. The different operators will appear before the Business Agents and before the Organization Committees and tell about the conditions in these shops and try to get the Business Agents to start something rolling; that is, to supply the workers in these shops with literature. To get dissatisfaction into these shops in order to scare the employer. Just about that time one of the managers of the detective agency will try to get an interview with the employer and tell him that we had the biggest man in the district in our employ and were able to hold things down.

He adds remarks on the way operatives' reports are prepared:

The operator is charged to visit as many possible meetings as he can. Report meetings all through the order of business. Report all what shops had been mentioned. Report his connection with the higher officers and Business Agents, and in my own experiences it often seemed peculiar to me how certain fellows tried to nestle close up to me to get news out of me, as up to that time I had been unable to get the name of any other operative, as they had been held apart from each other and do not know each other while they all get their instructions from the same place. Most of these reports are actually framed up, as it would be an impossibility for the operator to get all those notes.

. . . A well-trained operator will never go home without a good report, and so if he is not able to get one he is manufacturing one.

The affidavit gives the following as a typical example of the use to which reports are put:

How is a contract obtained? In December, 1917, I was called into the office . . . and asked if I could not travel down to Peoria, Illinois, under some pretext. I told them I could do so, as I was a member of a Committee appointed by the State Federation of Labor to investigate piece-work conditions throughout the State. The Company wanted to try and get a contract in the Holt Manufacturing Company in Peoria. I was to go down and find out conditions. Going into Peoria matters were ideal, for such a purpose as the Business Agent of Peoria is quite a talker, introduced me to the shop chairman of the Holt Company, who in turn again, after meeting me, and knowing I was a prominent member of the organization, just let loose and told me everything he knew about the organization in the Holt Company. I also attended a meeting of the Federation of Unions in Peoria, held on Sunday morning, and I was given the honorable chair. This report of mine was sent to the Holt Company just to show them what we were able to do, to get information without having our men in Peoria, and how much more we would be able to do if our men were in Peoria. I do not know if they did get a contract there.

The best light on the real purpose and method of this XX-Co. is in " S-32's " account of a strike:

About July, 1917, a strike took place in the Louis Wolf Manufacturing Company of the molders. I recall having heard P. O. say, " I must bring that thing up there (meaning the Wolf plant) to a pitch. I have got a few good fellows amongst the molders working on the inside and those fellows will stir up enough unrest, while I have Louis Wolf and his brother entirely in my hands." I told him straight forward not to give in one inch of ground, as he could win the whole shooting match without consenting towards the workers. " How are the machinists standing on that? " he wanted to know. I said as well as I know our Business Agents they certainly would pull the machinists out if the molders would go on strike. " Is there no possible chance of keeping the machinists at work? " I told him that I could not do anything in that matter. Anyway, the Wolf strike took place. P. O. had a bunch of guards, himself being armed with a blackjack, which is now in my possession as the XX-Co. turned the blackjack used on the Wolf strikers over to me to use during the election of Business Agents.

The Wolf strike had been going on for quite a few weeks and P. O. often told me how they had pulled in workers and beat them up; how they, with their hired guards, were instrumental in it and made it appear as if the strikers had done so. He went even so far as to make me take a day off and go to the Wolf plant and patrol along the Wolf plant and have the police officers arrest me and bring me into the plant and then, in good course, I was discharged after the interference of P. O., him telling the policeman that he could use that fellow to good advantage.

The method of labor detective concerns in quietly invading labor organizations is detailed by " S-32 ":

One morning P. O. told me that he had to have a Business Agent in District No. 8, in order to control the District. I asked him who was his candidate. He told me " that it was against the rules of the XX-Co. to give away the names of operators to another operator but to some extent I will have to take you in consideration. I have got an Irishman who is a District Delegate and who has worked for us faithfully for a long time and I will have him make a little speech the next District Meeting and then you will know who the man is."

Naturally I kept my eyes open the next District Meeting and I saw "BB" of Lodge 208 getting up and telling the District how the Business Agents were neglecting organization work on the South Side. I then knew my man. P. O. again called me in to give me instructions for the Business Agents' election. He said, " ' BB ' is a fine fellow but he needs a little education so you and he are just going to get together and make up the speeches which he is going to hold."

The time had come when the Convention of the Illinois State Federation of Labor started. Lodge 337 had declined to pay the expenses of a delegate. But the XX-Co. felt that it was necessary for me to go down there and that they also would send " BB " down there so I would have a chance to coach him on the Business Agents' election.

I arrived on Monday morning, that is the opening day of the Convention in Joliet, found " BB " sitting around at headquarters with his wife.

All through the sessions in the Illinois State Federation of Labor Mrs. " BB " would sit in a box and take notes and then tell me how interested she was in labor's work. I asked her what she was taking notes for and she said, " This is for my memory. I never knew what it meant to fight on the side of Labor." But of course I knew better, for P. O. had told me that he paid Mrs. " BB " for writing her husband's reports.

About the third day of the Convention "BB" approached me just as I had been told by P. O. and said to me that members of his lodge wanted him to run as Business Agent and what I thought of it. I looked at him as I said, "You have just as much chance as any one else. Why not go to it?" "Well, what I wanted to know is this, could I depend on your support?" "Why, if I can do something for you I certainly will." So for the next few days I was coaching "BB" how to win an election. I told him that he would have to slam as hard as he possibly could the present Business Agents. He would have to show off so they would believe he was a real fellow but I said to him, "You must use a little better language. I have got at my home some fine library and if you want to come over to my home you can take some of the books along and study, you are welcome to them." So the Sunday after Convention "BB" visited in my home and took a few copies of "Mental Efficiency" along. During that election time I happened to have the pleasure of getting acquainted with quite a few of the operators of the XX-Co. For instance, in the Joint Organization Committee, I noticed that a certain fellow by the name of "CC" of Lodge 229 was very active. I asked "CC" how he was at standing on the election of Business Agents and he said, "I think we had better keep what we have got." "I see 'BB' is running but nothing of that kind for me." I went back to the offices of the XX-Co. and I said to P. O. "You know there is one fine fellow in Lodge 229 and he could do a lot for 'BB' but he is entirely opposed to him." P. O. wanted to know who the fellow was and I told him it was "CC." "'CC,' he said, "I will fix him." I did not mention anything else but I noticed that a few days after that "CC" came out a hot supporter of "BB."

I heard "DD" of Lodge 338 making a similar speech. This pleased me very much because now I had really gotten to the point where I would get acquainted with the operators of the XX-Co.

Going back to P. O. I told him straight out that besides "BB," "CC" and "DD" were his men. He laughingly wanted to know how I told them and I told him they had repeated the speech I had written.

Naturally owing to my activity and the activity of the whole gang of operators in nearly every local, the business of the XX-Co. had been picking up until about in November P. O. told me that they were holding over one hundred contracts all over the country.

Business Agents' election came along and P. O. asked me if I could not stuff the ballot boxes in favor of "BB" and I told him that it was a hard thing to do. But he said, "You are chairman of the Election Board, you have access to the ballot boxes, you try your best and 'BB' will be elected." I promised him I would but of course would at no time attempt to do any stuffing. . . .

A day before the Business Agents' election I had a long conversation with P. O. and he asked me to get some police protection. I should go to First Deputy "EE" and ask for plain clothes men to be in the election hall. I did as I was ordered but "EE" said he would send no plain clothes men as enough of them had got shot. He would send uniformed men. . . .

The day of election came. "BB" having headquarters in the Briggs House, paid by the XX-Co., was defeated, and P. O. said, the day after election, it had cost him around $500.00 to elect "BB" and he could not see why "BB" was not elected.

The conclusion of "S-32's" affidavit names sixteen men on the payroll of the XX-Co. and prominent in labor organizations,—one as a local Union President, another as high as President of a State Federation of Labor.

ADDENDUM.[1]—These data on under-cover work within the unions were obtained by the investigator in the autumn of 1919. Particularly the assertion at the close of the preceding chapter by the Pittsburgh manager of the Corporations Auxiliary that they "controlled the situation" in Akron, Ohio, and that A. F. of L. organizers going to Akron "report to our man," was made in November, 1919.

In January, 1921, labor papers in many parts of the country carried accounts of the exposure of high labor officials in Akron, O. Ten officials, including men who had been president or treasurer of the city's Central Labor Union or had been candidates for city council in municipal

[1] Editor.

elections, were revealed as on the pay-roll of the Corporations Auxiliary, Cleveland office. They were expelled after months of careful investigation by members of the unions in Akron. Signed confessions from some were obtained, particularly by the machinists' union.

A " Who's Who " of these " renegades " reads:

William J. George—member bricklayers' union, member of Bricklayers Arbitration Board, Treasurer of Akron Central Labor Union 1920—Code No. A. 201. Candidate for City Council at last municipal election.

Michael Aikens, member of Moulders' Union—Recording Sec'y of this union, 1919. Delegate in Akron Central Labor Union, Code No. M. 205.

Floyd M. Burdick, member of Steamfitters' Union, elected vice-president Fed. 1920, business agent June 1920; Sec'y of Building Trades Council, 1920. Code No. K. 63.

C. L. Gaskins, member of Carpenters' Union, organizer for A. F. of L., Treasurer of Carpenters' District Council, 1918, Pres. Akron Central Labor Union 1918, Treasurer 1919, Chairman trustees Akron Central Labor Union 1920. Code No. K. 109.

R. D. Squires, member Carpenters' Union, President 1918-1919, Delegate Central Labor Union. Code No. M. 188.

Peter Christeson, member Akron Street Car Union, strike breaker in Cleveland, O. Code No. W. 90.

Herb Hazard, member of the Machinists' Union, on the Executive Board of that Union. Code No. K. 168.

Leo Riese, member of the Machinists' Union, on the Executive Board, Sec'y of I. W. W. Code No. E. 290.

Frank R. Moore, member of Machinists' Union. Code No. W. 171.

G. E. Clough, of the Machinists' Union, Delegate to Akron Central Labor Union, Secy.-Treas. of Akron Plum Plan League. Code No. W. 47.

The last four, all members of the Machinists' Union, had been under suspicion for more than a year before their final exposure. A special meeting of the local union was held on November 18, 1920, at which these men were dramatically accused. They broke down, made full admissions of guilt and signed written confessions. Leo Riese, " one of the most trusted of the spies, confessed with tears running down his face,—a good actor, but to no avail." So runs the report in the Akron *Herald* of December 31, 1920. Many offered to report on the detective organizations employing them; and handed over the contract which the Corporations Auxiliary Company required their operatives to sign, to the Machinists' Union together with other documents.

George evidently learned that he was under suspicion, for he hurriedly resigned his treasurership of the Central Labor Union—and left the city. He was trailed to Toledo, O., where his union card was taken, and he was forced to sign the following confession:

A CONFESSION BEFORE A COMMITTEE OF LOCAL NO. 3 OF OHIO

On or about seven (7) months ago I was approached by a man name Wallace, who put up a proposition to me. After thinking the thing over for a couple of days, and thinking I could get stuff to the bosses that would benefit the Association, I took on the proposition. The duties were to send in reports of things that happen in Bricklayers' Union to the contractors' Service Corporations. The mail was directed to Post Office Box 294, at Akron, Ohio; from there I do not know where the reports went. My services were disposed of on October 30, 1920, due to the stoppage of work. Mail was sent through Cleveland, Ohio, post office to Akron, Ohio. Salary connected with this was $110.00

per month, and when paid the paymaster would meet the man on the street or some appointed place. No checks were used, and the employees never visit to the office, as the company seldom used the same name any length of time. In fact, the men employed seldom if ever see men at the head of the company. Post cards sent from Toledo, Ohio, to Akron through Cleveland, directed to Thomas Young, 1922 East 18th Street. Monthly allowance of expenses were from $10.00 to $15.00 per month. After being dismissed or discharged was offered later a proposition at Toledo, Ohio, which I frankly refused. The directions of all mail are changed from time to time, also post office box. Wages are on a $3.00 a day basis; if same is earned, man gets the difference. All employes are numbered, as no names are used. While I was in the employ my number was 201-A.

(Signed) WILLIAM J. GEORGE,

Traitor.

Photographs of these spies show them looking like substantial labor men, well fed and well dressed, to fill the rôle of the trade-union leader-type, which appearance indicated the fidelity with which they followed instructions, for there are definite rules to guide under-cover men in assuming the appearance of members of any organization which they are ordered to join. A sample of such directions was given by another spy in his confession:

Spies in this organization (I. W. W.) were ordered to dress in old overalls and old shoes and not to shave. Spies in the various communist parties were allowed to dress somewhat better. Operatives specializing on the Socialist party were advised to dress like middle class folks and those working in the A. F. of L. unions to adopt the customs and dress of the craft to which they were assigned.[1]

[1] *The Forum*, (Spokane, Wash.) Feb. 23, 1921.

V—*Sherman Service*

The Corporations Auxiliary Company was by no means the only concern of its kind operating in the steel strike. The Sherman Service Company, with branches in most of the large eastern cities, also " aims to render service in bettering industrial relationships," by means of what it calls its " constructive handling of human beings in industry," yet its advisory director, R. V. Philips, was indicted in the Criminal Court of Cook County, Ill., for trying to incite to riot and for " fraudulent and malicious intent to unlawfully, willfully and with malice aforethought kill and murder divers large numbers of persons."

The indictment was found by the November, 1919, grand jury, but a year and a half afterwards Philips and his confederates had not been brought to trial. Original documents in the case remain in the possession of the State's Attorney of Illinois and of the War Department at Washington; parts of the record were made public during the strike.

Early in the strike officers of the Chicago Federation of Labor intercepted evidence against the Sherman Service of such a character that they took it and their witness, a Sherman Service operative, " No. 300," to the State's Attorney. Dissatisfied with the attitude of the State's Attorney, they later took the matter up with the United States Army, military intelligence division. Meanwhile the Federation's organ, *The New Majority,* published on October 11 the following:

"STEEL TRUST SPY CHIEFS TRY TO START RACE RIOT

Sherman Service, Inc., Instructs Sleuth to 'Stir Up Bad Feeling'
Between Italians and Serbians.

HERE IS A STORY OF A DELIBERATE ATTEMPT OF A DETECTIVE AGENCY, HIRED BY THE ILLINOIS STEEL COMPANY, A SUBSIDIARY OF THE UNITED STATES STEEL CORPORATION, TO CREATE RACE RIOTS BETWEEN ITALIANS AND SERBIANS:

"'There is enough ammunition stored in the plant of the Illinois Steel Company at South Chicago to shoot down every striker like a dog. It was done twenty years ago, it will be done this time. The minute any of them start toward the gate, they will be shot like dogs.'

"This statement was made to one of the sleuths employed by Sherman Service, Inc., 'Industrial Conciliators,' Room 1028, 208 La Salle Street, by the official who was instructing him in the performance of his duties. He was then assigned to go down to South Chicago, move about among the strikers and try to get them to go back to work.

"The next day, at his home, he received the following letter from Sherman Service, Inc., which he was to read and mail back to that concern the same day, as he was instructed to do always with the daily letter of instructions:

'A 563-D   OCTOBER 2, 1919.
Rep.——
DEAR SIR:
     WE HAVE TALKED TO YOU AND IN-
STRUCTED YOU. WE WANT YOU TO STIR UP
AS MUCH BAD FEELING AS YOU POSSIBLY
CAN BETWEEN THE SERBIANS AND ITALIANS.
SPREAD DATA AMONG THE SERBIANS THAT
THE ITALIANS ARE GOING BACK TO WORK.
CALL UP EVERY QUESTION YOU CAN IN REF-
ERENCE TO RACIAL HATRED BETWEEN THESE

TWO NATIONALITIES: MAKE THEM REALIZE
TO THE FULLEST EXTENT THAT FAR BETTER
RESULTS WOULD BE ACCOMPLISHED IF THEY
WILL GO BACK TO WORK. URGE THEM TO GO
BACK TO WORK OR THE ITALIANS WILL GET
THEIR JOBS.
DAILY MAXIM—SENT TO EVERY REPRESEN-
TATIVE TODAY:
CONSERVE YOUR FORCES ON A SET POINT—
BEGIN BEFORE THE OTHER FELLOW STARTS.
REMAIL.'

" So, having told the ' representatives' that there was enough
ammunition 'to shoot the strikers down like dogs,' the Sherman
Service ordered him to stir up bad feelings between Italians and
Serbians—taking advantage of the Fiume incident—to tell the
Serbians the Italians were getting their jobs and start them, angry,
towards the gates behind which was the ammunition to shoot
them down like dogs.

" The ' representative' got his job by answering an advertisement for a machinist in the Chicago Tribune. He went to the
office of the Sherman Service, Inc. There he met Mr. W. J.
McKee, superintendent of the Chicago office; June Tudor, in
charge of the spy system the Sherman Service maintains at South
Chicago; W. K. Lunt, vice-president and assistant general manager of the Chicago office, and F. G. Booth and R. V. Phillips,
captains of the spies and ' agents provocateur.'

ANOTHER SECRET LETTER

" Then he got the Italian-Serbian letter dated October 2. He
thought it was time to spill the beans on his 'industrial conciliator' employers. Before he could do this, however, he received
from them another letter of instruction, dated last Saturday, of
which the following is a copy:

' A 563 D   October 4, 1919.
Number——
DEAR SIR:
YOU WILL, NO DOUBT, APPRECIATE BY
KEEPING CLOSELY IN TOUCH WITH THE SITU-

ATION THAT THERE IS AN UNDERGROUND
MOVEMENT IN REFERENCE TO THE MEN GO-
ING BACK TO WORK. WE, THEREFORE, WANT
YOU TO SPEND SUNDAY GETTING OUT
AMONGST THE MEN AND DOING EVERYTHING
YOU POSSIBLY CAN TO URGE UPON THEM TO
GO IN A BODY AND APPLY FOR WORK MON-
DAY MORNING.

WE WANT YOU TO SPEND THE ENTIRE SUN-
DAY OUT AMONGST THESE MEN, LINING THEM
UP, SO THEY WILL START TO WORK MONDAY
MORNING. LEAD A DELEGATION OF THEM
WITH YOU. POINT OUT TO THEM THAT BY GO-
ING INTO WORK THEY ARE GOING TO GET
THE BEST JOBS.

DAILY MAXIM: SENT TO EVERY REPRESEN-
TATIVE TODAY:

YOUR SUCCESS IS NOT A GEOGRAPHICAL
POSITION, A CONDITION, OR A DATE. SUCCESS
IS IN YOU.

REMAIL '"

The military intelligence went ahead with an investigation
and made such discoveries that it took up the evidence with
the War Department at Washington. As a result the State's
Attorney, on November 1, raided the headquarters of Sherman Service, Inc., 1026-28 Continental and Commercial National Bank Building, 208 La Salle Street, and their branch
offices in the city, seizing fifty officers and employees and
several truckloads of files and documents. The resultant
indictment of " advisory director " Philips specifies con-
spiracies of " riot," " insurrection " and " murder," plotted
on October 17 (a week after the *New Majority* exposure).

The character of the offenses of Sherman Service, as described by the State's Attorney (Maclay Hoyne), was published in the newspapers' accounts of the raids. The following is from the *Chicago Herald* (November 2) :

Mr. Hoyne charges that the Sherman Service, which describes itself as "Industrial Conciliators," was employed by various companies against which strikes had been called, and that its operatives committed sabotage, assaulted persons, attempted to stir up class and race prejudice, and so foment disorder that strikebreakers and troops would be thought necessary. No evidence that the employing companies connived at these methods has been obtained.

Mr. Hoyne said H. V. Phillips, advisory director for the Sherman company, "gave instructions, not only verbally, but over the telephone and in writing, to commit violence." . . .

"There is no doubt in my mind that the Sherman Service was engaged in stirring up riots," said Mr. Hoyne. "Its operatives destroyed or advocated the destruction of property, aroused antagonism between different groups of strikers, and employed sluggers—all the time professing to be engaged in conciliating troublemakers."

Mr. Hoyne said complaint had first been made to him by Ed. Nockles, secretary of the Chicago Federation of Labor, who had as a witness Charles Stern, formerly Operative No. 300 for the Sherman Service. . . .

Mr. Hoyne said Phillips "was particularly active in arranging for the use of sluggers, breaking of windows, cutting of auto tires, burning of buildings and stirring up racial hatred and prejudice."

"I believe there is ample evidence," Mr. Hoyne said, "to convict Phillips and a number of other officers and employes of the agency of a number of crimes. I shall go to the bottom of this matter and prosecute the offenders, whoever they may be. . . ."

When Nockles lodged his original complaint he charged that the Steel & Tube Co. of America and the Illinois Steel Co. had hired the Sherman Service.

Concerning the last paragraph, the Commission of Inquiry in December, 1919, put the matter before the President of the Illinois Steel Co., which is the United States Steel Corporation's largest subsidiary in the west. He denied that the Illinois Steel Co. hired Sherman Service and was "confident that at the trial no evidence involving the Illinois Steel Co. would be brought out."

At the same time C. E. Russell, business director of Sherman Service, with offices in the same building as the Illinois Steel Co., declared to investigators that Sherman operatives were hired by the Illinois Steel Co. He added that Philips was still in the employ of Sherman Service, but no longer on active duty. Like Mr. Dewson of Corporations Auxiliary, he declared that his company was not a detective agency.

Sherman Service, on the occasion of the Chicago raids, published half-page and full-page advertisements, self-proclaimed as "published at tremendous expense." They appeared for days in the newspapers not only of Chicago but of other cities, asserting the loftiest principles and frequently ending thus:

Postscript: Sherman Service is not a detective agency. It renders no detective service of any description whatsoever.

A house organ, entitled *Industry, Society and the Human Element,* which is copyrighted 1917, by "Sherman Service Detective Agency" (p. 2), describes the "Sherman Detective Agency" (p. 9) and says, "Sherman Service is real detective service" (p. 13). "It has been customary for years to seek the aid of private detective service in legal and criminal matters—either municipal or private. A new field has recently presented itself—*the human element in industry*" (p. 13). Again (p. 27): "Enter Sherman Service, a secret service that represents what real detective agencies should," etc.

But in the suit brought by John Francis Sherman, "sole owner and proprietor of Sherman Service," against a former employee in Philadelphia in April, 1920, "We have never held out to be a detective agency," said Mr. Sherman on the witness stand. He put in evidence, as against the name "Sherman Detective Agency," new incorporation papers dated January 1, 1918, of "Sherman Service," as "Industrial Conciliators."

But in another court, in a suit against another former employee, in his complaint dated March 8, 1919, Sherman describes his business as "industrial education, conciliation, harmonization, *private detective* and industrial efficiency business for pay."

The employee, Frank G. Taylor, manager of Sherman Service's St. Louis office, joined a rival organization, the "Railway Audit and Inspection Co." of Norfolk, Va. Sherman's signed complaint declares that Taylor was diverting business to the Railway Audit and Inspection Co., a corporation "engaged in the conduct of a detective business, secret service agency or bureau" and "engaged in the business of industrial education, conciliation, harmonization, private detective and industrial efficiency business for pay and in a business the same" as Sherman Service. He complains that his "special and unique methods" of business were being endangered.

The architectural masterpieces of advertisement in Chicago newspapers after the raids included the following (*Evening Post,* November 5) under the cornice:

HOW CAN SHERMAN SERVICE BE MISUNDERSTOOD?

and signed——

SHERMAN SERVICE INC.
Industrial Relationships
New York City, Boston, St. Louis, Chicago, Philadelphia, Cleveland, New Haven, Providence, Detroit, Toronto.

Extracts read:

Sherman Service has recently been attacked by the radical element of labor, who are opposed to the Americanization of industrial forces of this country and to the maximum and uninterrupted production which is so essential to the continuity of national progress.

Our successful activities along constructive lines in harmonizing the relationship between employer and employee wherever we serve, and in developing a spirit of whole-hearted co-operation, is the greatest stumbling block which the recent-day agitator is forced to overcome—consequently the attack. . . .

We are not opposed to the basic principles of unionism in any way, shape or manner. We are opposed to any idea which seeks to disrupt our nation and our industries, through pulling down the productivity and earning power of management and men.

Through earnest endeavor we are applying our knowledge and experience to eliminate, in so far as we can, unrest in industry, which has caused exorbitant labor turnover cost and tremendous waste due to the discontented mind.

Our endeavors are overcoming a continually manifested ignorance of the fundamentals of the Constitution of the United States, which should be known and understood by every man and employee in our land. We do not oppose collective bargaining by and with the parties vitally interested.

We aim to have the square deal understood by employer and employee. We are opposing anything which tends to disrupt those ideals laid down by our forefathers who established the government of, for and by the people of our great country. . . .

HOW CAN SHERMAN SERVICE BE MISUNDERSTOOD?

The advertisements reproduce letters of Sherman's clients, " including many of the country's most prominent citizens," recommending Sherman Service to the War Department for " efficient war work " in their plants. A cablegram from Sir Douglas Haig " to a representative of Sherman Service " is flourished before the public.

The house organ, *Industry, Society and the Human Element,* hitherto mentioned, is not flourished and copies are now hard to obtain. The booklet, more elaborate and substantial than the " constructive propaganda " pamphlets of Corporations Auxiliary, displays on the cover the generous sentiments and aims proclaimed in the newspaper displays.   Inside one reads:

" We are striving to accomplish these ends by first gaining the confidence of the employer to the extent of establishing the service in his plant—community as well, sometimes—and then applying our constructive forces by personal contact and suggestion to employee and employer alike.   This is done through the representatives of Sherman Service, carefully selected, trained and directed, working with employees,—*invisibly so as not to be misunderstood;* and through other representatives, also carefully selected, trained and directed, working with the *employer-visibly.*"

The house organ details the sort of thing "invisible service" actually is.   Under the heading " Sherman Strike-breaking Service " one reads:

Not long ago the employes of a manufacturing house of national prominence submitted demands for a fifty-four hour week and ten per cent wage increase.   The company offered a five per cent advance, but, after several conferences without avail, the help, numbering over twelve hundred, went out on strike.

Plant Shut Down.

As only about ten or twenty workers remained loyal, the factory was soon obliged to shut down entirely. . . .

Strikers Affiliate.

There has been no union among that particular trade, and inasmuch as there are over two hundred thousand in the trade employed throughout the United States, a certain union made a very concerted effort toward having the strikers organize and affiliate with their association.   It would mean the unionizing of every plant in that industry throughout the country.   The company on the other hand being one of about fifty others controlled by one corporation, were equally persistent in preventing the above-mentioned union from being successful in this instance, they too, realizing that it would mean the organizing of all of their employes throughout the land.

Enter Sherman Service.

Simultaneously with the shutting down of the plant we were called in and practically given *carte blanche*. Keenly appreciative of the confidence rendered, and having at all times the full co-operation of our client, we were enabled to cope with the situation in a sympathetic, scientific manner, and to give our clients the full benefit of the experience and knowledge at our command on such matters.

Method of Operation.

Six secret operatives, two of each nationality which was most prevalent among the strikers, were detailed in order to learn the inside conditions—the acts and contemplations of the strikers and their leaders—who the most violent of the agitators were—the moral and financial support of the strikers and the organization, and primarily, to gain positions of confidence and influence among the men so as to be enabled to render an effective service at the psychological time. . . .

The book tells how the mill was reopened and strike-breakers were imported.

Proper Protection.

These workers were not delivered to the plant until the second day after the mills had re-opened so that the importation did not affect those of the strikers who desired to go into work of their own accord, but as no more than one dozen went in, fifty workers were delivered on the second day. Accompanying these workers were ten able-bodied guards of commanding appearance. The workers immediately went into the factory and proceeded to work, the regular foremen of the plant acting as their instructors. The appearance of the workers, and the manner in which they were protected, amazed the strikers.

The book details how " all conferences with the labor leaders were refused " and the episode's next step:

Strike Declared Off.

After eight weeks of careful painstaking analysis, all of our operatives were instructed to make one more concerted effort, and to influence all classes and nationalities to demand a secret ballot at the next meeting of the union, and to vote to have the strike declared off. The leaders, recognizing the sentiment among the strikers, loudly declared against a secret ballot, but an operative of each nationality and class presented strong arguments, declared that a secret ballot was the only method whereby a frank expression could be secured if it was a popular vote that was desired, and their followers helped them in their plans.

Result.

The ballot was cast and there was over a four fifths vote in favor of declaring the strike off and returning to work. All hands went back in a body the following day.

After the strike the job was finished as follows:

Organization Efforts.

Upon the return of the workers the leaders argued that they were not sufficiently organized to have won out at the time, but urged the men to continue to remain loyal to the organization and secretly organize from within the plant so that later their demands might be renewed and with the solid backing of all the workers, they would be able to obtain any demands which might me made.

Dis-Unionizing of Workers.

The weekly meetings of the local union discontinued. The leaders of the strike were gradually discharged for one reason or another, and upon almost every occasion their activities were easily disclosed by their association with the leaders outside of working hours. By a further concerted effort upon the part of our operatives in surrounding themselves with as many of the former strikers upon meeting days, and going away upon recreation trips with them, the attendance at the meetings gradually diminished, and at these a sufficient number of operatives were detailed to use the proper influence to promote necessary legislation that would be favorable to our client.

Meeting Dates Extended.

As the meetings diminished, we made a further successful effort to declare them to be held monthly. Then it was comparatively easy to start dissension among the leaders, which increased to the extent that each gathering resulted in a fight. These occasions allowed our secret operatives to further illustrate the fact that the leaders were out for personal gain, more than to help them, and finally by properly applied methods the charter of the union was returned and the local abandoned.

Corporations Auxiliary employees are " operatives "; Sherman Service's are " representatives." Both call their men " the professional staff," and Sherman Service's has included college men, ex-officers of the army and a college professor or two.

Business Director Russell explained to investigators that he " presents the findings and recommendations of the professional staff to the clients. These findings and methods are not those of theories of employment management or scientific management, for Sherman Service does not believe in these theories." Sherman Service recognizes the importance of " doing things from below," and believes that improvements in production, in spirit, etc., must be made from below. " Hence they engage intelligent mechanics," Mr. Russell went on, " who have been workers all their life and who generally do not aspire to be anything else but workers. They are generally the pick. They are put through a three months' train-

ing and are required to study certain assigned lessons on
their own time.   Only about four out of a hundred pass the
test. . . . Among them all they speak thirty-seven languages.
. . . It is also often necessary for them to be ' apparent reds.'
Wherever such organizations exist in the community and try
to influence the workers, it becomes the duty of the Sherman
representatives to pretend sympathy and join, so as to learn
who the leaders are.   Such information is then supplied to
the government."   He added the assertion that Sherman
representatives were hired by the government during the war
to find " reds."

Much more frequently it is necessary for the under-cover
representatives to be " apparent union men."   In explaining
the objects, Mr. Russell merely repeated Mr. Dewson of
Corporations Auxiliary.   " Sherman Service," he said, " believes in collective bargaining by associating the workers in
a plant, but it does not believe in outsiders interfering. . . .
Sherman Service is not opposed to trade unions as they
originally were understood.   The trouble at present is that
trade unions are grasping and unfair and are really working against the interest of the workers. . . . The steel strike
has thrown thousands out of work in other industries. . . .
Strikes only hurt the worker."

Like Mr. Dewson, Mr. Russell explained the Sherman
Service " renders service to corporations outside as well as
inside the plant "; in other words, in time of strike, the
operatives mingle with the strikers, spy on them and urge
them to return to work, as were the duties and activities of
" Z-16," " X-150 " and " X-199 " in their reports.   Both
companies " work in the interest of the wage earner as well
as the employer," suggest improvements, report wastage,
watch the foremen, and see that the men are not underpaid,
or even that they secure a raise.   And as they " serve the
worker as well as the employer," neither company seeks to

" disrupt unions," but each tries, and very thoroughly man-
ages, to have their men join the union, where, working " invisibly," but for the good of all, since "most of the labor
leaders are agitators and self-seekers," they can " prevent
them from misleading the workers and making unfair demands on the firm," and " guide the union's policies and
actions so as to protect the employer and the worker."

Like the Corporations Auxiliary, Mr. Russell asserted that
Sherman Service " representatives are encouraged to get
themselves elected to office in the labor unions "; and added
that they do " hold the highest positions " in unions.

VI—*Anonymous " Report in re Interchurch "* [1]

How high up in a great corporation's hierarchy are spy reports sent? Are labor spies used outside the steel towns?

Can so extensive a system fail to contaminate social organizations far removed from industrial precincts?

For whatever light it may shed on these questions, herewith is reproduced the anonymous " special report " on the Interchurch World Movement in which a spy investigated the investigation of which the present study is a part.[2]

The setting should be kept in mind:—a publicly announced Commission of Inquiry for a great movement was openly conducting hearings, openly approaching the leaders on both sides of a great controversy with requests for data and freely utilizing the services of investigators whose qualifications were easily verifiable and whose pursuits in life were traceable in open records. All these people, from bishops to statisticians, were making hopeful progress in fact-gathering, despite the troubled conditions of a strike, doubly troubled by a sort of hysteria over " reds " and " bolsheviks," principally a hang-over from the world war. It was then popular with men high up in industry and even in the government to cry " radical " in regard to the strike, but the inquirers had so far gone their way untroubled by criticism, meeting with tolerance, indeed sometimes with welcome. Then came the following:

(Document A)

" November 12, 1919.

Special report in re Interchurch World Movement of America, of 111 Fifth Avenue, New York City.

[1] Chapter rewritten by editor to include later data.

[2] This is the document referred to in the Steel Report, pp. 28, 233-234.

After an investigation of this movement I find that there are a large number of radicals in it.

First, the man in charge of the Publicity is Mr. Robert Bruère, who is the same party that wrote a book called " On the Trail of I. W. W." This book was a sob story about the way that the I. W. W. had been treated in the West. He also was a member of the I. W. W., belonging to one of the New York locals.

A Mr. Soules who is now in Pittsburgh, having an office in the Smithfield Street M. E. Church Building, corner Smithfield Street and Seventh Avenue, is another Radical, and was a member of the National Liberties League, of New York, and also a member of the I. W. W. He is now here for this organization investigating the Steel Strike and carrying a small kodak, making pictures around the Steel Districts. These photographs are to be used in the coming investigating work which will be conducted in Pittsburgh in the near future.

Another one of the party here is a Miss Savage, and also Mary O'Brien, or Mrs. Van Vorse, both of them are radicals. Mrs. O'Brien was a former member of the I. W. W. and took a very active part in the Range strike several years ago, assisting Gurley Flynn and Joe Etter on the Range to carry on the strike there. She has been active in a large number of the I. W. W. strikes and other radical movements, acting as a special writer for newspapers and magazines she gets away with a lot of propoganda for the I. W. W.

Miss Savage has been a member of the radical organizations in the East for a number of years and has always been active, she is now assisting in the work of getting evidence for the Interchurch World Movement on the steel strike.

Another fellow, named Joe Epstein, who has been a member of the I. W. W., The People Peace Council, and the Socialist Party and who is also James Maurer's right hand in getting out articles against the Pennsylvania State Police and the Steel Trust. This fellow is nothing more than a radical Red Jew, and should not be allowed to have any information at all. He and J. Maurer were both taken off the boat on which they were to sail to Europe.

In fact none of these people that are now here in Pittsburgh investigating for this Church movement should be told anything at all, nor should they be allowed to get any information from the Mills in any manner.

After paying a visit to their offices in New York and talking to a large number of the officials there I find that this organization could be used to a very good advantage if handled by the right parties. This organization could become a power in both the Industrial Field and the Church Field.

There are a large number of the men and women connected with this organization that are known as Pink Tea Socialists and Parlor Reds, and are not considered dangerous. I would suggest that these kind of people be weeded out of the organization. These are the worst kind of Reds to be connected with as they are to a certain extent high up in circles that are hard to reach and they can spread propoganda that hurts the work of others.

I found that this Organization is now making a canvass for money among the rich and the Corporation in the East, and that they have already had a Committee see Judge Gary, asking for money to carry on their work with.

A Mr. Blacenhorn will arrive in Pittsburgh on Thursday morning to assist the ones that are already here on the Steel Strike investigation.

No money should be given or any assistance granted this organization until they recall all of the ones that they have in the Pittsburgh District, and further more if there is any way at all of forcing them to get rid of the ones that I have mentioned they should be let go.

One of the things that this organization is going to do is to show the general living conditions of the workers of the country. The people that they have here now representing the organization are looking for nothing but the worst kind of hovels and conditions to represent the homes of the Steel Workers. While with the right kind of men and women doing the investigating the real homes of the workers would be shown. Unless they will consent to that kind of propoganda there should positively be no help given them.

I find that some of the personell of the office and some of the officers of the organization are very fine men and women, and these Reds have gotten in on them and now see a fine chance to carry on their own propoganda.

Something must be done at once about this, for these people are getting ready to put out a pamphlet on the general conditions of the Steel Workers and Miners, and they are not showing anything that is a credit to the employers.

Some of the homes that have been photographed to represent the homes of the steel workers, I find after investigation, are owned by men who do not even work for Steel Company.

All of the names mentioned in this report are of persons who have been and still are active in the organization known as the Peoples Print, located at 138 W. 13th Street, New York City, and formerly known as the Peoples Peace Council, better known as the National Civil Liberties League, with Roger Baldwin at the head. Later on Louis P. Lochner, former Secretary of the Ford Peace Ship, became the head of this organization. They are also known by the name of Peoples Freedom of New York City. They held a meeting in Madison Square Garden last Sunday afternoon, a report thereof being hereto attached, as is also various leaflets sent out from 138 W. 13th St.

All of these Reds are in favor of this Church movement as long as they have control of the outside working forces. As the organization now stands the radicals are in control, and they thus prevent any good that the organization might be able to do.

These fellows will not allow the truth to be told, as they are in control. James Maurer, the President of the State Federation of Labor is one of the men that is assisting the ones at Pittsburgh to get data on the steel strike."

This production bears the earmarks of a labor spy of much the same caliber as the other spies considered in this study. There is one marked difference: apparently being pushed for time, this detective made free use of pure invention in filling up his " special report."

The point of the matter is this: the " anonymous special report " became a serious episode in the Inquiry not because any of its allegations were true, but because it was received as true by powerful men who were not unaccustomed to a system of spy reporting.

It cost the Interchurch, by diverting resources and officers' time, thousands of dollars in the mere task of meeting this document in the many important places where it bobbed up. It hampered the inquiry not because of any truth in the " charges," but because great laymen in several states and in various industries received and weighed spy reports much as they took a newspaper.

The Steel Report relates the contemptuous indifference with which a copy of the document was first read by the investigators and members of the Commission of Inquiry.[1]

Document *A* was circulated first by steel company officials in Pittsburgh and shortly in steel cities outside of Pennsylvania.

Next, on December 5, 1919, at the conference in the offices of the United States Steel Corporation, at which the Commission of Inquiry discussed informally with Mr. Gary a possible plan for ending the strike, Mr. Gary insisted first

---

[1] Steel Report, (pp. 6-11) outlined the methods of the investigation and (p. 1) gave the correct list of investigators.—H. B.

on questioning the Commissioners concerning this document. While he rang for his copy, one of the members of the Commission supplied another from his own coat pocket. No one at the conference offered any suggestion as to the origin of the report. Mr. Gary's secretary said that their copy had been received in a plain envelope without signature. About the same date the Interchurch investigator of under-cover men was sitting in the office of a steel company in Monessen and at the request of the manager of the concern was opening recently mailed plain envelopes and taking out unsigned spy-reports. The manager explained that this was an operative's usual method of reporting.

Later, in reply to a letter from the Interchurch officials asking for information concerning the origin of the report, Mr. Gary wrote that he knew nothing about it and was surprised that inquiries should be addressed to him concerning a document which he had shown to the Commission " in confidence." The report was dated November 12, two days after the Commission's first interview with Mr. Gary.

Next, the material in the report appeared as an official "Notice" on the letterhead of the Ohio Manufacturers' Association under the heading "The Anarchists and the Interchurch Movement," dated December 9, 1919. Beginning with the statement:

People who have been looking with some degree of earnest hope to the Inter-Church World Movement of America, have been dismayed to find that the radical Reds have wormed their way into the organization and are preparing to use it for propaganda purposes.

the "Notice" went on to declare that:

The Inter-Church Movement, which, properly organized and wisely directed, should be able to do such a tremendous amount of good; the results cannot be other than evil unless there is a prompt and vigorous housecleaning.

The *"Notice"* included in detail the false assertions of Document *A*. The Executive Secretary of the Ohio Manufacturers' Association, Mr. Malcolm Jennings of Columbus, Ohio, acknowledged responsibility for circulating these statements among the association's seven hundred members, though he later preferred to refer to the *" Notice "* as a " personal bulletin."

It became necessary for the Interchurch executives to seek legal counsel. Full specifications concerning the Commission and its investigators were furnished and the position of the Interchurch defined in the following letter to the Ohio Manufacturers from Dr. S. Earl Taylor, the Interchurch General Secretary:

I am perfectly certain that the group of strong, Christian leaders represented by the Interchurch World Movement, of which the Honorable Robert Lansing, Secretary of State, is the Chairman of the General Committee, and Dr. John R. Mott, is chairman of the Executive Committee, will not permit such libelous statements to go unchallenged, and in behalf of the organization I hereby demand a retraction which will receive as wide circulation at your hands as did the original document. Surely the world is in a shell-shocked condition when reputable business men will give themselves over to the circulation of defamatory statements of this kind, whose only foundation is an anonymous document, the statements of which were instantly challenged and effectively disproven the moment they came to the attention of our Committee.

During the ensuing month of stubborn controversy occurred the Atlantic City Conference of the Interchurch Movement; the Interchurch appointed a special committee to investigate Document *A* and the facts. They heard witnesses, examined documents and reported back to the conference as follows:

> We have carefully considered the evidence submitted to us by officers of the Interchurch World Movement; we have read the documents circulated by the Ohio Manufacturers' Association, as well as the statement submitted by the Interchurch World Movement in reply to the charges of the Ohio Manufacturers' Association; we have had before us certain members of the special investigating commission and the director of the field work of the commission who is in charge of the investigators. On the basis of the above evidence we are fully satisfied that the charges made by the Ohio Manufacturers' Association are false and without foundation.

Finally the following retraction resulted and was circulated:

> Some weeks ago I sent out a personal bulletin to the members of the Ohio Manufacturers' Association under the caption ' THE ANARCHISTS IN THE INTERCHURCH WORLD MOVEMENT.' I wrote the bulletin in perfect good faith and upon what I regarded to be reliable and accurate information. I did not, however, before preparing the bulletin, bring the matter first to the attention of the Interchurch World Movement, giving them opportunity to confirm or deny. I understood that that had already been done. The officers of the Interchurch World Movement challenged the statements made in the bulletin and have furnished a statement containing a specific denial of the specific assertions made. I unreservedly accept their denial and make it mine, withdrawing the assertions of which they complain and asking the members of the Ohio Manufacturers' Association not only to take note of such retraction, but that they will bring the correction to the attention of any others to whom they referred the bulletin.
> I regret making any misstatements or doing any injustice to anyone.

(Signed) MALCOLM JENNINGS

Nevertheless, Document *A* was rehashed along with other spy products, in a manufacturers' organ called *Industry*,

reprints of which were anonymously circulated all over the
country. As late as June, 1920, typed copies of the original
were circulated by the managing director of the National
Industrial Conference Board to all members of the Board
with the statement that it came into his possession from an
unknown source, but was sent out "for information." A
member of the Board (which represents the country's largest
manufacturing interests) noted at the time that, if true,
the information would cause the withdrawal of financial
support from the Interchurch "by many prominent individuals."

Nor was the "special report" the only product of this
system of doing things. Another secret report, more elaborate and less illiterate, was being circulated by big business
men in steel centers and out. At the time, spring of 1919,
decision on the fate of the Steel Strike Report was passing
from the Commission on to the Interchurch Executive Committee. The new secret document purported to find " Bolsheviks," not among the Commissioners or their investigators,
but in the Interchurch Movement to whose hands the Report
was then being transmitted. It came out that the author-
agent was working for the National Civic Federation and
his report was sent with a covering letter by Ralph M.
Easley, Chairman of the Executive Council of that organization, to the offices of the United States Steel Corporation
on March 29, 1920.

Mr. Easley denied the act and the letter in a long conference with officers of the Interchurch some weeks later.
He insisted that if any such letter existed he had not signed
it. In June, however, the New York *World* published the
results of an inquiry conducted by it into the "undue delay
or suppression" of the Steel Strike Report and Mr. Easley
at this time gave out the text of the letter, admitting its
authorship. The letter as published reads:

I am inclosing copies of interviews with four gentlemen in important positions in the Interchurch World Movement, the Federal Council of the Churches of Christ and the Y. M. C. A. You will be particularly interested in what they have to say, because at this time they are proposing to raise hundreds of millions of dollars for their work. As a churchman and a business man, I am sure you and your friends will be interested in this matter. There certainly ought to be no trouble in having the loyal American members of the Protestant churches have these men kicked out of their positions, or at any rate put in places where they cannot poison any one but themselves. Please return the inclosure.

Mr. Easley's public explanation included the assertion that his action in sending the report to the Corporation was his own, not that of his organization, although the secret agent was working for the organization. The National Civic Federation includes some of the highest labor officials and some of the largest employers in the country.

Copies of the transmitted " interviews " (known as Document *B*) had long before been shown to Interchurch officers by manufacturers who had received them from the secret circulators but who revolted at the spy-methods used. None of these documents reached the Commission by under-cover methods. Document *B* is just as full of falsehoods as Document *A* and has the same purpose, to show that " Reds " made or backed the steel strike inquiry. For example it reads:

Rev. Dr. F. M. Crouch, Episcopal minister is in charge of the *Industrial Relations Department*. He has prepared for the Ind. Rel. Dept. an extensive report on conditions among the Steel workers in Pittsburgh. . . .

Then it denounces Dr. Crouch as " rabid."

Now Dr. Crouch was the only man named in Document *B* who was an employee of the Interchurch and he was not in

charge of the Industrial Relations Department and had noth‐
ing to do with the making or accepting of the Steel Report.

Another of Document *B*'s " analyses " concerned Dr.
Harry F. Ward, noted thinker and professor of Christian
Ethics at the Union Theological Seminary, but who was not
an officer or employee of the Interchurch. He was " proved "
a Bolshevik and his face described as follows:

> Mr. Ward has a receding chin . . . and a low broad receding
> forehead, generally indicative of the laboring class.

This and similar revealing statements in the copy of Docu‐
ment *B* as forwarded by Mr. Easley to the United States
Steel Corporation offices were edited out of the same docu‐
ment as later furnished by Mr. Easley to the Interchurch
officers. At the 1921 session of the Civic Federation, it is
interesting to note, all mention of the Interchurch was
dropped from a general attack on " church radicalism " spon‐
sored by the Federation.

Again, as in Document *A,* the importance of Document *B*
lies in the fact that business men gave it weight, circulated
it and privately quoted it with other spy-documents as basis
for not making future subscriptions to the Interchurch World
Movement.

After Document *B* came Document *C,* twenty-six type‐
written pages, circulated in steel centers as " extremely con‐
fidential " and described by laymen as " the thing responsible
for the failure of the Interchurch financial drive in Pitts‐
burgh." This document details events,—which never took
place,—and reports on men,—who never had anything to do
with the Steel Report. It tries to prove that the steel strike
investigators were " utilized by W. Z. Foster, the confessed
syndicalist anarchist." It is a curious mixture of accurate
statements and of most inaccurate deductions presented as
facts. For example, it describes an address by Dr. Ward:

In other words he intimated that the teachings of Jesus Christ should be brought into the industrial fields and that the cardinal principles set forth in the Sermon on the Mount should be injected by the churches into industrial relations.

This true quotation is then put with quotations from men who have proclaimed themselves radicals and the conclusions are used to " prove " the Interchurch and the steel inquirers " Bolshevik."

Document *C* is more astute than either of the others. It dwells on what is an undoubted fact, the permeation of the church (and of most social institutions today) by Christian theories and viewpoints which are revolutionary to reactionary minds; but it cannot resist going on to demonstrate a plot of dark and dangerous minds as responsible for the steel inquiry. Document *C* was used, without attribution, as part basis for the attack on the Interchurch World Movement in the organ called *Industry* and reprints of this were mailed anonymously to newspapers and persons in every part of the nation.

Three documents emanating from an industrial spy system or habit, therefore, were circulated with the objects of damaging the Steel Report and the Interchurch Movement. Others were heard of, but only these documents and their histories were furnished to the Interchurch. In addition the files of a high official in the Interchurch offices were ransacked.

Any future investigation of the matter will have to include the details of how the wrecking opposition functioned through an industrial spy system as here set forth, for the first time where they belong,—in a study of under-cover men in the strike.

The methods used against the church were methods used in opposition to workingmen. The sweep of the industrial spy system was simply extended to cover the " intruding "

church. The same sort of documents were used—and in
one case apparently the same man—to report on clergymen
as on labor in steel towns. The documents which went to
Mr. Gary are of the same stripe as the documents which the
———— Company of Monessen paid under-cover men to make.
How much wider and higher the contamination of the under-
cover system may extend is indicated in the full Steel Strike
Report,[1] but remains still to be studied out.

The newspapers do not always keep clear of the infection,
according to editors who tell how under-cover products are
sometimes transmitted to them from responsible sources.
Were spies at the other end of the chain which resulted in
the *Hartford Daily Courant* (March 2, 1921) printing the
following on its editorial page?

> People wondered how it [the Steel Report] came to be written
> and now we read in the "Wall Street Journal" that two of the
> "investigators" employed by the Interchurch reformers have
> been deported with the Bolshevik Martens.

The *Wall Street Journal* of New York (March 1, 1921)
in a long article declaring that "the Bolshevist nature of
the inquiry and its findings was pointed out in these columns," had actually added:

> This was amply confirmed by subsequent disclosures and two
> of the investigators employed are said to have returned to Russia
> with the deported Bolshevist envoy, Martens.

Did the *Wall Street Journal* get that additional whole-cloth
invention from somebody who got it from a labor spy? A
letter to the paper's managing editor asking for the source
was received back with these words typed in the margin:
"Your bureau will get no deadhead advertising from the *Wall
Street Journal*."

[1] Steel Report, pp. 18, 221-226, 229.

An experience of the Commission on January 27, 1921, suggests that the infection is beyond the control of those responsible for it. On that date the Commissioners appeared before the Senate Committee on Labor and Education by request of the Committee at a hearing in the Capitol. The Senators suddenly put before the Commission a seventy-eight-page mimeographed document, a " confidential communication," which the officers of the National Association of Sheet and Tin Plate Manufacturers had formally filed against the Report. It purported to be a " review and criticism " of the Report, prepared by C. L. Patterson, secretary of the Association's Bureau of Labor, and sponsored by W. S. Horner, president of the Association.[1] The senate committee invited the Commission to file a brief in reply.

The " review " turned out to be in considerable part the same spy material quoted before. Following is an extract from the Commission's reply sent to the senators:

Let us examine the 32 pages attacking the Commission. Its data are made up of secret reports sent in by spies or under-cover men. The " Review " does not tell the origin of its " charges "; in all sincerity these misled manufacturers offer to the Senate the reports of spies.

For a year past steel manufacturers have circulated secretly, in typed documents or in reprints, three separate reports by spies. We have seen these things before, forced men to apologize for them, but here they are again, as false as ever and still credited by manufacturers accustomed to relying on spies in the

---

[1] This remarkable production quotes from an editorial criticizing Bishop McConnell in the N. Y. *Christian Advocate*. When Senator Kenyon read the quotation at the hearing, Bishop McConnell remarked that it sounded inaccurate. The original editorial (Nov. 13, 1919) reads, " If the multitude who listen possessed the bishop's rare ability to discriminate," etc. The quotation furnished by the steel men to the senators reads ". . . possessed the bishop's wild inability. . . ."

The document (p. 19) also changes the spelling of the name of the prominent Interchurch official, Dr. Fred B. Fisher, to Fischer in support of its charges of pro-Germanism among those responsible for the steel report.—H. B.

steel industry. On p. 15 of this "Review" the argument that the Report is not of the Commission's authorship comes to climax in a paragraph printed in capitals thus:

WILL THE INTER-CHURCH WORLD MOVE-
MENT DENY THE STATEMENT OF THIS MAN,
REV. F. M. CROUCH, THAT HE IS THE MAN WHO
WROTE THE REPORT OF THE INTER-CHURCH
WORLD MOVEMENT ON THE STEEL STRIKE,
OR THAT HE COMPILED THE REPORTS PRE-
PARED BY THE SEVERAL INVESTIGATORS
AND PRESENTED IN COMPLETED FORM TO THE
COMMISSION OF INQUIRY, THE REPORT AS
PUBLISHED, FOR THEIR APPROVAL?

Certainly the Interchurch will deny that Dr. Crouch wrote the Report.

The Report explains its own authorship, and if these manufacturers had any doubt they could have dropped a letter at any time to the Interchurch or the Commission. What misled them into this particular solemn idiocy?

It was a spy document, dated March 22, 1920, forwarded by Ralph M. Easley of the National Civic Federation to the offices of the United States Steel Corporation on March 29, 1920. The spy reports on an interview with Dr. Crouch as follows:

"Rev. Dr. F. M. Crouch, Episcopal minister, is in charge of the *Industrial Relations Department*. He has prepared for the Ind. Rel. Dept. an extensive report on conditions among the Steel workers in Pittsburgh, Pa. and among the Coal miners in the middle west.

"Dr. Crouch said the report he was preparing on the situation in the Steel Industry to be presented to a Commission for O. K. before a final publication by the Interchurch World Movement for distribution was seven-eighths completed. Five-eighths of the report had been already O. K.'d by the Commission.

"So far as I could see there was about 1,000 pages of closely typewritten paper in the bulk which he said was the report. The final eighth will be completed within a few weeks."

On this basis the manufacturers' association assures the Senate that Dr. Crouch wrote the Commission's Report. If they had asked Dr. Crouch they would have been freely told that what he was working on was something entirely different, and that the Commission's Report had already been finished and that Dr. Crouch never saw it until it was finished. Instead, on the word of a spy, they " accuse " Dr. Crouch as the author, they take the spy's word that Dr. Crouch, a well-known scholar, " believes Bolshevism is preferable to capitalism."

Let it be clearly understood that most of the persons " accused " in this " Review " were known to members of the Commission, and respected by them, but these named men, it so happens, knew no more of what was in the Commission's Report until it was finished than did the steel manufacturers.

The Commission ought not to be expected to go on forever demolishing the straw men set up by spies who have to invent things to earn their pay.

The Commission certainly will not stoop to answer such questions as (p. 32), " Why did the greatest Christian organization in the world employ as investigators men and women of pronounced *liberal* if not radical views on social and industrial problems?" Must the Commissioners enter a formal plea of guilty on the count of " liberal "?

So in the Capitol, the Senate convening overhead, the Supreme Court in session down the corridor, the Commission with its recommendations on a menacing situation in the steel industry sat with the senators and on the table between them lay—spy stuff. Certainly to be so self-pilloried was not the prime intention of American industrial leaders when embarking on business enterprise. Manufacturers were caught in that plight because their industrial spy system got out of their control.

RECOMMENDATIONS

1. In 1913, by the United States Commission on Industrial Relations (Final Report, vol. I, p. 57):

In view of the endless crimes committed by the employees of the so-called detective agencies, who have been permitted to usurp a function that should belong only to the State, it is suggested that the commission recommend to Congress either that such of these agencies as may operate in more than one State, or may be employed by corporations engaged in interstate commerce, or may use the mails, shall be compelled to take out a Federal license, with regulations to insure the character of their employees and the limitation of their activities to the bona fide business of detecting crime, or that such agencies shall be utterly abolished through the operation of the taxing power or through denying them the use of the mails.

2. In 1920, by the Commission of Inquiry, Interchurch World Movement (Report on the Steel Strike of 1919, p. 18):

Inasmuch as—
(a) the conduct and activities of "labor-detective" agencies do not seem to serve the best interests of the country, and—
(b) the Federal Department of Justice seems to have placed undue reliance on cooperation with corporations' secret services, therefore—

It is recommended—

(a) that the Federal Government institute investigation for the purpose of regulating labor detective agencies; and for the purpose of publishing what government departments or public moneys are utilized to cooperate with company "under-cover" men.

II

THE PITTSBURGH NEWSPAPERS AND THE STEEL STRIKE

By M. K. Wisehart

CONTENTS

FOREWORD

" THE failure of the press was one of the reasons for an Interchurch investigation of the steel strike ":—so ran some of the comment after the publication of the Steel Report. A great bulk of the facts in the Report was " news " to the newspapers. Those facts, gathered during the strike, could have been in the newspapers and were not.

Among the facts collected during the strike were certain relating to the newspapers. They are presented in the following analysis of the press of Pittsburgh and seem to be the first detailed study of the press of any city during a strike.

The analyst was a newspaper man of long experience as a reporter of national politics and investigator of industrial problems in America, and as a special writer abroad.

The method outlined for the study was designed to answer the following questions:

What was the sum-total of actual information on the strike printed by the Pittsburgh newspapers ? What judgments on the causes and events of the strike would be formed by logical readers relying principally on Pittsburgh newspapers for their information?

Comparisons between the Pittsburgh press and the press of other cities were not made in detail, but sufficient examination was made to indicate the main similarities and salient differences. The differences turned out to be of degree, in some cases of very great degree.

Pittsburgh was selected, of course, because half the steel industry of the country centers in Pittsburgh and because the developments of the strike around Pittsburgh were decisive for the result of the strike in the whole country. Pittsburgh's preeminence, moreover, as a typical product of American large-scale basic industrial development, gave the study more than local significance. It was found that while the Pittsburgh newspapers, like newspapers of smaller towns, had relatively less decisive influence in the community than have the newspapers of larger cities, nevertheless a marked agreement existed between the viewpoint of Pittsburgh newspapers and the viewpoint of Pittsburghers, "the Pittsburgh mind." The Pittsburgh mind, in turn, weightily influenced national opinion by influencing newspaper and news association correspondents in Pittsburgh.

The public opinion studied here is, naturally, but one of two separate entities. The division is visible on Pittsburgh news stands; beside the half-dozen English newspapers there are often displayed over half a dozen foreign newspapers, largely out-of-town publications. To one-half the population of Allegheny County the English headlines are quite as unintelligible as are the Polish, Croatian, Italian, Russian and Magyar characters to the "American" half. But the public opinion here analyzed is indisputably that of the ruling fraction.

The analysis must be read as a sub-report to the Main Report of the Commission: that is, statements made herein

as the facts of the strike, with which the newspaper reports
are compared, are formulated not as the press investigator's
own research, but as the findings of the other investigations
of the Commission. The press investigator worked with the
other investigators and sometimes personally checked up details. But his main duty was getting the facts of the press,
theirs the facts of the strike, which he utilized for the comparisons.

Immediately after the steel and coal strikes there was
quickly established the first national news service owned by
labor unions, the Federated Press. In Pennsylvania the
unions began raising $500,000 to found a labor daily. In
other states efforts were made to start newspapers. The few
labor dailies in existence banded together to buy their own
paper mill. The following analysis sheds light on these
phenomena.

—H. B.

THE PITTSBURGH NEWSPAPERS AND THE STEEL STRIKE

I—*The Seven Newspapers*

FOUR hundred issues of the seven daily English-language newspapers in Pittsburgh were examined as they appeared during the first two months of the steel strike (September 22 to late November, 1919).

The seven papers have circulations running from 60,000 to over 100,000 each, and together constitute the dominant press influence for a large area around Pittsburgh, extending north to Erie, Pa., west to Youngstown, O., south to Wheeling, W. Va., and each toward the center of Pennsylvania, where the circulation of Philadelphia papers is more important.

Their names, hours of issue and ownership are listed as follows:

1. *The Gazette-Times* (morning)

2. *The Chronicle-Telegraph* (afternoon)
    Both owned by the sons of the late Senator George T. Oliver, colleague and co-worker of Senator Boies Penrose and head of the Oliver coal and steel interests. The sons are George S. Oliver, president of the Chamber of Commerce in Pittsburgh and Augustus K. Oliver, of the city council.

3. *The Post* (morning)

4. *The Sun* (afternoon)

    Both owned until his recent death by T. Hart Given, president of the Farmers National Bank; now by Arthur Braun, business associate of Mr. Given.

5. *The Dispatch* (morning)

Principal owner, Col. Charles A. Rook.

6. *The Leader* (afternoon and Sunday)

Principal owner, Alexander P. Moore.

7. *The Press* (afternoon)

Principal owner, Oliver S. Hershman; William S. Haddock, sheriff of Allegheny Co. during the strike, was former circulation manager.

The following analysis of the acts and tendencies of these seven newspapers, as shown by their news and editorial columns, is based upon one general test as standard: what might have been expected of a public press during an industrial crisis?

It is not a study of the press in all sections of the country involved in the steel strike, but particularly of those newspapers which, by location and familiarity with conditions, had the best facilities and opportunities for investigation and for presenting impartial news from the decisive area of the strike. A less extensive examination of the newspapers of other cities, especially New York and Chicago, indicated, however, that the attitude and reports printed by the Pittsburgh newspapers were more or less typical of the press as a whole. The Pittsburgh papers are not a special genus in American journalism.

What might have been expected of the Pittsburgh newspapers during the steel strike in view of well-established and generally accepted traditions of newspaper policy?

The first assumption in answer to this question must be that the Pittsburgh newspapers would have started with the determination to "cover" the event as one vital to the community, and this determination would have involved the obligation not to slight the event because it was "dangerous" or "ticklish," not to skimp it because it was difficult, and not to ignore it because it was inimical to owners' interests or to the local pride of the community.

Secondly, the determination to cover the event adequately as news would have involved the necessity of independent investigation, particularly if there were contentions as to conditions and discrepancies in the statements made by both sides of the strike, such independent investigation resulting in:

(a) Exercise of judgment and analysis in considering conflicting statements.

(b) Reports adequately conveying to the public a record of actual happenings.

Third, it might properly have been expected that there would be investigation of phases of the strike concerning which information was not being acquired by any governmental or social institution.   There was at least one such obvious phase of the strike—the attitude of mind of the foreign workers.   Concerning their attitude there was much vehement assertion, but little definite knowledge.

Fourth, such procedure might logically have been expected to lead to a conviction of opinion on one side or the other of the dispute or on a third position, and to the open editorial promulgation of it.

The policy actually followed by the Pittsburgh papers regarding the strike as a whole and regarding special phases of it will appear on perusal of the sub-divisions of this report.   Three general conclusions after examining the four hundred issues, however, can be set down now.

First, there was no marked change in policy by these papers from the beginning of the strike to the end, nor any marked difference in the attitude of any one paper compared with the others.   People did not point continually to any one paper as " telling a different story."   They all assumed a definite attitude to the strike, quite from the beginning, and stuck to it.

Second, in the four hundred issues only one example was

found or first-hand independent investigation. One paper printed one story of research by an eyewitness (dealing with the " foreign " workers and the state constabulary), but did not repeat the performance.

Third, while the papers' news columns contained altogether a considerable quantity of material on the strike, the editorial columns were very reticent. For weeks the strike was a principal topic of opinion in private conversation in Pittsburgh, but days would pass without a reference, let alone a discussion, in Pittsburgh editorial columns.

One characteristic of the treatment of the strike in the news columns was more apparent to visiting newspapermen's eyes, perhaps, than to Pittsburgh readers. It is good newspaper practice, at the beginning of a great event, to collect and summarize for the benefit of the public accounts of the precedent circumstances. " What's back of it all ? Who are in it ? How did it come about ? " To answer such questions newspapers on the eve of an election give columns to refreshing the public's memory; on the eve of a baseball " world's series," columns go to every feature of past or present interest.

No Pittsburgh newspaper gave, or pretended to give, any such account at the beginning of the steel strike. There were no general stories detailing the companies and mills in the industry, the numbers or characteristics of the workmen, their hours of labor, their wages, their living conditions, no history of the year's organizing campaign, no detailed lists of strikers' " demands," no summary of efforts to avert the strike. These things, which were more or less accurately discussed, or asked about, by most Pittsburghers in the last week of September, were not " news " so far as the Pittsburgh newspapers were concerned. Special correspondents sent in later from other cities found in a single issue of one weekly, *The Survey,* published in New York, more actual news of

the above sort than in all the files of the Pittsburgh newspapers.

General Impressions

A " head-line reader's " impressions of the strike as gained
from the seven newspapers would be hard to analyze with
any certainty. The later pages of this study concern instead
those features of the papers which gave the more careful or
" consistent newspaper reader " his total of information or
misinformation. However, because more superficial or
" head-line " impressions are all that a great body of readers
usually obtain, a summary is noted here of the impression
created by " running through " all the papers.

At the beginning readers would have learned that a large
number of men quit work, a larger number perhaps than had
been expected. They would then have received the impression that within a day or two the employers had no trouble
getting large numbers of men to go back to work so that operation was " almost normal" and before one week was up they
could have obtained no other impression than that the strike
was practically at an end. On this point the public might
have been somewhat confused for the reason that for several
weeks, beginning as early as September 24, two days after
the strike, the newspapers kept reporting that great numbers
of men were " flocking back to work," while at the same
time telling of mills which were to open on a certain day
in cities outside of Pittsburgh and on subsequent days ac-
counting for the fact that these mills had not opened; that
the strike continued to be " practically over " and " coming
to an end " even through December; that the large number
of men who went on strike did so for reasons connected
with W. Z. Foster's early beliefs in Syndicalism and his booklet on that subject; that the strikers were foreigners striking
in support of demands which would enable them to get control of the steel industry; that they were violent and seeking

opportunities to do violence and that their gatherings in and around Pittsburgh had to be suppressed for fear of this violence; that for any violence which occurred the strikers were at fault, while the public authorities and State Constabulary were never at fault.

Undiscriminating readers must have gained the impression that the men on strike in the steel industry were disloyal and un-American by virtue of entertaining some revolutionary economic theory. Had readers sought to find out what this theory was they would have had little trouble in finding in the newspaper columns extracts from Foster's "red book." Had they sought from the newspapers information of the actual demands of the strikers, they would have found from September 22 to the end of December scarcely a reference beyond statements to the effect that the demands amounted, according to Mr. Gary and other Steel Corporation officials, to "the closed shop." They would have learned nothing of the resentment which stirred a good many citizens of Pittsburgh against the suppression of free speech and other constitutional guarantees. Incidentally readers would have gained the impression that the clergymen of the district were opposed to the strike because almost all comment from clergymen quoted by the newspapers had this aspect.

Undiscriminating readers must have come to the conclusion that the district was being saved from a revolution by the efforts of the local authorities and the State Constabulary.

The investigator came into contact with a number of discriminating Pittsburgh readers, however, who had reached the conclusion that they could not learn from their papers the true facts regarding the strike and must rely on newspapers and magazines published elsewhere than in Pittsburgh. The features which gave rise to such beliefs will now be analyzed.

II—*The Advertising Campaign*

On September 27, the fifth day of the strike, an advertising campaign was begun to induce the striking steel workers to abandon their protest. While the advertisements were apparently intended for the strikers themselves, they had, unquestionably, by reason of their prominence, an important influence in forming public opinion on the causes and issues of the strike. Between September 27 and October 8 over thirty full-page advertisements denouncing the leadership of the strike and calculated to undermine the morale of the strikers, appeared in the various Pittsburgh newspapers. They were printed in English and generally in four or five foreign languages as well. In sum, the purport of these advertisements was that it was *un-American* for the steel workers to be on strike.

These advertisements, obviously prepared by competent professional skill, were carefully designed and were characterized by an effective display. A number of them contained a half-page cartoon of " Uncle Sam," garbed in stars and stripes, with his hand to his mouth calling in the direction of steel mills pictured in the background: " Go back to work!" This exhortation was printed in eight languages. The page-wide streamer line in heavy black type at the top read: " America is calling you!" The line at the bottom read: " Go back to work!" All the advertisements were characterized by a similar effectiveness in presenting the point of view of those who paid for this costly method of reaching the strikers and public opinion.

Coming as early in the strike as they did, these advertisements constitute a factor of considerable importance.

They are worth attention especially from two points of view: first, they represent in crystallized form the misinformation concerning the strike which was persistently circulated in the news columns of the Pittsburgh press and elsewhere; second, the point of view taken in these advertisements was *exactly the point of view which dominated the news and editorial columns of the Pittsburgh papers from the beginning to the end of the strike,* and it should be borne in mind that no Pittsburgh papers pretended to offer at any time a consistent and thorough examination of the causes of the strike from any other view.

The full-page advertisements as carried by the *Leader* on October 5 and 6 and by the *Chronicle-Telegraph* on October 6, exhibited in heavy type in the body of the advertisement the following statements:

The steel strike can't win. It is uncalled for and un-American. It is led by men who apparently are trying to establish the " red " rule of anarchy and bolshevism in this land of opportunity and liberty. The American institution of majority rule is threatened by a malicious, radical group of agitators. They are trying to throw hundreds of thousands of wellpaid, prosperous workmen out of employment because of the whims of a very small minority.

Don't be fooled any longer. Stand by America and all that America means. Stick to your job and keep up " good times."

" GO BACK TO WORK."

On Saturday, September 27, the *Chronicle-Telegraph* carried a page advertisement with a slogan three times repeated across the full width of the page in large type: " GO BACK TO WORK MONDAY." Besides quotations from the booklet " Syndicalism," by W. Z. Foster, the advertisement displayed such statements as these:

Yesterday the enemy of liberty was Prussianism. Today it is radicalism.

Masquerading under the cloak of the American Federation of Labor a few Radicals are striving for power. They hope to seize control of the industries and to turn the company over to the "red" rule of Syndicalism.

Among the slogans presented in the advertising campaign were the following, printed in type an inch to two inches high:

AMERICA IS CALLING YOU
THE STEEL STRIKE WILL FAIL, BE A 100% AMERICAN, STAND BY AMERICA.
THE STEEL STRIKE CAN'T WIN, BOYS! LET'S BE 100% AMERICANS *NOW,* EUROPE'S NOT WHAT IT USED TO BE, MAYBE THE DOORS OF THE OLD U.S.A. WILL NOT AGAIN OPEN TO THEM IF FOREIGN BORN NOW HERE RETURN TO EUROPE AND WANT TO COME BACK.

Almost invariably with others appeared the slogan, "GO BACK TO WORK." This was varied by the slogan which appeared on Saturday, "GO BACK TO WORK MONDAY."

In connection with the advertisement "GO BACK TO WORK MONDAY" instances were noted of newspapers which printed on Saturday or toward the end of the week news articles predicting the opening of mills on the following Monday.

The representations in the following advertisement are a fair sample of those to be found in all. That they are misrepresentations will be seen by comparison with the Main Report of the Commission.[1] The English part of the advertisement (half the page was given to translations into seven foreign languages) is quoted in full:

[1] See "The Steel Strike of 1919."

THE STEEL STRIKE CAN'T WIN.

Here are ten reasons why the strike will fail: ten reasons why you and every other man who is loyal to America will go back to work:

1. There is no good American reason for the strike.

2. A very large majority of the workers did not want to strike.

3. The strike is not between workers and employers, but between revolutionists and America.

4. It is becoming more and more apparent that the strike is merely the diabolical attempt of a few Radicals to seize industry and plant Bolshevism in this country.

5. The strike is doomed to fail, just as all unpopular and unpatriotic movements have failed in this country.

6. Public sentiment is against the strike; Americans have great sympathy for genuine wrongs but they have neither sympathy nor tolerance for Radicals who seek to use organized labor as a tool in their nefarious campaign against industry and American liberty.

7. The strike is an economic failure and the loss will be felt by everyone including you.

8. America will never stand for the "red" rule of Bolshevism, I.W.W.ism or any other "ism" that seeks to tear down the Constitution. Radicalism must be put down.

9. There is a strong possibility that the Huns had a hand in fomenting the strike, hoping to retard industrial progress in America.

10. Keep America busy and prosperity will continue.

The source of these advertisements was obviously one whose interests were in accord with those of the United States Steel Corporation. It appears that they were not paid for by money from the steel companies, but by business men who conceived that their interest would be best served by the acquiescence of labor in whatever conditions were meted out to it regardless of whether these conditions favored an American standard of living, of education and of opportunity.   In reality such appeals as appeared in these advertisements urged labor to submit to un-American conditions in the name of " Americanism."

III—" Radicalism, Disloyalty and Un-Americanism "

The strike of the steel workers was conducted under the sanction of the American Federation of Labor with leaders acceptable to and endorsed by that organization.[1] Despite the fact that the demands were for better working conditions, a six-day week, eight instead of ten, twelve or fourteen hours a day, and for recognition of labor's right to organize, etc., the newspapers before and during the strike asserted and re-asserted in various direct forms and in various ways of impli-cation that the objects of the strike were " revolutionary " and " Bolshevik " and that the strikers were " disloyal " and " un-American." Approximately 300,000 strikers were out during the first fortnight of the strike, but instead of this fact and the conditions and causes which had produced the strike, the Pittsburgh newspapers as well as most of the press of the whole country found space for extracts from the reprint of Foster's " Syndicalism," as distributed to the newspapers by persons interested in the steel companies.[2]

In the Pittsburgh district, most of the strikers were for-eign born, low-skilled laborers. This fact was used con-stantly with the implication that the strike as a whole was an "alien" strike. The term " alien " had acquired a pecu-liarly ugly significance in the war. That the American workmen near Pittsburgh were not out, partly because they held the coveted skilled jobs with better pay and working conditions and had not been reached by the organizers, was

[1] See " The Steel Strike of 1919 "; Organizing, p. 180
[2] No copy of the original book, out of print for several years, was found in the possession of any striker or strike leader. A reprint, which was a facsimile in everything except the price mark and the union label, was widely circulated by the officials of the steel companies. " Steel Strike of 1919," p. 34.

101

not discussed in the press, but the fact that these skilled workers were not out was used as a basis for the representation in head-lines and articles that the unskilled workers had no just grounds for complaint. Moreover, terms such as " reds," " alien," " Bolshevik," " un-American " were used in such a way as to prejudice public opinion and to stigmatize the strike as a whole in spite of the fact that in the Chicago, Colorado, Wheeling and Ohio districts skilled American workers had largely joined the strike.

In the Pittsburgh papers there was nothing to disclose what appears to be the fact, namely, that " loyalty " was made an issue in the strike as a means of winning public sentiment to the support of the position taken by the head of the United States Steel Corporation.

While the Pittsburgh papers were daily charging the foreign born population with disloyalty, violence and other infractions of the law, there was no corresponding protest against the methods practised by officials in depriving unions of their rights to hold meetings.[1]

It would appear that the Pittsburgh papers had at no time made a critical examination of the charge of disloyalty and radicalism as it concerned the rank and file of the men on strike.[2] As a result all " aliens," except those willing to work in the steel mills under conditions prescribed by their employers, were placed under suspicion. This disposition to charge " red radicalism " indiscriminately characterized most American newspapers in October and November. The New York *World* in an editorial on November 26 was one of the first to re-examine the charges of a Bolshevik or I.W.W. menace to the United States, as follows:

In spite of the poses of the professional politician and platform orators, there is no Bolshevist menace in the United States and

[1] See " The Steel Strike of 1919 ": Social Consequences, p. 236.
[2] *Ibid.*, Ignorance: Bolshevism, p. 38.

there is no I.W.W. menace that an ordinarily capable police force is not competent to deal with. There is a great deal of Bolshevist agitation, which is mainly rhetorical, and the I.W.W. leaders are trying to capitalize industrial discontent for the benefit of their peculiar economic theories. But the American people are not fools and they have not gone crazy. They do not need a nurse to take them to work in the morning and bring them home at night lest they be corrupted by the seditious doctrines of soap box orators.

But even this paper earlier in the autumn had stigmatized the steel strike, in editorial and cartoon, as " revolutionary."

An instance which will illuśtrate with what. irresponsibility the newspapers of Pittsburgh led the public to the belief that the steel strike was connected with the activities of the I.W.W. or other organizations of the same type appears in connection with a prominently displayed first-page article in the *Post* on December 10. This article appeared under the headline, " TWO KILLED, ONE SHOT BY WAITING POSSE, OFFICER JOINS MONESSEN GANG, LEADS THEM TO OHIO BANK, WHERE SHERIFF'S MEN SHOOT THEM DOWN. STORY READS LIKE WILDEST FICTION."

After explaining how the detective had worked to trap the culprits, the article continued:

The slaying of the safe crackers had its origin with the big steel strike and was hatched in the headquarters of the I.W.W. and Reds in Monessen. . . . The plans for the series of bank robberies that was to make those participating in them independently wealthy so they could return to their native lands in affluence were first taken under advisement a short time after Detective Marczewski had been sent to Monessen to conduct an investigation by the Railway and Industrial Protective Association.

Marczewski had been in Monessen but a few days when he was approached by John Zneskzki, 25 years old, and requested to be-

come a member of a secret organization that worked within the
ranks of the I.W.W. but which had a limited membership. All
of them were employees of a steel plant there and were on strike.

An attempt was made by the investigator to discover what
connection the burglars might have had with the " I.W.W.
and Reds " in Monessen. Inquiry was made of two editors
of the *Post* concerning the source of the information. It
was explained that the story had been brought to the office
of the *Post* by a detective connected with the Railway and
Industrial Protective Association of Philadelphia. This
detective was said to be unknown to the editors, though he
was a friend of a member of the *Post's* staff of reporters.
When asked whether the evidence seemed to be substantiated
that the bank robbery had originated in I.W.W. headquarters
in Monessen, one of the editors said:

" As a matter of fact I don't think the I.W.W. had anything to
do with it. I know something about the I.W.W. and I know they
haven't any headquarters in Monessen, and I know that the
I.W.W.'s were scared away from this section at the beginning
of the strike."

The editor was then asked if he did not think that before
such statements as those quoted above were printed, the matter should have been investigated to ascertain the truth. In
answer he said:

" Not under the circumstances. The detectives wouldn't care
if such a statement were printed. The statement wouldn't hurt
them. It couldn't hurt the two men who are dead. As far as
the I.W.W. is concerned, that organization is in disrepute anyway."

On October 31 an editorial appeared on the front page of
the *Leader,* under the title " Man's Extremity God's Oppor-

tunity." While an appeal for divine guidance in human affairs is natural to all reverent men, the sensational character of this editorial and its application to the steel strike then in progress as well as to the coal strike just beginning, would seem to merit severe condemnation from the point of view of policy, patriotism and justice. The columns of the *Leader* had found room almost daily for the charge that the steel strike was of Bolshevik origin. Many of these articles were signed by the Rev. L. A. Carroll of East Pittsburgh. It was inevitable that the *Leader's* sensational editorial should be connected locally with the tendency displayed in the Rev. L. A. Carroll's articles. Among the statements in the editorial were the following:

There appears to be NO MAN OR MEN BIG ENOUGH in this land to stay the rising tide of disaster.

The president of the United States has FAILED to bring order out of disorder.

No public man possesses power or influence sufficient to allay the turmoil.

Employer and employee cannot reach that mutual understanding, that necessary harmony, upon which the livelihood of ALL OF THE PEOPLE is dependent.

An industrial warfare is being waged behind whose lines lurks ANARCHY.

Famine, destitution, bloodshed and misery fringe the battlefields.

The AMERICAN FLAG is no longer reverenced by all of the people.

American institutions, American traditions, American hopes, American aspirations are no longer respected by many Americans.

RAUCOUS VOICES RAIL AT PATRIOTISM'S PLEA.

The American Republic is already in the twilight of its DARKEST HOUR.

It would be FOLLY TO DENY the desperate conditions that exist.

It would be CRIMINAL TO CONCEAL the deadly peril of the nation.

The people of the United States MUST AROUSE THEM-
SELVES to a realization of the growing menace before they are
annihilated by the power of evil. . . .

It is a sane and serious KNOWLEDGE OF CONDITIONS
that all who read a newspaper today must admit are not ex-
aggerated, that obliges the Leader to speak with truth and candor.

The labor strikes, existing and to come, are NOT ORDINARY
LABOR DISPUTES. The world has known nothing like them
and their effect upon mankind may plunge the world into hor-
rors that history has never recounted.

On October 3, page 1, the *Gazette-Times,* under a three-
column headline reading " ALIEN STRIKERS' DEPOR-
TATION URGED BY WALSH TO CRUSH RADICAL
TENDENCIES HERE," printed the following statements:

Deportation of striking aliens is part of a punitive plan
evolved by Commissioner Peter P. Walsh of the fifth police
district, to end their efforts to terrorize American and foreign
workmen who refuse to join the strikers. Statistics compiled by
the commissioner, which show that of 106 foreign-speaking strikers
arrested, only two possess the rights of citizenship, are the reasons
offered by him for the need of such drastic action. These facts
and figures, he avers, closely corroborate the evidence offered by
millmen before the Senate Committee inquiring into the walkout of steel workers that " the strike is not one of American
workingmen, directed by sober-minded heads, but is a strike of
the foreign-speaking element, led by the most radical leaders."

On October 3, page 9, the *Leader* gave publicity to the
same subject under the heading " URGES DEPORTATION
OF FOREIGNERS TAKEN BY POLICE IN STRIKE."
The first statement under this headline reads as follows:

Declaring that of 106 strikers arrested in his district only
two of them possessed the right to American citizenship, Police
Commissioner P. P. Walsh, of the fifth district South Side, has
announced a drastic program, which, if carried out, will mean

immediately deportation of all foreign-speaking unnaturalized steel strikers in the Pittsburgh territory who in the future are taken by the police.

On October 7, page 7, the *Chronicle-Telegraph* printed an article with the headline " ALL ALIENS NOT RADICALS RETURN TO MILLS, REPORT. OFFICIALS SAY ONLY CITIZENS OR THOSE READY TO BE NAT- URALIZED ARE WANTED—STRIKERS' JOBS ARE FILLED." The article contains the following statements:

Virtually all steel mill laborers in the immediate Pittsburgh district who walked out of the mills two weeks ago yesterday are back today, steel manufacturers announced, except the extreme radical foreign element holding union cards. For instance, in the Sharon-Farrell district, where between 5,000 and 7,000 men were out the first day, not more than 200 real strikers, it was averred today by a mill head, remain idle in that territory. Ow- ing to the un-American principles, which some of these men are known to have expressed, it was declared perhaps some would not be re-employed. From all sections comes the information that there is a disposition to employ only those foreigners who have taken out naturalization papers or expressed their willing- ness to become American citizens.

On October 29, page 9, the *Gazette-Times* printed an article under the headline " DRASTIC STEPS DEALING WITH ALIENS ASKED. HOMESTEAD CHAMBER OF COMMERCE URGES RESTRICTION OF IMMI- GRATION, WANT UNIONS CURBED." This article reported the action of the Homestead Chamber of Commerce in appealing to the Pennsylvania Senators and Congressmen. While the headline shows the usual tendency to stimulate public sentiment against aliens, it is in this case fairly based upon the contents of the article. It might have been ex- pected that such opinions as were expressed by the Home- stead Chamber of Commerce, since they seemed to deserve

such notable publicity, would have elicited some judicious
or analytical comments from the same newspaper editorially.
There was no such editorial comment from the *Gazette-Times*,
though the Homestead Chamber of Commerce had gone to the
extent of making the following suggestion:

"5, Forbid their (aliens) belonging to any organization public
or private, except well-recognized religious organizations for public
worship."

While the Pittsburgh papers were especially inclined to print
articles that the strike was of Bolshevist origin, they were
apparently much less inclined to display to the same extent
news showing that the strike was characterized by any traditional practices of American trade unions.   On October 30,
the *Leader* printed a small item on page 24, which would
seem to have deserved much greater prominence as a truer
indication of the unrevolutionary character of the strike:

STRIKERS WHO BROKE CONTRACTS ORDERED TO RETURN BY UNION.

Youngstown, Oct. 30—The national strike committee at Pittsburgh has indorsed the stand taken by the Amalgamated Association of Iron, Steel and Tin Workers, that contracts with steel
plants made before the strike shall be held inviolate, and all
Amalgamated men under such contracts have been ordered to
return to work, it was announced today by B. J. Davis, vice-
president of the Amalgamated, who is here to-see that the orders
are carried out.

It might have been expected that charges of German designs and German influences behind the strike would have
been the last raised even by a hostile press.   The charge was
given prominence, however, by the *Chronicle-Telegraph* on
October 2 and by the *Gazette-Times* on October 3.

The story was attributed to an anonymous "well-known steel head" and in this case as in many others, no matter how irrelevant or irresponsible, nor how prejudicial to a fair understanding of the issues, the newspapers seemed to welcome them for purposes of display.

Under a sub-head, "GERMAN DESIGNS SUS-PECTED," the *Gazette-Times* in a long first-page article on October 3 carried the following:

Investigation of the influence behind the strike call has developed the possibility of interests outside of the United States which involve American trade throughout the world being concerned. By obstructing the largest industry in the United States, its iron and steel trade, foreign markets would be directed to European nations at a time when America is seeking to expand its international trade following the war. The suggestion was advanced yesterday that Germany, in its designs upon American trade, would attempt to hamper it by spreading its sinister influence among foreigners to cause frequent strikes, calling some of the radical element here to its aid. Considerable attention is being paid to this angle of the strike by the numerous agencies at work investigating in this Pittsburgh district.

On October 2, the *Chronicle-Telegraph,* under the headline "INSPIRED WALKOUT TO REGAIN TRADE, STEEL MAN ASSERTS," carried prominently on the first page the following:

Numerous steel men today expressed themselves as believing the strike of steel laborers, which they say is now positively on the wane here, with the Russian Slav as the obstinate radical still out, was started either deliberately or otherwise in the interest of the Central Empires to get back their trade.

"Even if the effort was not deliberate" said a well-known steel head today, "the effect on the steel makers would be just the same if it should last long enough. A prolonged strike would enable Europe to get our market and in the end the American workman would be the sufferer. No matter how you look at it, if the radical foreign element in this country is to be countenanced, the effect will be the same."

Numerous strikes are in progress in this country in all lines, it was pointed out today. It is declared this situation is most significant. It also is averred hands may yet be exposed that will show an international conspiracy to stir up trouble in America for the purpose of benefiting the countries that were enemies of the United States in the world war.

IV—*Silence on Grievances*

Before and during the strike the Pittsburgh newspapers maintained an almost unbroken silence regarding the actual industrial grievances of the steel workers as to hours, pay, working conditions, and the lack of means to confer with employers concerning such matters, not to mention housing and social conditions. These newspapers, however, not only published grossly inaccurate underestimates of the number of men on strike, but gave no informing account of the conditions responsible for such a protest.

The policy characterizing the Pittsburgh newspapers developed first in connection with the attempt of the National Committee for Organizing Iron and Steel Workers to confer with the head of the United States Steel Corporation. Not one editorial or news article in any Pittsburgh paper frankly questioning Mr. Gary's refusal to confer with labor could be found. The tenor of all news articles, editorials and headlines in the four hundred newspapers examined implied approval of his course. The matter printed at the time of Mr. Gary's appearance before the Senate Committee in Washington was especially marked in this regard. Numerous articles, editorials and headlines gave unquestioning support to his opinions.

The policy of two Pittsburgh newspapers—the *Dispatch* and the *Press*—has been in the past such as to indicate that under ordinary circumstances they are inclined to treat matters concerning organized labor with greater frankness and fairness than the *Gazette-Times*, the *Chronicle-Telegraph*, the *Post*, the *Sun* and the *Leader*. Especially the *Press* has had a tendency to recommend " social justice " in rather vague

111

editorials.   In the case of the organizing steel workers, however, the *Dispatch* and the *Press* took no definite position.

Regarding wages, hours, treatment, working and housing
conditions among the steel workers, the Pittsburgh papers
made no effort to give the public information based on independent investigation.   Only one article in the four hundred
issues examined gave any details of a first-hand observation
of the immigrants' loss of civil rights.   As to the number of
men who struck, the results of only one independent investigation was published, and that, made by a news agency in
late November, was based mainly on company figures and it
confirmed the figures given out by the strikers two months
before.   As to conditions in the mills the only attempts to
investigate by Pittsburgh newspapers were made when visiting correspondents tried, vainly, to get from the companies
passes into the plants.

The most casual inquiry would have sufficed to develop the
fact that the steel workers felt that they had actual grievances; [1] that they complained of the conditions under which
they had to live and that many of them were living in con-
gested and intolerable surroundings; that for the most part
they were working ten to fourteen hours, many of them with
a twenty-four-hour shift every fortnight, while many worked
seven days in the week.[2]   It would have been found, too,
that while most of the strikers knew little or nothing of any
particular economic theories, some of the more intelligent
were expressing anxiety for improved conditions in order
that they might have more time for home life,[3] and might
avail themselves of opportunities for night schooling and the
education required to become real American citizens.[4]

During the strike the newspapers printed a few statistical

[1] See " The Steel Strike of 1919 "; Grievances, pp. 137-43.
[2] *Ibid.*, The Twelve-Hour Day, pp. 44-51.
[3] *Ibid.*, p. 65.
[4] *Ibid.*, pp. 82-84.

items on the wages of steel workers, generally after their publication in other cities. The statistics quoted always omitted comparisons of steel workers' incomes with standards of living whether a minimum standard or an " American " standard.[1] Moreover, such statistics were generally those compiled by bodies connected with employers' organizations. (The fact that the strikers' leaders had no statistical information whatever on wages and hours did not induce the newspapers to compile them for the information of the community.)

Without a single exception worthy of note, the statements, demands, grievances and testimony from the side of the strikers were printed under headlines or in a context tending to give the impression that what the striking steel workers sought was something unwarranted and that their grievances were unfounded. While evidence from the strikers' side of the case was effectively discountenanced by methods habitual to at least five of the Pittsburgh newspapers, publicity without question was given to statements from Boards of Trade. The following is an extract from resolutions of the Monessen Board of Trade which appeared in the *Sun,* September 29 :

Be it resolved, that the Monessen Board of Trade of Monessen, Pa. an organization now over 10 years old and comprising more than 250 members from both business and mill men, go upon record condemning such misrepresentation (referring to the testimony of John Fitzpatrick of the National strike committee regarding the " reign of blood and iron " in Monessen and regarding the fact that the wages received were responsible for the deplorable housing conditions among a large element of the steel workers) of actual conditions as misleading to the public and damaging to workmen and employees alike; it is the sense of this body, which always has been actively concerned in living conditions, uplift movements and charity work in the community, that the workmen in the steel industry have been better paid than other occupations for similar service and that they have lived just as well as they knew how or desired.

[1] *Ibid.,* pp. 92-100.

One method of treating news when the events happened to be undeniably favorable to the strikers' side was exemplified by the *Leader* on Sunday, October 12. On October 11 the United States Senate Committee investigating the strike at the hearing in Pittsburgh had heard as witnesses representative strikers, union organizers and members of the community. On Sunday the *Leader* printed a long account of the previous day's proceedings. The testimony of some of the witnesses was summarized and some of it quoted, but the " lead " of the article, which occupied all the front-page space and was carried under an emphatic black headline, was devoted to Senator McKellar's condemnation of the men who called the strike. The day's proceedings actually amounted to an arraignment before members of the Senate of the United States, not only of conditions in the steel industry, but of conditions in Allegheny County on account of the not impartial activity of officers of the law. The *Leader's* " report " appeared under a three-line display head, reading: "McKELLAR SCORES CHIEFS FOR NOT DELAYING STRIKE."

The *Gazette-Times'* treatment of the proceedings of the Senate Committee on October 11, when chiefly strikers' witnesses were heard, was conspicuously biased against the strikers.

Although many witnesses testified concerning the industry's long hours, the arbitrary treatment, the tactics of police and officials, the desire of foreign workmen to become Americanized and of their difficulty in learning English after a twelve-hour workday, only a short portion of the *Gazette-Times'* article toward the end was concerned with this testimony, while the headline and " lead " of the article made no reference to this significant phase of the day's hearing.

The following is the headline and " lead " of the *Gazette-*

Times' article on the steel strikers' October 11 testimony
without mention of the grievances cited:

STEEL STRIKE PREVENTABLE, SENATORS HEAR

Walkout in Opposition to President's Wish, Witnesses in
Local Probe Say.

ORGANIZER GRILLED

Statements of Strike Leaders Are Occasionally Resented
by Investigators.

SESSION FOR TODAY

That the steel strike could have been prevented and it was called
by organizers, regardless of the request of President Wilson, was
drawn out by the United States Senate Committee on Labor and
Education, investigating the strike situation in Pittsburgh during
hearings in the Federal Building yesterday. J. G. Brown, one of
the organizers in the Pittsburgh district, virtually admitted, when
closely interrogated by the Senators, that there was no effort or
disposition on the part of those in charge of the strike to heed the
President's wish for a postponement until after the conference
now in progress between representatives of capital, labor and the
public.

In summing up the testimony of Brown in the form of an in-
terrogation, Senator McKellar said during the examination of the
witness, "What you mean to say, then, is we will pay more attention to Mr. Gary's silence than we will to the President of the
United States, who has always been fair to us." Several questions
of this nature were turned by the witness, with the assertion that
the strikers could not hope to obtain a satisfactory settlement of
their demands through means of the conference.

QUESTIONED ON HIS RECORD

Brown occupied the witness chair during a large part of the
afternoon's session. He was questioned by the members of the

committee on his record, and particular attention was paid to the alleged part taken by him in radical disturbances in Seattle and other parts of the State of Washington. The witness was asked if he belonged to the I.W.W., the Socialists or any of the radical organizations.

The Senate Committee examined several witnesses during morning and afternoon sessions. Testimony was heard from strikers and strike leaders and from representatives of the steel companies. The committee pursued lines of questioning into the conditions in the mills and of the proportion of foreigners in the steel industry. They announced their purpose of sifting to the bottom of the matter, to hear "the bald truth," as it was expressed.

The following is the headline and "lead" of the *Gazette-Times'* article dealing with the steel companies' October 13 testimony:

SENATORS FIND MILL WORKERS HERE SATISFIED

Steel Strikers at Hearing Yesterday Unable to Give Cause for Walkout.

DOMINATION CHARGED

Organizers Conducted Movement, Forcing Men to Leave Plants.

FOREIGNERS TESTIFY

A general satisfaction with conditions and wages in the steel industry prevails among the workers, judging from testimony given by employes of long service during yesterday's sitting, in the Federal Building, of the Senate Committee on Education and Labor investigating the steel strike situation.

The committee was told that American workmen in the main remained at work and that the striking element was made up of foreigners.

The domination of the hastily constructed unions in many places by the strike organizers was shown by testimony of strikers and workers who had been almost coerced into the movement. A number testified that no balloting had been done prior to the strike call and that they were unrepresented in the conduct of the walkout.

REASONS FOR STRIKE UNKNOWN

An ignorance of their position and of the reasons for the strike was displayed by strikers. Many of them recited a catechism of demands which would impress a close observer as having been learned by rote. One witness, employed in the Pittsburgh Steel Company plant in Monessen before the strike, asserted E. H. Gary's refusal to meet with strike organizers as his reason for striking.

On October 12 the Senate Committee heard witnesses brought by steel company employers, including the superintendent of the American Steel and Wire Company at Donora. A considerable part of the *Gazette-Times'* article was devoted to the testimony of this Superintendent that the steel workers preferred a longer day with higher wages to an eight-hour day with reduced wages and to the testimony of non-striking skilled workers that they were not dissatisfied.

The two days' hearings by the Senate Committee was the only occasion that forced the local newspapers to print anything that showed the strikers actually had a case meriting a hearing.

During the strike most Pittsburgh newspapers printed editorials and articles dealing with the problem of " Americanization." The same papers, however, gave no space to the Americanization demands of the steel workers. Without a single exception their articles overlooked the issues of the steel strike as constituting any phase of the problem of Americanization and forbore even to discuss the question so vigorously raised by the strikers at the Senate hearings, " How I go learn English when work twelve hours ? "

V—*Civil Rights and the Press*

A feature of the strike was the fact that no newspaper in Pittsburgh took a stand for freedom of speech and a just enforcement of the law by the regularly constituted authorities. The Pittsburgh newspapers' silence in the past regarding the discriminatory conduct of officials of the city and the county has been interpreted by many residents of Allegheny County to mean that there exists a fundamental solidarity of interest between the media of public opinion, the officers of the law and the steel industry, such that even flagrant violations of the rights of individuals belonging to labor unions can occur without awakening protest or effective comment. The following editorial from the *Gazette-Times* of October 11 is typical of printed comment during the strike:

AN IMPUDENT PROPOSAL

No American can read without indignation the proposal submitted by Samuel Gompers that the Industrial Conference shall declare for " Freedom of speech, of the press, and of assemblage." The implication that this American right, guaranteed by the United State Constitution, has been abridged to the disadvantage of any respectable and worthy element of the public cannot be assented to. If anything, it has been too liberally construed in favor of organizations and agitations hostile to the common weal. Abuse of constitutional privileges, misuse of inalienable human rights, is a crime against the people. It is not to be tolerated in any intelligent and law-abiding community. Freedom of speech and of assemblage will be preserved. The American people will see to that. And they will also see to it that there shall be no unlawful activities promoted and carried on under the impudent claim that the ambitions of some may be pursued contrary to the rights and safety of all. The question raised should have no place on the program of the Industrial Conference.

Concerning the suppression of civil rights the newspapers of Pittsburgh did not lack information. Much of that furnished them by the union officials was of a character to warrant not only publicity, but further investigation. The policy actually followed, however, gave tacit approval to the conduct of Mayor E. V. Babcock and Sheriff William S. Haddock, and the public was not allowed to suspect the extent to which persons in western Pennsylvania were living under a régime calculated to support steel company policies while undermining the organized protest of workers.

The following is a résumé of four efforts to put before the public charges involving civil liberties.

(a) At a special meeting at the Labor Temple on October 10, the Pittsburgh Central Labor Council, a long established, traditionally trade union body, passed a resolution including the following charges:

That the United States Steel Corporation and its subsidiaries, and all other steel companies aligned with it in their un-American war upon organized labor have instituted a campaign of vilification and libel through the medium of their subsidized press, in purchased advertisements and editorials and slander by their paid officials and hirelings.

That they have inaugurated a state of terrorism as their sole method and hope of breaking this strike.

That in their attempt to break the strike they have procured the assistance of various state, county and city officials and police, together with the hired police, private detectives and thugs and strike breakers of said company, and have—

(a) Made numerous unwarranted arrests and numerous assaults upon a helpless and defenseless people;

(b) Denied union men the right to hold meetings either on the public commons or in private or rented halls, by threats directed against the owners of such halls and by refusing to grant permits therefor;

(c) By invading such assemblies as were had with their constabulary, detectives and sheriffs, intimidating, assaulting, dispersing and arresting those in attendance;

(d) By denying unions their sacred right of holding regularly constituted chartered union meetings without the presence of intruders and constabulary sitting on the platform and therefore invading the privacy guaranteed to any fraternity;

(e) By the Mayor of Pittsburgh refusing to the strikers hereafter places, except at the Labor Temple and one other small hall, notwithstanding he had admitted that such assemblages have been peaceable and law abiding, and in spite of offers on the part of labor unions to pay for any police that may be delegated to attend said meetings if any were necessary for the purpose of preserving order;

(f) By the Sheriff of Allegheny county refusing to permit interpreters to translate by word of mouth any message conveyed to them by their English speakers and by refusing distribution of any literature.

The whole list of charges received scarcely a mention in print and so far as could be learned no newspaper was stimulated to investigate what foundation might exist for such charges.

(b) A petition of Pittsburgh labor unions asking the privilege of placing before the City Council the strikers' grievances against the police department, Mayor Babcock, magistrates and sheriff's deputies, was denied on October 14 by a tie vote. The petition, citing specific counts and signed by the presidents of seven local labor unions, was not generally printed in the Pittsburgh press, except in the *Leader,* which on October 15, page 1, printed a fair brief report of the proceedings of the council and the petition in full. No criticism of the council followed on the part of the Pittsburgh press, except in the *Leader,* which had been leading in denouncing the strike as Bolshevist, disloyal and un-American, but now took a firm position editorially with regard to the council's action after the action had been taken. The *Leader's* editorial of October 15 reads:

STUPIDITY IN COUNCIL

When city council, by a tie vote, yesterday refused to grant to local labor leaders a hearing on alleged discriminations and abuses, it displayed A LACK OF INTELLIGENCE VERGING ON SILLINESS.

The men who appealed to council were ALL PITTSBURGHERS.

None of the outsiders, against whom there is just resentment, appeared among the appellants. Had the request been made by these outsiders, there might have been some logic in city council refusing to deal with them.

But it was PITTSBURGHERS who asked for the investigation—CITIZENS AND TAXPAYERS—and they have the RIGHT of petition and the RIGHT to courteous treatment from their representatives in council.

And the people of Pittsburgh, too, have the RIGHT TO KNOW whether any or all of the charges of the labor men are true or false.

A REFUSAL to investigate will be accepted as a plea of GUILTY.

Suppression of the facts is not a boost for Pittsburgh—it is a BLOW to Pittsburgh's reputation for just dealing.

The workers' complaint was that police officials, magistrates, deputies and others are given the authority to arrest strikers in the city without just cause; to prevent public and private gatherings of union labor men and to imprison strikers and their sympathizers without hearings.

These charges are serious, and no matter how individual members of council may view the labor movement, they have no right to be a party to ANY OPPRESSIVE MEASURES, if such exist.

PITTSBURGH HAS BEEN PUBLICLY ACCUSED.

If there is no investigation of the accusation, Pittsburgh's NAME IS STAINED just as much as if a conviction were had.

An investigation would prove the falsity or truth of the charges.

If they are proven false, NO HARM CAN COME from an investigation.

If the charges are shown to be true, MUCH GOOD WILL COME in the remedying of a great wrong.

Council is acting STUPIDLY, and contrary to Pittsburgh's best interests.

ONLY THE COWARD FEARS TO LEARN THE TRUTH.

No names were named in the above firm stand and no results followed. Not even the *Leader* attempted the investigation, lacking which, it said, Pittsburgh stood convicted. This was the only article in four hundred issues of seven newspapers in which sentiments for fair play were expressed with conviction by any Pittsburgh paper.

(c) A delegation of eighteen representatives of organized labor of Pittsburgh and Allegheny County, representing 150,000 workers, left Pittsburgh on October 28 to go to Washington to protest to officials of the Federal government against the denial to labor in Pennsylvania of the constitutional rights of free speech and public assemblage and to place before the executive authorities specific complaints regarding various towns and districts. Notice of this action and copies of the specific complaints were sent to the newspapers on October 27. As news the event was ignored and the complaints received only the most meager notice.

(d) The most flagrant instance of press partiality was shown in the news treatment of the special convention in Pittsburgh of the Pennsylvania State Federation of Labor on November 2. This convention representing 500,000 union members, after hearing evidence of the denial of civil liberties in western Pennsylvania, voted unanimously to call a state-wide general strike unless the Governor should call a special session of the legislature or take other effective steps to restore normal conditions. The news was of sufficient importance to be displayed at length on the front pages of the New York *Times* and the New York *Sun*. One of the Pittsburgh morning papers mentioned the convention on page 6 and devoted almost its entire article to a quotation from the sole speaker against the general strike. One other morning paper printed a brief mention on page 9.

The true state of civil liberties in Pittsburgh and the vicinity could not have been discovered by the most discriminating reader through perusal of the Pittsburgh newspapers. Even the formal requests of respectable national organizations to the proper authorities were in most cases suppressed completely by the newspapers of Pittsburgh. The following item, for instance, appeared in the New York *Times* of November 23, but while it appeared in the monthly *Pittsburgh Christian Outlook,* it could not be discovered in any Pittsburgh newspaper:

ASKS RIGHT OF FREE SPEECH

CHURCH COMMISSION CHARGES DENIAL TO PENNSYLVANIA STEEL WORKERS

Governor Sproul of Pennsylvania was urged yesterday by the Church and Social Service Commission of the Federal Council of Churches of Christ in America to secure to the people of his State the right of assemblage and free speech. This action was taken, it was said, after the commission had carefully considered evidence gathered by its investigators in various steel towns in Pennsylvania. A letter sent to the Governor by Rev. Worth M. Tippy, Executive Secretary of the commission, said in part:

" In various steel towns in the State of Pennsylvania the right of assemblage and free speech, even within buildings, has been and is being denied by various authorities. The consequences of such denial are to discredit the institutions of the United States among immigrant workers, and to weaken the leadership of those who seek needed industrial change by constitutional methods."

VI—*Strikers' Violence and Officials' Violence*

Affidavits and statements gathered by investigators and analyzed elsewhere reveal the extent to which the striking steel workers and unions generally were deprived of their right of speech and assembly throughout western Pennsylvania by town, city, county and state officials.

In this conduct the officials had the active approval of most of the Pittsburgh papers, the tacit approval of all. Proprietors, editors and reporters of these papers must have had knowledge of the fact that in Cleveland, O., Youngstown, O., Steubenville, O., Wheeling, W. Va., in Indiana, in all of Illinois except Gary for a period, in Minnesota, in Colorado, strikers' meetings were freely allowed and that violence and rioting did not result. In this, nevertheless, the papers of Pittsburgh found nothing to impel them to question the policy of the officials of their own community. While refraining from public examination or criticism of official acts and the use of the State Constabulary in patrolling and raiding, the papers printed in great number articles designed to prove that " an emergency existed." The evidence consisted of headlined stories of " riots."

Affidavits elsewhere show to what extent residents of Clairton, Weirton, Braddock, Homestead, Donora, Monessen, Farrell and New Castle suffered from the strike-breaking activities of State Constabulary and deputies. Bulletins by the national strike committee emphasizing that the strike was being conducted within the law and that strikers' acts must be lawful, were suppressed by the newspapers, in favor of stories implying that the various communities were in danger because "local authorities could not handle the situation." [1]

During the strike not less than 150 articles and items appeared in the Pittsburgh papers tending to support the contention that the strike was fraught with disorder on the part of the strikers. Over articles which themselves showed an obvious lack of investigation and first-hand information, such headlines appeared as follows:

ONE MAN SHOT; Constables and Strikers Hurt (*Dispatch*, October 22);

1 SHOT, 20 HURT IN BRADDOCK STRIKE RIOTS, MANY HURT IN CLASHES BETWEEN STATE POLICE AND FORMER MILL WORKERS (*Gazette-Times*, October 22);

RIOTING AT BRADDOCK IS QUICKLY SUPPRESSED (*Sun*, October 21);

EIGHT SUSPECTS ARRESTED IN RIOTING AT BRADDOCK (*Gazaette-Times*, October 24);

STEEL WORKERS' HOME BOMBED AT DONORA; FOUR ARE ARRESTED (*Press*, November 30);

FOUR FOREIGNERS HELD ON DYNAMITE CHARGE (*Dispatch*, November 8);

DONORA RADICALS TRY TO BLOW UP HOME AND BRIDGE (*Press*, November 11);

NEWSPAPER AT DONORA THREATENED (*Leader*, October 12);

2 SHOT IN STRIKE RIOTS AT DONORA; SEVERAL INJURED (*Chronicle-Telegraph*, October 9);

DONORA AND ENVIRONS TERRIFIED BY BOMBS—REIGN OF TERROR EXISTS FOLLOWING DYNAMITING OF HOMES AND STREET CAR—FOUR ARRESTED ON 12-YEAR-OLD BOY'S TESTIMONY (*Sun*, November 7).

The contrast between reports of violence as they appeared in the newspapers during the strike and accounts obtained from witnesses is so marked that a few cases should be cited in full. The following citations give first, accounts in the

[1] See "The Steel Strike of 1919": Ignorance; Bolshevism, p. 36.

newspapers and next, the accounts of the same incidents obtained by investigators for the Interchurch Commission. Several of the wildest stories simply evaporated on investigation, no person being found who would vouch for the printed accounts. A " Donora bomb outrage " turned out to be a stick of dynamite exploded under the porch of a striker, not a " loyal worker," apparently in a personal vendetta.

From the *Chronicle-Telegraph* (September 25) :

FARRELL STRIKER KILLED BY POLICE

STATE TROOPERS LOCATE ALLEGED SNIPER'S HOME AND SHOOTING FOLLOWS

Sharon, Pa., September 25 (Special)—Nick Grata was shot and killed shortly after 11 o'clock by state troopers, and his brother, Dan Grata, was shot in the right leg. The troopers had gone to the men's home at 108 French Street, Farrell, Pa., near here, in an attempt to locate a sniping post from which numerous shots had been fired at the troopers and men at work.

According to the state troopers, many shots have been fired from the French Street house to the American Steel and Wire Plant, a short distance away. A careful watch has been kept to ascertain from which house the shots came, and they were finally traced to the one occupied by Grata. This morning four troopers, armed with Springfield rifles, were stationed at different points about the house. Shortly before 11 o'clock a foreigner was arrested when he appeared on the porch of the house. A trooper approached and told him he was under arrest. The man immediately put up a fight but he was overpowered.

A moment later a shot rang out from a window of the house, just missing the trooper who was taking the foreigner to jail. A short time later Nick Grata stepped to the porch and cautiously peered around the corner in the direction where one of the troopers was standing. As he did so another trooper fired.

Dan Grata ran into the yard at the same time and was struck in the leg by a bullet fired by another trooper. He sustained a flesh wound.

Account of the same incident, according to the signed statement of witnesses:

On September 23, about 10:00 A. M., Dominic Gratichini, of 108 French St., was in his own house when he heard shots fired outside. His brother, Nick Gratichini, was at that time near the smokehouse in his yard fixing some tools while Dominic's four-year-old child was sitting on his knee. Dominic Gratichini then came out of his house to get his child, and when he came out he saw state Troopers coming out from the gates of the American Steel and Wire Co., firing shots in all directions. As he approached his brother he found his brother struck down with a bullet in his leg and lying on the ground. He grabbed his little girl and tried to take her into the house when he, too, was shot with a bullet in his leg. His brother then struggled to get inside the house, and as he was half way in the door, he was shot again and killed instantly. Dominic was taken to the company hospital by William Maxwell, foreman of the plant, and his wounds were dressed there by the company doctor. Before he was taken to the hospital his house was searched, and the police would not allow him to attend to his dead brother. Dominic Gratichini has seven children. His wife was about to give birth to a child.

Mr. Frank Weber, a U. S. citizen, of Spearmint Ave. testifies that he had seen the state troopers firing at the above men while they were in their yard.

his

(signed) Dominic (X) Gratichini.

mark

(signed) Frank Weber.

From the *Leader,* October 9, page 1:

TWO MEN SHOT DURING A BATTLE AT DONORA MILL

Donora, Pa., Oct. 9—Two men were shot and a number suffered severe bruises about the head and body today when a mob, attacking a negro mill workman in Eighth Street, this city, was charged by a squadron of state police.

Twelve men were arrested by state troopers after a half-hour of fierce rioting. Several others were rushed to the local hospital to have their wounds dressed.

When the negro workman was attacked, a large number of other negroes came to his rescue and the riot resulted.

State troopers who were hurriedly summoned broke up the fighting, but not until a number had been injured.

The two men who were shot were foreigners and received their injuries previous to the arrival of the state troopers, who, it is claimed, had nothing to do with the shooting.

Neither of the foreigners who received bullet wounds is in a serious condition, it is said.

The rioters refused to disperse upon the appearance of the troopers, and the latter then started using their riot sticks freely, soon forcing the fighters to flee.

None of the troopers was seriously hurt, although many missiles were thrown at them, according to spectators.

Today's rioting was the culmination of a series of near-riots which have occurred here this week since the resumption of work at the plant of the American Steel and Wire Company.

Foreign strikers, it is said, have attempted to congregate daily about the entrances to the plant in an effort to prevent workmen entering the plant.

On several occasions state troopers have been summoned to disperse these gatherings.

The following accounts of the affair were given to an investigator for the Commission on October 11:

Andy Zubchich and John Harashinsky, both of Donora, Pa., and at present at the Monongahela hospital, were standing on the corner of Eighth and Allen Streets on October 9th, about 7:30 A. M., when four negroes came along. Upon seeing them, one of the negroes approached them and the men asked him where he was going. He said: "Follow me and you'll know," and walked on. Then the three other negroes came to them, and, when they were asked where they were going, one, by the name of Lightfoot, drew his gun and began firing shots at them while the men were scattering away. The negro kept on shouting: "Come on, boys, I'll kill every one of the white folks in Donora." More shots were then fired by the negroes, although not a single shot was returned.

The two men mentioned above were shot in the legs and were taken to the hospital. Many witnesses were present who saw this absolutely unprovoked shooting, among these witnesses are: Mrs. Stovicki, 451 Eighth Street, Donora; Mrs. Shefsky, of the same address; Theodore Horich, 82 Allen Place, Donora, and his wife; Mike Holdnick, 72 Allen Place, and Stanley Stryhosfski, 450 Eighth Street, Donora.

The negroes who did the shooting are reported to have been seen walking the streets, and it is also reported that they have been deputized since.

John Karandyewski, Allen Place, Donora, Pa., on October 9th, about 7 A. M., he was crossing the street to buy something when he saw three men standing on the corner of Eighth Street. He then saw three colored men coming up the street. He heard a white man asking the colored men where they were going, the negroes answered: " None of your business, we will shoot you, damn you," and immediately started to fire from their revolvers. One of the white men was struck and fell, while Mr. Karandyewski was struck in the hip. The latter then started to run to the office of Dr. Heatter, while blood was streaming from his leg. While at the office of the doctor, Borough Policeman Magee came in and arrested him and took him to jail. He did not know what he was charged with. Was kept in jail for three days, and although he asked for a doctor to rebandage his wounds several times, which was needed, he was only treated by the jail doctor once, and they would not call his own doctor. After three days in jail he was brought before Squire Ford and released on $500 bail. He claims he still does not know the charges against him.

John Koza, Moralda Street, Donora, saw the above person on the morning of the ninth of October as he was coming down to the station to see a friend of his off to Canada. He advised the wounded man to go to the doctor. Two deputies immediately came over and arrested him. He was kept in jail for three days, after which he was released on $500 bail. He was charged with participating in the riot.

(signed) John Karandyewski,
John Koza.

The following excerpt from a long article lauding the constabulary appeared in the *Press,* page 2, under a three-line, two-column display headline on September 30:

Many interesting stories are told around here of the state troopers. O. J. H. Hartsuff, Superintendent of the Carnegie Plants in Farrell and Sharon, is authority for the following:

"When rioting first broke out here eight days ago a sniper was located in the rear of a building overlooking the plant. It was at night and we could only see the flame spit from a revolver, but the shooter was invisible. The man had to be driven from the place and it was up to Sergeant Jacob Smith, leader of the constabulary, to do it. Smith placed a trooper across the road from the building and then walked under an arc lamp. He was in full view of the sniper, and the latter was not slow to take advantage of it.

"As his revolver rang out a similar flame shot from across the road, and upon examination it was found that the supposed striker had been killed. The trooper had fired at the flame and had driven a shot through the eye of the man with the revolver. Smith was not hit. But the whole affair was ruined the next day. I was walking through the plant with the sergeant when he discovered that he was standing under a crane with a large block of steel attached. Fearing it might break, Smith turned and ran. He was not afraid of a mob or of a shot, but would not take a chance on the crane under which hundreds of workmen walk each day."

The following signed statements were given by witnesses of the affair in question, to an investigator for the commission.

On September 23d, about 7 P. M., John Bauzdak, of 2 French Street, was standing on the corner of Greenfield and Stanton Streets, talking to a few friends. State troopers were chasing up the streets at that time and were firing from their guns. Hearing the shots, Bauzdak turned his face to the street below to find out what it was. As he turned a bullet struck him in the eye and he fell dead instantly.

Jacob Notz, of 610 Louisiana Street, who stood near the dead man, testifies that he had seen the man standing peacefully on the corner and that he was not provoking any disorder whatsoever.

John Bauzdak left a wife and two small children.

(signed) Jacob Notz.

Helen Jesko, 1108 Darr Avenue. On September 23d, about 7 P. M., Helen Jesko went out from her home to go to the butcher shop. When she was returning from her purchase she heard firing up the street. She was running into the yard of a neighbor when she was struck in the leg by a bullet, fired by a state trooper. She was then taken to the hospital in an ambulance and kept there for two days, after which she was cared for by a doctor in the house. Mrs. Jesko has six children. The oldest thirteen years, the youngest one seven months. During her mother's illness the oldest child cared for the youngest.

(signed) Elli Jesko.

During the period of the strike but one article appeared which showed unequivocally that an attempt had been made at first-hand investigation of the disorder and riots. Ordinarily, the cause of the riots was attributed to the strikers as a matter of course. It is significant that the writer of this article, which appeared in the *Press,* page 1, October 8, should have written that the facts in the case were " startling." The article told with some approach to candor how the writer had seen arms and hands and heads plastered up and how she had heard apparently reliable stories of unprovoked assaults by troopers upon both men and women. It is regrettable indeed, that no other Pittsburgh newspaper, followed the example of the *Press* and that the *Press* should have limited its enterprise and candor to one example in three months.

The newspapers of Pittsburgh were the principal means by which color was lent to the claims of public officials and steel mill officials that there was necessity for the suppression of free speech and assembly. If it was to the interest of the steel companies to have the rights of unions and of strikers denied and to have the strikers themselves accused of violence and to have disorder actually created in many instances by officers of the law, then it can properly be said that the Pittsburgh newspapers cooperated to the fullest extent both in the matter they suppressed and in the tendencies of the matter they printed.

VII—*Strike News Colored*

A reader of the Pittsburgh newspapers from September 22 to October 10 must have gained the impression that the large number of men conceded to have gone out on September 22 had done so with no other intention than that of turning round and flocking back to their jobs beginning September 23. The impression that the strike was having little effect on steel production and that the men were returning to work in great numbers as soon as the strike began, was created by printing hundreds of items—quoting named or unnamed mill officials or merchants remotely connected with the strike and items without other cited authority than the newspaper itself. So far as these articles had to do with the number of employees on strike their tendency was the same—to minimize the number of men out and to circulate information that from the employers' point of view the situation was " improving," " satisfactory," or " almost normal."

On the other hand few of the statements issued by the National Committee for Organizing Iron and Steel Workers were given any space at all and only two were quoted at length. Usually such statements, if referred to at all, were mentioned in the body of the article after the headline and lead had made emphatic statements effectively discrediting the strikers' side.

Had the facts been in accord with the impression created by the newspapers, no criticism could hold merely because this impression was favorable to the employers. During the first three weeks of the strike, however, the facts were far different. The best available estimates are that on September 22 about 280,000 men went on strike. During the following week the total exceeded 300,000. By October 7 this number

132

seems to have increased though the estimates of 500,000 increase from strike headquarters seem to have been too high.

During the time that the strike was increasing, the Pittsburgh papers gave the impression that it was waning. Within three days after the strike began they printed articles that the strike was broken. Throughout the strike the newspapers continued to print articles that purported to tell of the number of men who had returned or who would return. Some of the mills which the papers specified as operating " almost normal " within a few days after September 22 were again specified by the same newspapers as gaining large accessions of men a month later. By adding the newspaper estimates and predictions of the " men who had returned to work " a statistically-minded union official of Youngstown, O., at one time proved that the newspapers of the Pittsburgh district had informed the public that 2,400,000 men had " gone back to work " in the steel industry, in which about 50,000 are normally employed.

Owing to conditions in the Pittsburgh district it was difficult for newspapers or any other agency to obtain an accurate count of the men on strike. It would seem therefore that a policy of fairness would have required publication without prejudice of the claims made by both sides. At a time when estimates from strike headquarters were being suppressed and when employers were giving out information that the strike was over, one article appearing in the Pittsburgh *Dispatch* (October 1) gave some inkling of the true state of affairs. It was headed:

ONLY NOISE, STRIKERS SAY OF ACTIVITY

It included the following statements:

Meanwhile, newspapermen were negotiating with Carnegie Steel Company and Jones and Laughlin officials for permission to **tour** the Homestead Steel Works and Jones and Laughlin plants to view conditions within the big plants. Efforts also were being made to gain entry into one or two other large plants, but the desired permission was held in abeyance. By some company spokesmen it was held that the presence of visitors in the plants might be demoralizing. There are said to be 15 correspondents of newspapers and news-gathering agencies from outside Pittsburgh here. Apparently they made no better headway than the local talent yesterday in getting at the facts concerning the strike. . . .

Despite the claims of " 100 per cent operation " made by officials of the Jones & Laughlin Steel Company, Foster and several other strike leaders at headquarters yesterday declared the big " J. & L." plants were not operating at more than 50 per cent of normal.

These statements, together with all that could be observed of conditions from outside the plants, indicated that the situation about the mills was not as " rosy " as some steel mill officials have asserted they were.

Two days after the strike, on September 24, the *Leader* printed a first page article under a big display head two columns wide with three lines of type, PITTSBURGH MILLS RUNNING FULL; UNION MEN MEET. The article carried no statement that the Pittsburgh mills were running in full, and the mills were in fact not running in full six weeks later. The article did carry the following statements which were widely at variance with the headline:

In practically every district large numbers of men who were idle during the first two days of the strike returned to work, and some of the steel manufacturers were optimistic enough to declare that the backbone of the strike in the Pittsburgh district had been broken. . . .

The situation this morning, in the view of the operators, was the most hopeful since the inauguration of the strike.

While no reports were received of any large numbers returning, the mill officials asserted that the outlook was promising and they indicated a " walk in " was under way.

On September 24, in the *Chronicle-Telegraph,* page 1, the following statements were displayed in a box with the head-line:

SITUATION GRATIFYING, SAYS CARNEGIE OFFICIAL

In some manner it has got to them (the foreign workmen), that the American workman has not gone out, as the foreigner had been told, and the latter has given expression to the desire to be an American, and in some instances to have resented being called 'un-American.' If this sentiment proves to be general, it cannot but be very hopeful to the entire situation, and that it is at least growing and spreading would apparently be indicated by the gradual return to work.

On September 24, the *Chronicle-Telegraph, Leader* and other newspapers, printed a substantially identical article, containing the statements:

Ninety percent of the Americans employed by the Allegheny and West Penn Steel Companies at Brackenridge were "on the job" early today when the morning shift started to work on the third day of the national steel strike. Less than one percent of the foreigners employed in the plants were at work. . . .

Merchants in the valley town are optimistic today. They de-clare the strike situation to be unusually favorable. Some of them were predicting the complete resumption of the mills *before the week-end.* It was said many of the foreigners, seeing the ac-tivity of the plants and realizing jobs at which they made large salaries, since the start of the world war, were to be taken from them, might desert the union organization.

Here again the point of criticism rests, not in inaccuracies, but in the simultaneous suppression of statements made on the other side. The papers continued to give the impression that there was no other side.

On September 25, page 4, under the headline, WORKERS FLOCK BACK TO JOBS, BRADDOCK REPORTS

THREE TIMES AS MANY WORKING TODAY AS YESTERDAY, MANY PLANTS OPEN, the *Leader* printed the following:

> So well has the question of labor been met, officials say, that another furnace will be put in operation this afternoon or tomorrow morning. . . .
>
> The streets of Braddock and Rankin are practically deserted of strikers, it was stated, and there was no disaster.

On September 27, the *Chronicle-Telegraph* and *Leader* also printed the following:

> Local mill officials expressed the belief that the strike was over so far as this district was concerned, and predicted that Monday would see practically all strikers back at work.

On the same day the *Chronicle-Telegraph* also printed under the headline, REPORT LABORERS GOING BACK ALL THROUGH DISTRICT, the following:

> With breaks in the ranks of the steel laborers being reported all along the line, one of the most prominent steel officials in the Monongahela Valley said today:
>
> "If we start off tomorrow night in as good shape as now the strike is shot."

On October 1 under the headline, STRIKE CRUMBLING, STEEL MEN SAY, the *Chronicle-Telegraph,* page 1, printed the following statements:

> Countless numbers of men today again walked into the mills of the Pittsburgh and Western Pennsylvania district, according to manufacturers, who declared the steel laborers' strike is slowly but surely crumbling.
>
> One leading manufacturer put it in these words: "Resumption of some of the steel plants may be slow, but it is absolutely resistless."

This article was a marked exception to the general rule because it did make some reference to a bulletin issued from strike headquarters. It first made the statements cited above and others showing that the strikers were returning to work in great numbers and farther along in the article printed the following brief summary of a statement, the original of which was itemized by towns and districts:

A bulletin issued by the strike committee here today, for the benefit of strikers, claimed 370,000 men in the industry are on strike. The bulletin asserts the correct view of the situation is not being given by steel manufacturers, and attacks the United States Steel Corporation, which, the bulletin says, is attempting to be bigger than the United States Government. Mills in many places, the bulletin says, are down.

As early as September 27 the *Leader,* page 1, had printed the following prediction:

Local mill officials expressed the belief that the strike was over so far as this district was concerned, and predicted that Monday would see practically all strikers back at work.

The disregard of accuracy and the ready acceptance of information from the employers' point of view with or without prejudice to the striking employees is illustrated by matter published at a later date concerning the situation in Johnstown. On November 12 the Cambria Steel Company posted notices that the plant at Johnstown would resume operations the following Monday. Some of the newspapers printed the information that " 7,000 men had registered their willingness to go back to work. On November 17 articles to the effect that the strike had collapsed in Johnstown appeared in most of the Pittsburgh newspapers under such headlines as these: *Post,*—CAMBRIA STEEL MILLS RESUME TO-DAY, MORE THAN 7,000 MEN RETURNING (this article was from Johnstown, dated November 16, when the mills had not yet opened). *Chronicle Telegraph:*—8,000 JOHNSTOWN STEEL STRIKERS RETURN TO WORK. *Sun:*—8,000 MEN BACK AT CAMBRIA MILL JOBS. *Press:*—8,000 STRIKERS RETURN TO WORK IN JOHNSTOWN STEEL MILLS. On November 19 the *Post* printed another article on the Johnstown situation with this headline, 10,000 CAMBRIA STEEL MEN RETURN.

The whistles of the Cambria steel mills did blow on November 17 for the first time since September 22. An investigator participated in the count of men returning to work. The following is the substance of the observations made:

By count, about 900 men went to work Monday morning. This may be an overestimate; on account of the Sheriff's " strike zone " orders it was not possible to get near enough to the gates to be sure that all the men counted were actually going to work. During the day nearly half of these came out. On Tuesday between 3 and 3:45 P. M. (when the 8-hour shift came off, of which there are normally 3,000 to 4,000), at the subway gate, 35 men came out, 5 entered; at the lower gate, same time, 3 came out, none went in. Between 5:15 and 6:15 (when the 10-hour day and 14-hour night shifts change, of which there are normally 8,000 to 10,000 coming off), at the subway gate, 87 left and 20 entered; at the lower gate 106 left and a few entered, about 12 to 15. Observers reported that the other gates to the mills were not in use.

It appeared that a considerable number of men were being kept in the mills at this time, and an approximate estimate of the men, foremen, bosses, office help and workers of all kinds actually at work in the mill on Tuesday, amounted to about 600.

Two incidents in December illustrate the inaccuracy of the Pittsburgh newspapers in attributing statements to union officials, and it is to be noted that such attributions were never of a sort to give encouragement to the strikers. On December 5, the *Gazette-Times* printed a " Special Telegram to the *Gazette-Times* " under the headline, CONBOY AD-

MITS DEFEAT; QUITS JOHNSTOWN. The article carried the statement, " Conboy admitted the strike was lost." The article carried a dateline of December 4, which was Thursday. On the following day, December 5, a conversation was held with Thomas J. Conboy, the strike organizer at Johnstown. He was still in Johnstown and while he was contemplating a trip to Pittsburgh on Saturday, he was determined to stay in Johnstown as long as the " Citizens Committee " was " trying to run him out of town." Regarding the statement attributed to him that the strike was lost, he said:

" I made no such statement. I have not seen a newspaper man in eight weeks."

On December 5 the *Press* carried on the first page under a Wheeling dateline an article sent out by the Tri-State News Bureau. This article had the headline, REPORT STEEL STRIKE WILL BE CALLED OFF, and carried the statement that the National Committee of the steel strikers had decided after a two-day meeting to call off the strike. The article cited John M. Peters, secretary of the Wheeling strike committee, as authority and quoted him as saying he could not give out anything further till evening. Over the telephone from Pittsburgh on December 5, Mr. Peters said that he had not made any such statement, that he had no information whatever that the strike was to be called off, and that he did not know that the National Committee in Pittsburgh had held a two-day meeting.

The *Press* and the *Dispatch* may be regarded as exceptions to the statement that the tendency of the Pittsburgh papers as a whole was to help break the strike by printing opinions overwhelmingly on one side. Neither of these papers appears to have been active in printing articles designed to discourage the strike. At the same time they did not, with the exception of one article in the *Press,* show an inclination to investigate independently. While the *Press* and *Dispatch* showed less initiative in getting " news " and printing articles favorable to the employers they did print a good many such articles and the strikers' side found little, if any, more space in their columns than in the other newspapers. *The Gazette-Times,* the *Post* and *Sun,* were not far behind the *Leader* and the *Chronicle-Telegraph* in printing that the strike was ineffective.

VIII—*The Press and the Pulpit*

During the strike the newspapers of Pittsburgh prominently displayed the sermons, addresses and statements of both Protestant and Catholic clergymen when these utterances were in accord with the policy of the United States Steel Corporation and especially when they alleged that the strike was of Bolshevik origin. At the same time the papers had opportunity to, and did, suppress preachers' statements and sermons which criticized civil officers in Allegheny County and appealed for fair American treatment of the foreign born. It would have been difficult for the public to believe that there were many clergymen who were not in accord with the views favored by the press.

On October 6 under the headline, SAYS RADICALISM IS MENACE TO FREEDOM, DR. ALEXANDER IN FIRST POST-VACATION SERMON DECLARES IT DESTROYS IDEALS, the *Chronicle-Telegraph* printed the following:

Radicalism is a menace to freedom and is destructive to all the ideals toward which men must strive.

This was the central idea which the Rev. Dr. Maitland Alexander elaborated in his first sermon in the pulpit of the First Presbyterian Church, since his vacation. The sermon was preached last night.

The rest of the item, about twice as long as the foregoing, was devoted to news of church anniversary celebrations. This particular item is important only in showing that the tendency of the press was to give space to all matters big and small which might discredit the strikers' cause.

On September 22, under the headline, MINISTER IN-DICTS STRIKE LEADERS, the sermon of the Rev. P. Molyneux, pastor of St. Brendan's Roman Catholic Church at Braddock was quoted at length. The sermon denounced the strike and strikers. Subsequently Governor Sproul wrote an approving letter to the Rev. P. Molyneux. This, too, was given considerable publicity. In a circular letter to the strikers, the Rev. Adelbert Kazinci, pastor of another Roman Catholic Church in Braddock, approved the strike, called upon the steel workers to support it and criticized the statements of Father Molyneux. This circular letter received no publicity.

On October 6, the *Chronicle-Telegraph* printed statements opposed to the strike by the Rev. Father Henry Geibel, pastor of the St. Charles Roman Catholic Church at Donora under the headline, STRIKERS URGED TO RETURN TO WORK BY DONORA PRIEST. Previously the same newspaper had printed a long letter from the Rev. Thomas Devlin in which Father Devlin denounced the strike. This letter was carried under the headline, ORGANIZERS OF STEEL STRIKE ARE BRANDED AS RADICALS BY LOCAL CATHOLIC CLERGYMAN. At about the same time Catholic priests were expressing equally strong views in support of the strikers' cause, but these were not reported in the Pittsburgh press. [1]

Throughout the period of the strike one of the features of the *Leader* were the articles appearing at intervals from the pen of the Rev. L. A. Carroll, of St. William's Church, East Pittsburgh. These articles carried big display headlines such as:

BOLSHEVISM MEANS CRUCIFIXION OF OUR AMERICAN LIFE.

WITH STRIKE ENDED PUBLIC OPINION WILL FORCE REAL LOVE FEAST.

[1] See "The Steel Strike of 1919": The Twelve-Hour Day, p. 83.

MUST BEAT BACK THE RED VISION OF BOL-
SHEVISM HERE.

LOOK BOLSHEVISM SQUARE IN THE EYES AND
MEET IT WITH AN OFFENSIVE.

The effect of these articles was invariably to encourage the
belief that the main issue of the strike was the question of
Bolshevism.

Though apparently it did not appear in the Pittsburgh
press it should be noted that an article by the Rev. William
M. Woodfin, of the First Presbyterian Church at Homestead
appeared in the New York *Tribune* on October 2. In this
article Mr. Woodfin defended the position of the United
States Steel Corporation under the text, THE ALIEN
STEEL STRIKE.

The Pittsburgh newspapers gave no hint of the fact that in
some localities, notably McKeesport, mill officials had taken
occasion to present to the preachers the point of view of the
employers and to ask that sermons be preached from that
point of view. [1]

A final example of partiality shown by the Pittsburgh press
appears in connection with " An Appeal to Americans " issued by the Pittsburgh Council of the Churches of Christ.
The Pittsburgh Council embraces the Protestant Churches of
all denominations in the district, and is an old established
organization which had been silent throughout the strike.
The appeal was adopted by the Council on November 28. It
was read from nearly every Protestant pulpit in Allegheny
County on Sunday, December 14, and it was sent to all the
newspapers of Pittsburgh with the request that it be published Monday.

Mention of this appeal appeared in only two morning
newspapers of Pittsburgh. The *Dispatch* printed a large
part of the appeal, in small type on the fourth page and with-

[1] See Report on the Pulpit and the Strike.

out the introductory paragraphs, perhaps the most important of all in view of conditions in the district. The *Post* reduced mention of the appeal to a few paragraphs which appeared on the fourth page and concluded its article with paragraphs about the denunciations of radicals by Congressman S. D. Fess in the First Presbyterian Church, Wilkinsburg.

The " Appeal to Americans " is here given:

We appeal to you in behalf of our neighbors of foreign birth.

They are among us in large numbers. Thoughtless and mistaken policies toward them at this time will bring grave consequences, both for them and for us. Unfortunately the evidence is unmistakable that some erroneous policies are being followed.

These people in the main are open-minded, honest, industrious, peace-loving. They are mostly from the peasantry of Europe, a stock possible of development into excellent citizenship.

But they have come from a culture foreign to American ideals and customs, and so cannot be expected at once to understand our ways or accommodate themselves to our manner of life. The fact that they have voluntarily come to us, shows a desire on their part for our culture that merits constant patience on ours.

Many of them have come as refugees, seeking freedom from various forms of oppression in other lands. To them America has been an idealized country, a land of freedom, of opportunity for all, a government by all people in the equal interest of each, a place where all the people meet on a plain of mutual helpfulness.

A tragic feeling of disillusionment is now sweeping over great numbers of these people. They are saying: " We have been deceived. The American people do not want us to have opportunity for the best things, they want us to be their hewers of wood and drawers of water. The American Government is like in kind to those from which we have fled, there is not equal justice at court for the poor man. Let us go back to the lands from which we came. America has proven a disappointment. There has been a change at home, it may be better there! "

If these people thus go, it will be a tragedy, both for them and for us. For them in further disappointment they will encounter; for us in the loss of those who might have become good citizens here, and in the scattering thus throughout the world of people filled with embittered feelings toward our country.

It is idle for us to condemn foreigners for misunderstanding us and our institutions. The only wise thing to do is humbly to examine our own record to find wherein we have made this misunderstanding possible.

We have done so by herding these people in separate settlements, in communities apart. Towns have been built with separate sections for foreigners and Americans; foreigners have generally been discouraged from dwelling in American communities; they have seldom been welcome to our gatherings.

We have done it by our civic neglect. We have left these people to receive their interpretation of America from the lowest type politicians, saloon keepers and dive keepers, who seek them only to exploit them.

We have done it by our industrial policies. We have put these people, coming from the farms of Europe, at the menial tasks of our great industries, and we have not made it easy for them to rise out of that condition.

We have done it by the condemnation of all foreigners because of the wrong-doings of comparatively few. When Radicals among them, burning with hatred for their home governments, have turned against the American Government, many of us have condemned foreigners as a class and treated them in a way that made vastly more easy the course of the Radical in winning them.

We have done it by a hysteria which, acting in the name of the law, has sometimes made the law itself hateful to them. Mobs of so-called "best citizens," in the sacred name of patriotism, have taken the law in their own hands against Radicals, and thus set glaring examples of anarchy by their own actions. Testimony before the Senate Committee investigating the Steel Strike, led that committee to say of some things done here in the name of the law, that "Treatment by the officers has been brutal, and their treatment in the courts does not accord with the high ideals of American democracy."

We recognize the presence of some aliens in our midst who have come wholly for selfish purposes and as enemies of our American institutions, and we would have no one misconstrue this statement in such a way as to soften our utter condemnation of their treasonable and insidious attacks upon that which we hold most dear.

Yet the church would be derelict and censurable if it were to remain silent at a time like this, making no protest against these errors so fraught with potencies of evil. We therefore appeal to our fellow Americans for a different course and for prompt and earnest efforts to correct the evil already done.

We appeal to civil officers to be exceedingly careful not to be unjust.

We appeal to employers to give to their employees time and encouragement for cultured life.

We appeal to the public to treat foreigners with the same courtesy shown to an American, and to be real neighbors to them, patiently helping them to learn our language and to arrive at all that is best in our American life.

We appeal to members of the American churches that they manifest a real Christian attitude toward these people, many of whom have revolted against churches which they considered tools of tyranny in other lands, and in so doing have swung far into hostility against religion itself. This state of mind cannot last. Let us, by act and word, so interpret to these people the mind of God that, when their fundamental religious nature shall again assert itself, we shall be in position to help them find Him and find peace and joy for their souls.

IX—*Conclusions*

It is inconceivable that the public which relied on the Pittsburgh newspapers could, by any human method of reading newspapers and allowing both for exaggeration due to bias and inaccuracy due to haste, have understood either the causes of the steel strike or the significance of its incidents.

Readers were well informed of the position taken by the chief spokesman for the United States Steel Corporation, and the newspapers never questioned the impression that the only "moral" issue favored the side of the Steel Corporation.

The effect of the "news" treatment of the strike was to create the overwhelming impression and prejudice that the strike came about through the pursuit of unreasonable demands, inspired by revolutionary motives. The real issues of the strike were not printed. Extensive space was given to the "red book" of Foster, which was in no sense an issue or a factor in the organization of the strike.

A policy of antagonism to the strike was adopted by the Pittsburgh newspapers without a pretense of previous investigation. It was sustained mainly in the following ways:

(a) by the acceptance of impressive and lucrative advertisements without regard to the merit of statements contained in them.

(b) by representing that the men on strike were chiefly radicals or revolutionists, whereas sections of the main report show that the strikers had almost no understanding of economic theory but a desire to better their immediate industrial status.[1]

(c) by silence as to actual industrial grievances and by publishing statistics in a misleading way.

(d) by silence on the issue of free speech and assembly after ac-

[1] See "The Steel Strike of 1919": Grievances, pp. 136-43.

cepting without apparent investigation the charge of local officials that repression and a denial of ordinary rights to strikers was necessary because of the existence of an emergency.

(e) by accepting and publishing accounts of violence and disorder from the employers' and officials' point of view without investigation of such incidents.

(f) by publishing inaccurate statements of the number of men on strike and of the number of men returning to work, thus giving the public and to some extent the strikers themselves the impression that the strike was so uncalled-for as to be misrepresentative of the steel workers; by encouraging the strikers to abandon their protest and to return to work through inaccurate statements and inaccurate predictions as to the mills that had already resumed operations and were about to resume operations; by "coloring" the news through the publication of statements issuing from one side chiefly.

(g) by effectual suppression of news whose tendency would have been to inspire a fair-minded examination of repressive conditions in the Pittsburgh district.

The policy of avoiding investigation was apparent even when the facts which might have been ascertained might have reacted against the strikers' side of the dispute. No investigation, for instance, was undertaken to establish whether or not there were cases of intimidation on the part of strikers in their efforts to keep those who wanted to work from returning to the mills. In this matter as in most others, the newspapers accepted such accounts as were given by the police or other authorities. Similarly, the press made no attempt to determine and to publish the point of view of the clergymen of Allegheny County. They gave much prominent space to such statements, letters, and addresses as came to hand, when these were in opposition to the strike. On the other hand, despite the generally accepted importance of the problem of the foreign-born, and despite the newspapers' own demand for "Americanization," the virtual suppression of the "Appeal to

Americans " of the Pittsburgh Council of Churches, marked a distinct departure from well-established newspaper policy, to the disadvantage of the public interest.

The Pittsburgh papers were not only a failure as a public institution during the strike; they committed overt acts of support for policies which were against public interest.

Comparison of the Pittsburgh papers with those of other cities may begin by showing certain differences which indicate how far the Pittsburgh papers departed from customary practice.

In many other communities, such as New York and Chicago, the newspapers did not go to the same extreme in suppressing actual news of the strike in favor of articles indicating that the strike had come to an end almost before it was under way. In such newspapers as the Chicago *News* and the Chicago *Tribune* the statements and protests of labor organizers were printed at least briefly.

A dispatch from Gary, Ind., in the Chicago *Tribune* on November 3 was of a kind finding no space in the Pittsburgh press. This quoted a labor organizer's speech telling the men that the strike would be won and that the strikers would get their jobs back while the " scabs " would be discharged.

Most Chicago papers printed the usual current reports about " reds " and " radicalism " in a way likely to prejudice the public against the demands of the strikers, but they did not withhold all the news which, if carefully read, might have enabled their readers to reach some understanding of the strike.

The New York papers also printed news which could not have obtained space in any of the Pittsburgh newspapers. The New York *World* printed an unusual series of news articles by a competent special correspondent. Its news columns contained, for example, an account of the testimony before the Senate Committee on Education and Labor during the sessions in Pittsburgh, which was described as follows by a member of the Committee for Organizing Steel and Iron Workers: " The account was fair and just. It was based on the evidence, not on what was in the reporter's mind. It might seem even that the heart of the reporter who wrote it had been touched by what our witnesses had had to tell at that hearing."

Both the New York *Sun* and the *Times* gave first page publicity to a mass meeting at Madison Square Garden at which $165,000 was subscribed by members of the New York City trades unions for support of the steel strike. No account of this meeting with details of what happened could be found in the Pittsburgh newspapers, and all news which would have given the Pittsburgh public intelligence of the fact that the strike was being supported either by the sentiment of mass meetings or by actual contributions was, as a rule, suppressed in the Pittsburgh papers. By way of illustrating the difference in the attitude of the press of Pittsburgh and of newspapers elsewhere (which were likewise against the strike in policy), the headline and "lead" of the *Sun* article is worth quoting. The headline was:

FOSTER'S PLEA BRINGS $165,000 — STEEL STRIKE LEADER STIRS 5,000 AT MADISON SQUARE GARDEN MEETING—UNIONS PLEDGE $315,000—RESOLUTIONS DENOUNCING DEPORTATIONS ARE ADOPTED—GATHERING IS ORDERLY.

The " lead " of this story read as follows:

William Z. Foster, the steel strike secretary, told 5,000 members of the New York City trade unions in Madison Square Garden last night the story of his ejection from Johnstown, Pa., on Friday, and then, with hands outstretched and his head thrown back, dramatically asked: " What are you going to do about it? "

In a remarkably short space of time the crowd gave in the neighborhood of $165,000 in actual cash and immediate pledges of $315,000. To augment the cash donations tin basins were passed through the crowd. Just how much this collection amounted to was not known. But the basins were spilling over and derby hats were rushed into the breach.

The New York *Sun* of October 8, 1919, printed the following special cabled interview with Lord Northcliffe:

CLOSED SHOP NOT AN ISSUE IN GREAT BRITAIN
By Lord Northcliffe

I can see no connection between the tremendous upheaval we have just gone through (the railway strike) and hundreds of strikes taking place throughout the United States. There is no question of the recognition of the labor unions in this country. Every skilled worker belongs to a union and his employers want him to. Ten years ago, when I acquired the control of the *London Times,* this ancient institution was what is known as an open shop. It had never allowed Trade Unionism. I expressed my urgent wish to the mechanical staffs that they should become members of the various labor unions to which they are attached, and there are now members of fifteen different labor unions working in this and every other newspaper office in Great Britain.

I believe that the labor unions make for smoother relations. Without the labor unions our strike last week would have been a civil war. It was the control of the men by their leaders which made it a peaceful struggle. . . . Any comparison between labor in the United States and Great Britain is irrelevant. That your men should be striking for the recognition of the labor unions seems to us like going back to the Middle Ages.

This dispatch in the opinion of Pittsburgh newspapermen certainly could not have been reprinted in Pittsburgh during the strike.

But these differences were not the main characteristic of the comparison. The general agreement betweeen the impressions conveyed by the Pittsburgh newspapers and the run of newspapers elsewhere was the more noticeable fact.   Pittsburgh editors during the strike did not, on the whole, feel themselves out of agreement with the rest of journalism in this country.   When certain specimens of steel news in outside papers were pointed out to Pittsburgh newspapermen and were conceded to be " too stiff for Pittsburgh," the Pittsburgh newspapermen were almost always able to point to Philadelphia, New York and Chicago headlines (and specially editorials) quite like theirs.   Readers of Pittsburgh papers, traveling out of town during the strike, did not immediately feel that papers elsewhere were giving a different impression of the strike or that readers elsewhere notably disagreed with Pittsburgh readers' conceptions.

Comparisons were made between Pittsburgh and outside papers' treatment of specific episodes in the strike.   When newspapers in Pittsburgh on the first two Saturdays of the strike were headlining that the mills would reopen full on the following Mondays, most newspapers in New York [1] had similar trends, though much more fairly put.   The New York *Times'* headline for September 27 read:

BREAK IN STRIKE
EXPECTED MONDAY
BY STEEL PLANTS

Carnegie Steel Reports Strikers
Returning   to   Work
In Larger Numbers

Union Still Denies Losses

Foster Disappointed Because
Organized Labor Withholds
Sympathetic Strike

[1] Again the *World* was the exception.

The differences were differences of degree. Similarly on October 6, the New York *Tribune's* headline ran:

6 MORE PITTSBURGH MILLS
REOPEN AS STRIKE SUBSIDES

State Police at Monessen Arrest
20 Pickets and Timid Workers
Are Regaining Confidence

All Plants Now Running

Effort at Resumption Not
Made in Ohio, Where
Strikers Are Armed

As a rule the news was of *the same general types.* There were no headlines such as: " Steel Workers say they work 7 days a week "; or " Half the Steel Workers are on the 12-hour day "; or " Steel Common Laborers declare they cannot earn enough for families "; or " Steel Workers Demand Way to present grievances in Mills "; or " Workers demand right to hold union meetings." And yet all these things were facts, they were news, they constituted the news which explained the strike, they were the " news peg " of daily happenings, and they were all more or less accessible to reporters. Too rarely were such facts gathered up and systematically and convincingly thrust upon reporters by the strike leadership; too often that leadership was merely helpless before the conditions imposed by newspapermen or antagonistic because the papers were perceived to be hostile. But the essential facts, *which were found by others during the strike,* could have been gathered at the time by investigating newspapermen, if searching investigation had been what the newspapers wanted.

First-hand investigation of phases of the strike by experienced observers appeared in the *Survey* (reports of Miss Adele Shaw and John A. Fitch) during the strike, and in the

Metropolitan Magazine (article by William Hard) after the strike. These did not at all agree on points of fact with the accounts in the run of American newspapers. The latter lent themselves rather to support of the very misleading editorials in the New York *Times*. When the *Metropolitan* afterwards advertised itself as having " torn the camouflage off the steel strike " it meant the camouflage put there by newspapers generally.

The Pittsburgh newspapers were simply a more emphatic example of policies which convince labor that the press is unfair to labor during a strike. The record of the Pittsburgh papers was not such that critics could point to most other papers of the country as a great contrast. The discrepancy between the accounts in the small labor press and the accounts in most of the daily newspapers was such as to accentuate divisions in American society. In many parts of the country labor papers began declaring that the steel strike " showed up the press " once and for all. To what extent such conclusions create division is illustrated in the following from the Wheeling *Majority,* owned by labor unions. It is taken from resolutions passed by the Wheeling District Mill Council at its meeting of October 18:

Whereas, We . . . believe that aside from stereotyped dispatches, misleading statements given the Press by those Employers who lose the most through this strike, Editors have clearly proven their partial and personal attitude in the steel strike, by a continual attack upon labor, its proven labor leaders of honesty and integrity, and the causes for the strike, never attacking the combination of men, pledged to control the steel markets, the labor market and even the Government itself, the unwarranted and brutal attack upon the men on strike, their wives and children, that they may hope to break the strike by, and

Whereas, We have knowledge that the Public Press fear to be impartial in this strike and give an unbiased, true account of actual conditions,—be it therefore

Resolved, That we, the affiliated Trade Organizations named below, representing the Wheeling District Allied Mill Workers' Council, which is also the General Strike Committee representing the twenty thousand steel workers on strike in this district vigorously protest against the partial attitude of the Press, and be it further

Resolved, That we call upon and urge our Constituents to sever their subscriptions to such unfair newspapers at once until such time as the public may be given the truth of an impartial nature towards the workingmen on strike, and be it further

Resolved, That these matters be immediately brought before the membership of the said named organizations and by unanimous action thereon, place such publications on the "We don't patronize" list and prefer charges against those found violating their obligations.

This was but one of many actions by workingmen in many parts of the country expressing hatred of the press in general, as a "natural enemy," again bared by the steel strike,—some like the above urging the boycott as a retaliatory weapon, others urging the founding of labor papers.

No summary of the policy and tendency of the press as a whole during the strike would be complete without reference to the fact that it was apparently influenced by the national "psychology" developed during the war. This solidarity of opinion, arising naturally from national efforts to "mobilize public sentiment" and to overwhelm obstructionists to the country's war policy, notoriously continued beyond the war and in behalf of others than the government. To it must be attributed in part the fact that many newspapers accepted, as a real issue of the strike, "loyalty," and forbore to make for the public a just examination of the actual causes. Had the strike come two years after the close of the war, it seems probable that the real issues could not have been so completely submerged.

ADDENDA

1. An important phase on which nothing is said in this report is the relation of the Associated Press.

In the past, local situations of national import have, through the dominance of a local press over the local A. P. correspondent, been " colored " for the whole nation. The local A. P. correspondent is generally the employee of a local newspaper. The only safe procedure for the A. P. in great controversial stories like the steel strike is to send in independently investigating reporters from the outside.

Many things indicated agreement between A. P. dispatches from Pittsburgh and the Pittsburgh newspapers. But because conclusions in such a matter should be founded only on detailed comparisons and because such comparisons were extremely difficult, due to inaccessibility of the original A. P. dispatches, no conclusions are stated.

2. An exception should be noted of certain newspapers which are found occasionally in smaller cities than those whose papers have been cited. Frequently they come nearer the old practice of the country's earlier independent press. The Johnstown *Daily Democrat* presented at times during the strike a very great contrast to the Pittsburgh papers. Another example of how different from the Pittsburgh newspapers could be a paper a few miles from Pittsburgh is cited in the following statement by S. T. Hammersmark, the local steel strike organizer at Youngstown, O.:

" There are two daily newspapers in Youngstown, the *Vindicator* and the *Telegram,* both printed in the afternoon. The *Citizen* is considered a company paper. The two daily newspapers were fair.

"No paper, unless owned and controlled by labor, can be expected to be absolutely fair to the labor point of view. There is no possibility of getting straight news from the labor standpoint in newspapers run in the usual way with dependence on advertisers for support, but the *Vindicator* and *Telegram* were independent enough to be fair on the whole.

"These two newspapers covered their front pages early in the strike with false statements that the men were going back to work. So far as the charges of revolution and radicalism were concerned, they printed only the Associated Press dispatches. News from that point of view they cut down a good deal. They did not try to incite to riot. They published a good many stories which were not true, as we knew, and which sometimes they corrected in later editions or concerning which they subsequently printed correct statements from us.

"They did not refuse to print statements issued from strike headquarters. During the first three weeks of the strike, we had a statement in the newspapers every day. They were published along with the mill owners' statements. Many of our statements appeared on the front page along with statements made by mill owners and their representatives. I should say that at least twenty-five or thirty statements from strike headquarters were published in full by these two newspapers, which were throughout so fair in presenting both sides that they were described as our "mouthpiece." In spite of this characterization, nevertheless, the *Vindicator* and *Telegram* printed a lot of matter early in the strike to give the impression that the strike was lost. . . .

Space permits only the mention of the existence of newspapers of this kind. In still smaller steel cities there are a great number of papers which are simply steel company organs. In many places they are the only newspapers. In such cities as Gary, Ind., the steel workers laid more blame for failure on the strike-breaking activities of these company papers than on anything else except the use of armed forces.

3. The so-called labor press of Pittsburgh comprises three weekly publications, the *National Labor Tribune,* the *Labor*

World and the *National Labor Journal.* They are not labor-owned papers.

The *National Labor Tribune* carries on its first page the mottoes: " The oldest and most conservative labor paper in America,"—" Indorsed by every labor organization of national importance,"—" Labor's fearless champion for nearly fifty years." Its November 20, 1919, issue was a fair sample of its " championing."

The full-page streamer headline across the front page was as follows: THE MINERS' STRIKE COMES TO AN END—THE GOVERNMENT STILL LIVES. One of the three leading articles on the front page had a three-line head in heavy type as follows: MINERS COMPELLED TO WALK OUT AND STRIKE WITHOUT ANY GRIEVANCE. Secretary of Colorado Miners Insists on Miners Quitting—Agreement with Operators a Mere Scrap of Paper—Miners Quitting—Miners Pass Resolutions Condemning Leaders—Some Men Average $9.65 per Day, or $2,741 per Year.

Regarding the steel strike the paper printed on the first page in this issue the following:

CARNEGIE STEEL PLANTS NEAR SHARON IN FULL
BLAST

SHARON, PA.—Blast furnace No. 4 of the Carnegie Steel Company was blown in Wednesday.

The Carnegie Steel Company now is operating its Sharon and Farrell works at 100 per cent. All other mills of the United States Steel Corporation are running in the Shenango Valley at full capacity. The Stewart Iron Company's stack here is the only furnace out of 14 still idle.

The advertisements of the *National Labor Tribune* are such as are carried by the daily press which does not pretend to represent labor. The advertisements are those of corporations.

The *National Labor Tribune* began as a genuine labor paper. It was once the official organ of the Amalgamated Association of Iron, Steel and Tin Workers. It ceased to be the organ of this association in 1899, when its policies were exposed at the Amalgamated Convention.

The *Labor World* was started as a private venture when it became known that the *Labor Tribune* would be discredited by the Amalgamated Association, in the hope apparently that it would be chosen as the successor. It was not chosen and has continued as a privately owned publication. It has never been endorsed by the Central Labor Union of Pittsburgh. It is commonly understood that the paper is prosperous with a large income derived from advertisements.

Under the title " The Situation " the *Labor World* printed in its issue of October 30, 1919, the following in heavy-faced type regarding the steel strike:

At present writing the industrial situation, while still menacing to a great extent, is becoming clearer of obstacles in the way of reaching a peaceful stage once again. The steel strike is subsiding rapidly, as the following press dispatch from Chicago a day or two ago would indicate:

Titus, member of the steel workers' council, labor leader and captain of the strikers' pickets at the Gary mills, today made official admission that the great strike has been lost to the union men.

" There is no use pretending." Titus said to Col. W. S. Mapes, in charge of the military occupation.

" The men are going back to work. The strike is lost and the army is responsible."

Reopening of the rail mill today furnished employment for several hundred skilled workers. In the first hour sixty tons of perfect steel rails were made, it was reported. Every department of the big steel plant is now in operation.

From every center of the strike there are daily reports being issued, stating that men are returning to work, and it is safe to say the vast majority of plants are in operation now, more or less.

The *Labor World* carries a weekly financial page largely devoted to advertisements of brokers, banks and dealers in investment securities. In the issue in question there were twenty-five such advertisements on the " financial page." The advertising of the *Labor World* is chiefly derived from financial institutions and corporations.

The following copy of a letter soliciting " patronage "— was sent by the *Labor World* to manufacturing firms in Pennsylvania. The reference to the " exposure " of W. Z. Foster is worthy of note.

Bell Phone 4195 Court   P. & A. Phone 1380 Main
  New York
  Chicago
  Philadelphia   NATIONAL AND RATIONAL
  Cleveland   Advocating a Square Deal Between Capital and
  Cincinnati   Labor
  Youngstown
  Detroit   T H E   L A B O R   W O R L D
  Indianapolis   TWENTY-EIGHT YEARS A SUCCESS
  Toledo
  Portland   General Office: 220-222 Third Avenue
  St. Louis   PITTSBURGH, PA.
  Seattle

Dear Sir:—
We notice that your firm is an extensive advertiser.

Will you support a weekly that is conducting the best directed campaign against RADICALISM, BOLSHEVISM and LABOR UNREST; that reaches more than 100,000 families of the better class of mechanics in the steel, coal and various other skilled manufacturing industries?

We enclose you our rate card, a booklet, and mail you under separate cover a copy of the *Labor World,* showing that we exposed the revolutionary leader, W. Z. Foster, as long ago as last April, and thus helped to avert a world-wide plot to create revolution in the industries of this country.

We are employing the ablest writers, authorities on these subjects, and expect to be reaching over 250,000 readers before the year is out.

We have supplements in foreign languages and make rates for subscriptions in quantities.

We solicit your patronage of our columns. Kindly let us hear from you.

Thanking you in advance for any courtesies extended to us, we are

Very truly yours,
THE LABOR WORLD,
Per ————————
Managing Editor.

The *National Labor Journal* was until recently the official organ of the Central Labor Union, the affiliated group of Pittsburgh labor unions. The endorsement of this paper was withdrawn by the Central Labor Union on November 20, 1919, because of the paper's hostile policy toward the steel strike and the Pennsylvania labor movement. The paper has been privately owned for a good many years. While a few unions have held stock in it, it has not been controlled by labor. The chief owner is David Berry.

The paper is well supplied with advertisements of the kind that appear in the regular daily papers. It did not print as many corporation advertisements during the steel strike as the other papers. Taking the issue of November 21 as a sample of what this paper prints in the way of advertisements, it may be noted that space was occupied by advertisements of corporations and public utility firms.

If the daily press was misrepresentative of the causes and facts of the steel strike, the so-called labor press of Pittsburgh was much more so in view of its pretended concern with the interests of labor.   Labor, in the city of Pittsburgh, has no paper devoted to its welfare and to constructive criticism and suggestion.   It does not appear that the so-called labor papers, in view of plentiful advertisements, are hampered in their activity by financial stringency.

III

CIVIL RIGHTS IN WESTERN PENNSYLVANIA

By George Soule

CONTENTS

INTRODUCTION

The evidence concerning the restriction of freedom of assembly in western Pennsylvania is of three sorts. The denials of permission to hold meetings are matters of public record. Material which bears on the reasons for these denials is partly of public record, partly in the form of testimony by public officials, mill officials and union members, before either the investigating committee of the United States Senate or this Commission, and partly in the form of personal interviews and observations gathered by this Commission and the investigating staff.

A—*Freedom of Speech and Assembly*

I. One of the most striking aspects of the situation in the steel towns has been the denial of free speech and assembly to workmen in Allegheny County and other parts of western Pennsylvania. This denial did not grow altogether out of the strike itself; it existed before the strike, and seems to have as close a relation to the acknowledged labor policy of

163

the employers as to any merely temporary crisis. Local public officials assert that it was necessary to prohibit meetings in order to prevent violence. This statement is open to question, but if it is accepted, still the connection between labor policy and absence of civil liberty remains. Whatever danger of violence there was during the strike arose from the industrial conflict. On account of the long-continued refusal of the employers to deal with organized labor, industrial conflict became inevitable the moment workmen began to assemble for the purpose of forming unions. If, therefore, the right to assemble led to the forming and strengthening of unions, and unions led to industrial conflict, and industrial conflict led to breaches of the peace, the only way to prevent violence was, in the minds of the local officials, to prevent meetings. In other words, if the officials were right, the industrial situation was such that civil peace could be preserved only by interference with the exercise of ordinary civil liberties on the part of a large proportion of the population. (See opinion of Judge Kennedy of the Allegheny County Court on the action of Mayor Crawford of Duquesne.)

The denial of permission to meet was exercised before the strike by the Burgesses or Mayors of the boroughs or cities. Most of these communities have laws prohibiting meetings, even indoors, without a permit from the authorities. Meetings in the streets or elsewhere outdoors can of course be broken up by use of ordinances forbidding the obstruction of traffic, or other similar ordinances common in American municipalities. Just before the strike was called, the action of the local officials was supplemented by a remarkable proclamation issued by Sheriff Haddock of Allegheny County. A well-known attorney has stated that there is no legal escape from either of these restrictions, since the city ordinances regulating meetings have been tested and found constitutional, and the Sheriff's proclamation can be attacked only on the ground that the situation did not warrant it. With the local officials of the same mind as the Sheriff, as they were in this case, it would be practically impossible to prove in court that the Sheriff's action was unwarranted.

AUTHORITIES' JUSTIFICATION FOR DENIAL OF CIVIL RIGHTS

II. The denial of the right of assembly is a fact concerning which no doubt exists; it is freely admitted by the public officials. Their justification for the denial is that violence might have resulted if meetings had been permitted. This assumption should be examined in more detail.

Did the refusals follow the commission of acts of violence resulting from meetings? Not in Homestead, Duquesne, McKeesport, Clairton, Monessen, Pittsburgh or most of the steel towns. In many of these places the privilege of meeting was refused at the very beginning of the organizing campaign; in none of them did the refusal follow the commission of any violent act. In one town alone—Braddock—where meetings had been allowed before and during the strike, permission was withdrawn after violence had occurred. This violence, however, was not the result of a meeting; it occurred at the gates of a mill when strikebreakers who had been housed on the mill property were let out for the first time. This event had been heralded in the papers, a crowd of strikers gathered at the gates, and a street fight with no serious consequences resulted. After this no more indoor meetings were held in Braddock, although for weeks before they had been permitted with no evil consequences.

In Duquesne, where no meetings were allowed either before or during the strike, Senator Kenyon asked Mr. Diehl, general manager of the Duquesne works of the Carnegie Steel Co., " Have you had any violence here? " Mr. Diehl re-

plied, " We have had lots of threatening, but no violence."
. . . *Senator McKellar,* " Was there any one seriously hurt or
killed ? "   *Mr. Diehl,* " I do not think so, sir; I do not know
of any."   *Mr. Wharton,* " There was not any one seriously
hurt in the town at all."

In McKeesport a riot resulted from the cancellation of
permission for a meeting on Labor Day, but no violence had
resulted from meetings which had been actually held.

Did violence occur in towns where permission for meetings
was granted ?   Only in the cases of Braddock and McKeesport, above mentioned.   In Homestead for several weeks
meetings were permitted, with certain restrictions.   Mr.
Oursler, general manager of the Homestead Steel Works,
was asked by Senator Kenyon, " Have you had any violence
from these people who are out on strike, Mr. Oursler ? "
Mr. Oursler, " I should say yes; we had a number of individual cases where a man was beaten up and of throwing
bricks through a window, but we have not had any serious
amount of violence."   *Senator McKellar,* " Has any one
been killed here ? "   *Mr. Oursler,* " No, nobody has been
killed."

It is evident from these statements that the sort of mob
violence for fear of which meetings were prevented did not
occur in Homestead.   When meetings were finally prohibited
there, it was on account of a technical objection to remarks
made by a speaker.   (See Homestead record.)

In Johnstown, Pa., where meetings were permitted with
no restrictions whatever, no violence occurred.   The first dangerous threat of violence came from a " citizens' committee "
opposed to the strike, who forced some of the union officials
to leave town.   And near Sharon and Farrell, where the
strikers marched in thousands across the state line into Ohio
in order to hold their meetings, no violence ever occurred during these assemblies.

That the claim of the public officials of Pennsylvania that meetings of strikers must be prohibited in order to avoid disorder and violence was not borne out by the facts is even more clearly brought out by a survey of the strike districts in the states of West Virginia and Ohio made by the Commission's representatives during the tenth and eleventh weeks of the strike.[1]

In Wheeling, W. Va., and its environs, there were about 15,000 strikers and at no time did the strikers have any difficulty in the holding of their meetings. No permits were necessary and no restrictions were ever placed by the authorities upon the kind and place of meeting or the nature of the speaker. Some of the business element protested against permitting Secretary Foster to speak at Wheeling, but the city authorities insisted that he had a right to speak and saw to it that he was protected in this right. Mr. Foster spoke before a large audience and perfect order was maintained, so much so that the city officials were prompted to commend publicly the peaceful and lawful attitude of the strikers.

During the first ten weeks of the strike there was virtually no disturbance in the Wheeling district even of a minor nature. Meetings were held throughout and picket lines were always maintained. Sheriff Hastings previous to the strike deputized a number of strikers as well as thirty-three delegates to the Wheeling Trades Assembly, under the laws of the state of West Virginia. The district organizer of the Wheeling district always wore the badge of the Deputy Sheriff. All meetings of the strikers were opened with religious service.

In Steubenville, O., where more than 8,000 men were out on strike, three or four meetings were held every week. No disturbance of any sort ever occurred in this town. Despite protest from the local Chamber of Commerce,

[1] See "Steel Strike of 1919": Social Consequences, p. 237.

"Mother" Jones was permitted to speak. Perfect peace was maintained throughout this district both in the public meetings and on the picket lines.

About 35,000 men went out on strike in the Youngstown district, and during the first six weeks of the strike—until the November election—the strikers were permitted to hold meetings in the public market. On an average nine mass meetings a week were held. At none of these meetings was there ever any necessity for police intervention, and at no time was there any disturbance at a meeting. Later on, after the arrest of a few of the organizers on charges of "criminal syndicalism," the police tried to forbid public mass meetings, although restrictions were not placed on indoor meetings. The labor people appealed to Governor Cox of Ohio, who immediately interceded in behalf of free speech.

At Canton, O., about 6,000 men responded to the strike call. No difficulties were placed in the way of holding meetings, which were held indoors as well as in the city parks. Among the speakers there were Mr. Wm. Z. Foster and "Mother" Jones, and at none of these meetings was there any necessity for police intervention, or did any trouble occur.

In Cleveland, O., where about 22,000 steel workers struck, from three to six meetings were held daily from the beginning of the strike. At no time was there any police officer present at any of these meetings. No trouble of any nature developed.

When facts such as the above were brought to the attention of Pennsylvania public officials or employers, they almost always replied by referring to the alleged "radicalism" of the "agitators." Was the nature of the agitation such that it made reasonable an expectation of violence?[1] The investigators have not been able to find traces of any such agi-

[1] See "The Steel Strike of 1919": Social Consequences, p. 236.

tation. A thorough examination of the complete files of materials sent out by strike headquarters has failed to reveal any incitement to violence. At the numerous union meetings which the Commissioners and the investigators attended, no inflammatory remarks were made. On the contrary, both literature and speeches frequently urged the strikers to obey the law and to be careful not to cause any trouble.[1] Perhaps more significant than all is the fact that in spite of the close watch kept by the authorities, none of the important union speakers or organizers has been convicted of incitement to riot or of any similar misconduct. That the character of the speakers had little to do with the privilege of meeting is demonstrated by the testimony of Mr. J. G. Brown, an organizer of the American Federation of Labor, before the Senate Committee. Mr. Brown had asked Mayor Crawford of Duquesne whether a permit would be issued for a meeting to be addressed by Secretary Frank Morrison of the American Federation of Labor. Mayor Crawford replied, " No, Jesus Christ cannot come in and hold a meeting here in Duquesne. It won't do any good to send anybody out."

STRIKERS' OPINION OF CAUSE FOR DENIAL OF CIVIL RIGHTS

III. The union officials and strikers, on their side, believe that the right of assembly was denied for the purpose of defeating the organizing campaign and helping to break the strike.[2] In any strike, morale is a highly important factor. If men cannot meet together, receive information and encouragement from their leaders, and make plans, their power of collective action is seriously impaired.

Where was the denial exercised? In western Pennsylvania, and chiefly in Allegheny County. Allegheny County

[1] See Report of Under-Cover Man, this volume.
[2] See " The Steel Strike of 1919 "; Social Consequences, p. 238.

produces a large proportion of the steel of the country; it is
there that the greatest basic mills of the United States Steel
Corporation are located.   In the early days of the strike,
news dispatches stated that both sides admitted that the cru-
cial struggle would be fought out in the Pittsburgh district.
It was generally reported that if the United States Steel Corporation could keep its great mills at Homestead, Duquesne,
Braddock, Clairton and McKeesport running at normal capacity, it would weather months of a strike successful in other
localities.   It was in these very towns that the most determined efforts to prevent meetings occurred, and toward the
end of the strike all meetings were prohibited in each of
them.

When did the denials occur?   As we have previously demonstrated, not as a rule following upon violence or threat
of violence, and not solely after the strike itself had created
a tense situation.   In Homestead no labor organizing meetings had been permitted since the union was destroyed in
1892, and it took a long legal fight to secure what limited
freedom of assemblage was eventually permitted there during the organizing campaign.   This was taken away after a
few weeks had failed to bring all the strikers back to work.
At Duquesne no meetings were permitted during the organization campaign or after it.   In McKeesport permission for
meetings was first denied months before the strike.   After
strong pressure a few meetings were allowed, but permission
was denied again before the strike was called.   At Clairton
similar difficulties were encountered by the steel workers.   At
Braddock more freedom was won, but it was taken away, as
previously related, after the strike had been in progress for
several weeks.

The way in which public officials and private interests
seemed to work together to prevent meetings also gives color
to the view of the union men that a concerted effort was be-

ing made to deny the right of assembly in their towns.   In Duquesne, for instance, the union received permission from the owner of a vacant lot to hold a meeting on it.   They then applied to Mayor Crawford for a permit, and the permit was refused.   The men, nevertheless, wishing to make a test case of it, went to the lot at the appointed time.   They found on it new "no trespassing" signs.   They were told the lot had just been purchased by the Carnegie Land Co.

In Homestead during the organizing campaign Mr. J. G. Brown, for the union, rented a hall, and then went to the borough authorities to see if a permit to hold a meeting there was necessary.   His story, in testimony before the Senate Committee, is as follows:

"I saw the Burgess in company with another man and asked him if we could hold the meeting. He said, 'Well, you cannot hold any meeting in Homestead.' I said, 'Why not?' He said, 'In the first place, you cannot get a hall.' 'Well,' I said, 'We have a hall, we have got a hall all right.' 'Then,' he said, 'what do you want of me?' I said, 'We want to arrange to have a band play on the street and distribute some advertisements.' He said, 'There will be no bands play on the streets of Homestead and no advertising done.' I said, 'Well, now, could we not pass cards around to the houses, or something of that sort?' 'No, sir,' he said, 'you cannot pass anything in any way.' 'Could we not advertise in the papers,' I said. 'Oh, yes,' he said, 'if you want to; if you can get the space. I don't think you can get the space.' So the matter dropped at that, and the next morning I was called and told that a mistake had been made, that the hall had been rented to some one else, and was rented to me by mistake, and they very much regretted the proposition, but they would have to cancel that lease."

Mr. Brown had paid for the hall, and held a written receipt.   The union men had a similar experience in Braddock.   They, therefore, decided to hold their meeting in the adjoining borough, Rankin.   The Burgess of Rankin gave his permission, but when the men arrived at the hall they found a placard on the door reading, " Closed by the Board of Public Health." After meetings had been forbidden in McKeesport, the men went across the line into Glassport, where the local authorities had no objection to meetings. Thereupon Sheriff Haddock of Allegheny County intervened and forbade meetings in Glassport on the ground that it would not be fair to the Mayor of McKeesport to permit meetings in an adjoining borough when they had been forbidden in McKeesport. Mr. Eugene Junker, who had charge of renting the Birmingham Turn Verein Hall in the South Side, Pittsburgh, told one of our investigators how pressure had been put on him to stop strikers' meetings there. First a large sum was offered him, he was then threatened and called pro-German and anti-American, and at length the interested parties tried to rent the hall through a third person. It was after every such effort had failed that Mayor Babcock of Pittsburgh prohibited meetings on the South Side. Mr. Junker said that there had been no disorder at the meetings or following them, and that the speakers warned the workers to obey the law.

It was such occurrences as these which led the union men to the conclusion that private interests and public authorities were working together to prevent meetings.

This conclusion was strengthened by a knowledge of the connections of many of the public officials. Sheriff Haddock of Allegheny County was a brother of the manager of the American Sheet and Tin Plate Company's plant at Farrell, Pa., a subsidiary of the United States Steel Corporation. Mayor Crawford of Duquesne was president of the First National Bank, and brother of the president of the McKeesport Tin Plate Co. Mr. Moon, president of the Borough Council in Homestead, was chief of the mechanical department of the Homestead mill. Burgess Lincoln of

Munhall, where the Homestead works are situated, was a superintendent in the mill.   The Burgess of Clairton was a mill official, etc., etc.

The absence of the right to assemble naturally had its result in the non-effectiveness of the strike.   In the Pittsburgh district, where civil rights were denied, many more of the highly skilled American-born failed to strike than in Johnstown, Wheeling, Youngstown or South Chicago, where civil liberties were not abrogated.   In Duquesne, where no meetings were held at any time, Mr. A. F. Diehl, general manager of the mill, testified that about 1,400 men out of 5,700 employees struck on September 22, and that most of them were back by September 26.   In McKeesport, where only a few meetings were held, the strike lasted a little longer and was of larger proportions, but collapsed after a few weeks.   In Clairton, Homestead and Braddock, the effectiveness of the strike was similarly proportional to the amount of civil liberty permitted.

LOCAL POLITICS

The question may be asked why local governments are so hostile to the workmen, although they are elected by popular suffrage.   The most important element of the answer is bound up with the question of naturalization.   Many of the workmen have never become citizens, because of their inability to learn English and attend to civic duties while working twelve hours a day, seven days a week.[1]

Often political candidates are themselves members of the mill management having the power of discharge, but in any case the superintendents and foremen take an active part in electioneering.[2]   The moment any subordinate in the mill begins actively to oppose the political machine, he becomes

[1] See " The Steel Strike of 1919," p. 12.
[2] *Ibid.*, p. 238.

a marked man.   Some one is likely to ask him why he is wantonly sacrificing his chances of preferment in the mill. If his defection is aggravated and important, he is likely to be discharged.   This is particularly noticeable in the case of candidates for Judge of Elections and similar offices.   No one has an interest in securing such office unless he is acting for a group who are concerned in the success of certain candidates; the remuneration itself is slight and the expense and trouble of being nominated according to law are enough to make an ordinary citizen reluctant to accept the nomination.   In the case of any votes of which the machine is not sure, another device is at hand.   According to the state law, any voter who says he does not understand how to mark his ballot may ask a bystander to help him, and the two men may enter the booth together.   There are always watchers from the mill lounging about the polls.   The chances of corruption—either through threat or through bribe—which are latent in this possibility are obviously large.   In short, the prestige and power of the dominating industry is so great that political opposition rarely grows beyond its primitive stages.   An observer of long residence in Pittsburgh declared that the only thing that would make the steel worker independent in politics was a union capable of protecting him from discharge.

B—*Arrests, Assaults and Police Brutality*

Aside from the larger issues of free speech and free assemblage involved in the steel strike-bound communities of western Pennsylvania, the strike also brought out more forcibly than ever before the actual status of the abstract individual rights to life, liberty and the pursuit of happiness, as well as the rights of self-defense, and the security of home and property.   At the very beginning of the strike, charges of brutal assaults and attacks were made by the strikers and their leaders against the State Constabulary, the Deputy Sheriffs and the Company Guards. The first audible protest against these violations from an outside person came from the Rev. A. Kazinci of Braddock, when he wrote to Governor Wm. C. Sproul and described in detail the assault of State Troopers upon his people as they were coming out of church; and the driving of horses by the same State Police upon little children as they were assembled in the school yard. Numerous charges of assaults and attacks were also brought out before the United States Senate Committee at its hearings in Pittsburgh, when scores of men and women under oath recited instance after instance of unprovoked attacks upon them by the State Police and mill guards.

A little later, President James H. Maurer, of the Pennsylvania Federation of Labor, denounced the action of the State Police in several public speeches. Governor Sproul challenged Mr. Maurer's assertions and the latter then sent a letter in which he repeated his charges and inclosed over one hundred sworn affidavits of men and women as proof of his charges. As the Governor made no reply, the Pennsylvania Federation of Labor called a special convention in Pittsburgh for the purpose of taking action looking to the restoration of civil liberties and to finding some means to put a stop to what, they were convinced, was an attempt to discard all law and order in the strike regions. This convention then declared for a general strike in Pennsylvania, if the state authorities failed to restore civil liberties to the strikers.

In these circumstances, it was obviously essential for the Commission to make first-hand study and canvass of the nature of these charges and the extent of such practices. Investigators as well as several of the Commissioners visited the separate communities in order to ascertain from the complainants themselves the nature of their charges. The towns of Braddock, Butler, Donora, Farrell, Homestead, Johnstown, McKeesport, Monessen, Natrona, New Castle, and New Kensington were visited, and for the purposes of comparison, Wheeling, W. Va., Steubenville, Youngstown, Cleveland and Canton, O.

The information obtained in Pennsylvania towns concerning police brutality and the action of the magistrates and justices of the peace, includes over two hundred affidavits and signed statements or statements made by strikers and eyewitnesses in the presence of investigators. Declarants generally wanted to swear to their testimony, but in several towns the only notaries were connected with the steel companies and no service was obtainable.

It was impossible to check up many of these statements against public records: in many cases no public records or merely perfunctory ones existed. Some of the statements deal with events covered by sworn testimony before the Senate Investigating Committee, some of them tell of occurrences described independently by a number of witnesses. With others the effects of the wounds caused by bullets and bruises on heads and arms were still visible, while many had certificates from their physicians corroborating their words.

Except in a single instance the strike leaders in the different communities never learned in advance of the coming of the investigators or of their purposes. Most of these affidavits were obtained by joining strikers' groups casually in the different communities. Other affidavits which were sent to Governor Sproul by President Maurer of the State Federation and were presented to the United States Senate Committee are included in the report, but only after re-examination of them in conference with Mr. Maurer's investigator. Not more than one day was spent in any of the towns by the investigators, and on several occasions two or three nearby towns were covered in the same day.

In most instances, a line of men and women ready to testify and swear to their accusations had formed and had to be broken up when the investigators left. This investigation took place over a month before the strike ended, and as arrests continued, it is obvious that the cases here reported by no means represent the sum-total of those who claim to have been maltreated.

The charges brought against the State Constabulary, Deputy Sheriffs, and Company Police, deal with the murder of men and women—one as he was in his own yard—and the wounding of hundreds of others; the clubbing of hundreds; the assaulting of men while lawfully and peacefully pursuing errands on the streets, and of prisoners while they were locked up in their cells; the arresting and holding of men and women for long periods in the jails and police stations without provocation, and even without definite charges being lodged against them; the excessive punishment meted out to these strikers by the different Justices of the Peace, Burgesses and Police Courts, and the frank discrimination in the courts between those who were at work and those who were out on strike; the frequent surrender of law and its administration by the public authorities to the local company officials.

In a few towns the public officials made flat denials of the charges of unwarranted arrests and assaults, as was done for example by the head of the State Constabulary at Braddock, to a member of this Commission; other officials such as the Sheriff and Chief of Police of Newcastle admitted that of about one hundred persons arrested during the first week of the strike at least forty were held without bail " as suspicious persons," and that these would be held " until the strike is over, even if we have to build a new jail to house them." Moreover, the same constabulary officer in Braddock who had asserted in November 19 that all acts were legal, was arrested the latter part of November and held for court under $2,000 bail on charges of assaulting arrested persons while in their prison cells.

In general, a survey of these affidavits by the individual towns reveals certain well-defined methods of procedure adopted towards the strikers by the local authorities. In a measure, those methods have been an indication of the effectiveness of the strike in these communities. In Monessen, where the strikers held out solidly for a long time, with the exception of the arrest of many Russians on vague charges of " radicalism," the policy of the State Police was simply to club men off the streets and drive them into their homes. Very few were arrested. In Braddock, however, where some of the mills were partly operating, the State Police did not stop at mere beating. Ordinarily, when a striker was clubbed on the street he would be taken to jail, kept there over night, and then the Squire or the Burgess would fine him from $10.00 to $60.00. In Newcastle, the Sheriff's deputies carried the Braddock policy much further. Many of those arrested in Newcastle, who had lived in the town almost all their adult lives, were charged with being " suspicious " persons and were ordered not to be released until the strike was over. Others were released in Newcastle after they furnished bail ranging from $500 to $2,500 each. The other towns in western Pennsylvania generally followed one of the methods described above.

The summary of these charges alphabetically arranged by town with a few typical affidavits are reproduced here:

Note: The language used in many of these documents is " interpreter's English." Many witnesses could not speak English. Generally after a lengthy examination of the witness, a brief statement, summary or affidavit would be written out in English, translated back to the witness by the interpreter and after final correction signed by the witness.

Braddock, Pa.

During the first few weeks of the strike, meetings were permitted in Braddock on certain days of the week. Although no trouble occurred at any of these meetings, the strikers were prohibited, by the middle of October, from holding any further meetings in either Braddock or the adjoining borough of Rankin. By the end of November at least one hundred and fifty strikers had been arrested in Braddock. Several men were shot, some badly wounded. The Braddock affidavits charge that men were clubbed over the head and arms, dragged from their own cellars, arrested without any provocation in their own homes, or while on their own porches, beaten while they were being taken to jail, and assaulted in the police station. Men and women, it is charged, were attacked on church steps; children were endangered by horses in the school-yard; men who were arrested were fined from $10.00 to $60.00 on the pettiest charges and even on no charges.

An Interchurch Commissioner spent half an hour talking with strikers in the little room used as an office for the union organizers. A moment after his departure State troopers rushed into the place demanding " that speaker " and threatened to close the headquarters because " a meeting " had been held.

Typical Braddock cases are contained in affidavits 1 to 24 inclusive, consisting of sworn and signed statements of strikers and witnesses as well as certificates of physicians who attended to the injured: of these No. 6 is given here. A transcript of part of the minutes of the Borough Council is also included.

COMMONWEALTH OF PENNSYLVANIA, } ss.
COUNTY OF ALLEGHENY,

Before me, the subscriber, a Notary Public in and for said State and County, personally appeared Benny Maiorowski who being duly sworn according to law, doth depose and say that he lives at 1024 Washington Avenue, Braddock, Pa., and that on Tuesday, 23rd day of September, 1919, about 8 o'clock in the morning, he was walking up Ninth Street from the American Steel & Wire Company after drawing his pay envelope, and while on the corner of Willow Way St., waited for another friend who was coming up with his pay. As he was standing there, a State Policeman ran up to him and ordered him to move on. As he was moving, the policeman started clubbing him over the back without any provocation whatsoever. After he crossed the street, another State Constabulary man run up and began to club him and as Mr. Maiorowski ran up to the steps he drove him off and continued clubbing him until the corner of Washington Ave., about a block away.

Mr. Thomas J. Petrovic of No. 30 Ninth Street, Braddock, Pa., a citizen of the United States, testifies that he had seen this clubbing as described by Mr. Maiorowski.

and further deponent said not.   (signed) *Benny Maiorowski.*
                                    (signed) *Thomas J. Petrovic.*

Sworn and subscribed to before me
   this 10th day of October, 1919.
      (signed) *Frank P. McBride*
         Notary Public (SEAL)

STATE OF PENNSYLVANIA, } ss.
COUNTY OF ALLEGHENY,   }

Before me, the undersigned, personally appeared Frank Bandursky, who being duly sworn according to law deposes and says that the facts set forth in the foregoing affidavit of Bennie Majorosky are true and correct and that deponent witnessed the attack by the State Police upon said Bennie Majorosky, as above set forth in the foregoing affidavit.

(signed) Frank Bandursky.

Sworn to and subscribed before me
this 1st day of Oct. A. D. 1919.

   A. F. Kaufman, Notary Public,
   My Commission expires February 24, 1923.

That the State Constabulary were not desired and were not needed in Braddock is evidenced from the following minutes of the Braddock Borough Council, held on October 6:

" Mr. Verosky (Member of Council) : ' Mr. Chairman, the Citizens of the borough wish to know by whose authority the State Constabulary were called into Braddock to take up their quarters here and to practically relieve the police of their duties, by patrolling the streets on foot, mounted, and always under arms.'

" Mr. Holtzman (President of Council) : ' Surely, I do not know who called them into town, but, were I the burgess, I would make it my business to find out, in view of the fact that the constabulary is neither wanted, nor needed, here.' "

Butler, Pa.

In Butler the authorities permitted the holding of a limited number of meetings indoors, but the speakers had first to be approved. The charges of assault brought against the State Police in Butler come not only from strikers but from non-strikers and business men as well. The State Constabulary are charged with molesting business men and invading their property. They are charged with attacking a crippled person on the street, who could not run fast enough to suit the pursuing officers; and with clubbing a man over the head because he did not move while a horse's hoof was on his foot. It is charged that an attempt was made to incite strikers to riot in order to find means of intimidating them. Strike organizers charge that they were arrested by company guards without warrants, robbed of their belongings and locked in cells without even the permission to consult their attorneys.

Typical Butler cases are contained in affidavits 25 to 31, which include some of the documents forwarded by James H. Maurer to Governor Sproul. Nos. 27, 28 and 31 are printed here:

October 3rd, 1919.

Jacob Saguta,
21 Bessemer Ave.,
Lyndora, Penna.

On August 25th 1919 after receiving my pay I was standing looking in a store window. State trooper No. 52 rode his horse

up on me the horse stepping on my left foot. Trooper ordered
me to move on, as the horse was on my 'foot I could not move.
He then struck me across the head with his club cutting a gash
in the left side of my head that the doctor took three stitches to
close up the wound. After hitting me with his club he kept
chasing me with his horse.

(signed) Jacob Saguta

Sworn and subscribed before me
this 3rd day of October 1919.

E. P. Peffer,
Justice of the Peace.

My commission expires January 4, 1920.

BUTLER, PENNA.

Butler, Pa., Oct. 3, 1919.

James Torok,
Store Keeper,
103 Standard Ave., Lyndora, Pa.

On about August 15th 1919 I saw State Troopers chase a crippled man who could not run, as fast as his horse, and run him
down, the horse bumping him in the neck with his head, knocked
him down; later three men were coming to my store to buy some
things, the State Troopers run their horses right on them and
chased them home; one of the men stopped and said; "I have to go
to the store," and the Trooper replied; " Get the Hell out of here
you — — — or I will Kill you," and started after them again, and
the people ran home and stayed away from the store.

(signed) James Torok.

Sworn to and subscribed to before me
this 3rd day of October, 1919.

E. P. Peffer,
Justice of the Peace.

My Commission expires Jan. 4, 1920.

(SEAL)

---

1 Andrew Binko,
33 Pierce Ave.,
Lyndora, Penna.

On August 25th, 1919, State Trooper No. 52 attacked me on
the street of Lyndora, was going from my home to the office of
the company to get my pay when State Trooper attacked me,

without even saying a word to me; struck me across the right
arm with his club, causing me to carry my arm in a sling for
several days, at the same time tried to ride over me with his
horse.

(signed) Andrew Binke (X his mark)

Witness:

Frank Guccy.

Sworn and subscribed
before me this 3rd day
of October, 1919.

E. P. Peffer,

Justice of the Peace.

My commission expires Jan. 4, 1920.

(SEAL)

Clairton, Pa.

In Clairton, on the Sunday before the strike, numerous
men and women were assaulted by the State Constabulary
and arrested while they were attending a mass meeting for
which permission had been given by the local authorities.
Workmen in the uniform of discharged soldiers were among
those at the meeting ridden down by the State Troopers and
an American flag carried by the discharged soldiers was torn
down and trampled by the State Police, according to the affidavits.   It is charged that men were beaten up while locked
in cells of the Clairton police station.

The cases are contained in affidavits 32 to 54, of which
Nos. 32 and 40 are printed here:

CLAIRTON

MR. P. H. GROGAN

Arrested on Sunday, September 21st, $1000 bail

Permission was given me to hold the meeting by Burgess Thos.
E. Williams, and he suggested the spot where the meeting was
to be held.   Six previous meetings had been held on the same
permit.

I was sitting listening to the speaker looking on the floor, when
all at once there was a commotion, and six policemen came gal-

loping up, beating people and cursing. One rode down to the front, but couldn't get onto the platform as the people were so thick he couldn't ride through. He didn't come up to where I was, but there was a flag in front and he (State policeman —— No. ——) grabbed the flag and threw it down on the ground. Just at that time there was a commotion back of the platform; women and children screamed; another state policeman came riding down on these people; they were standing against the fence and were pressed so hard against it that 50 or 75 fell through in all sorts of shapes. This drew my attention, and I saw how they were beating the people up with clubs. I again turned my attention to State policeman ——, who acted like he was either crazy or drunk. He started to shoot, and the people were scrambling as fast as they could get away. He emptied the gun more than once—I couldn't tell how many shots. His horse fell, perhaps the flag pole tripped him.

He got to shooting the people for trying to get up the hill and get away. A few tried to grab up something to throw. I walked back up on the platform and called to the people to cut out throwing and go away. The policeman pointed his gun at me, but I looked straight at him and told him not to shoot. He didn't shoot at me, but started to shoot in the other direction.

Horses were standing up on their hind feet and there was much confusion and noise. There were lots of women and children— many children in baby carriages.

When I got down from the platform I forgot about the flag, and someone said "there is your flag." It was about 20 feet away. I started to get it and Fred Young said "Where are you going?" Then he said he would get it for me, which he did. They then took us up to the Clairton police station.

We were at that station about 7 hours without anything to eat, although we asked for something several times. Then we were taken in a car to Pittsburgh. Several times we made requests along the way for something to eat, said we would pay for it, but the officer in charge refused to do so.

We were kept in the County jail until 10:45 Wednesday morning, and let out on $1000 bail each put up by the Union. I am an American citizen and was discharged from the Steel Company on account of joining the Union.

P. H. Grogan.

STATE OF PENNSYLVANIA,⎱ ss.
COUNTY OF ALLEGHENY, ⎰

Melon Terzich being duly sworn according to law deposes and says that at North Clairton, Allegheny County and State of Pennsylvania, on Sunday the 21st day of September, 1919, he was present at a meeting of steel workers held on a vacant lot between 3 and 4 o'clock P. M. and then and there saw State troopers rush on the lot and the people started to run away. But when the state troopers rushed to the platform and tore down our flag that the men became incensed and some ex-soldiers seeing our flag being insulted and defiled rushed at said troopers in defense of our flag, and started the excitement and almost caused a riot, and that all good and loyal citizens were greatly incensed. That there was no provocation for said interference and riding over women and children.

Melon Terzich.

Sworn and
Subscribed before me
this 29th day of September,
1919.

Charles A. Lewis,
Notary Public.

My commission expires March 31, 1923.

(SEAL)

Donora, Pa.

The Donora affidavits relate to men who were shot by armed negro strike-breakers who were later reported to have been deputized. Here also men were arrested and given excessive fines and prison sentences on petty charges or when no charges were booked against them. The affidavits charge that men were thrown into cells and kept there several days before they were given a hearing; that a man was robbed by State Troopers of his pay. The State Police are charged with attacking strikers while they were walking or standing peacefully on the streets or in business places. The State Police were also charged before the United States Senate Committee with the taking of a woman with her two little children to the police station from her own home. The arbitrary methods practised in this town may be illustrated from the arrests made on December 5 after an explosion was reported. The State Constabulary, the documents charge, rode into head-quarters of the strikers, drove the men out and placed the ninety-eight men present, including the local organizer, under arrest, and refused to release them on less than $500 bail each. The police then closed the strikers' commissary and soup kitchen. Typical cases are contained in affidavits 55 to 72 inclusive, of which Nos. 56, 60, 61, 69, and 72 are printed here: _____

October 9, 1919.

At about 7 A. M. this morning, Mrs. Kropik was standing on her property looking at State Trooper No. A 45. One of the Troopers followed this woman into the house which terrorized the entire family who had just got out of bed and were not dressed. This Trooper caught hold of Mrs. Kropik and the husband pleaded for him to not take Mrs. Kropik to jail. Then said Trooper used a club on Mr. Kropik's chin and injured him. He bled considerably. At hearing before Squire Ford the evidence was so scanty that Squire Ford acquitted Mr. & Mrs. Kropik and children who were taken along.

Signed, with other affidavits, by

Wm. Feeney and Louis Tomayko, organizers.

See also U. S. Senate Committee Investigation, v.II, p.789.

_____

William Tokos, Meldon Ave., Donora, says that on October the 29th about 4:30 P. M., he was coming out from a bowling alley, and stopped on the Street for a while. Two State troopers then came over and ordered him to move on; as he started to obey the orders the Troopers drove their horses upon them, and he ran back inside the bowling alley. The Troopers followed him inside, searched him and altho found nothing upon, took him to jail where he was kept for 38 hours and then fined $17.25. He was charged with "*Laughing at the State Police.*"

(signed) William Tokos.

DONORA, PA.

October 9, 1919.

Ella Syrko of 633 Third St. at about 7:15 A. M. told Trooper to go to bed and not bother around her house. Trooper swung her against the door breaking it in. This woman is in a delicate condition. Mary Tupiak, 605 Third St. and Elizabeth Sickles, Witnesses.

(Above signed by Wm. Feeney & Louis Tomayko, Organizers.)

Charleroi, Pa., October 11, 1919.

Before me personally came Louis Tomayko, and upon oath administered according to law deposeth and sayeth the within enclosed statement is true and correct in every essential to the best of his knowledge and belief.

(signed) Louis Tomayko.

Attest:

Paul R. Nutt (signed)

Justice of the Peace.

(SEAL)

My commission expires first Monday in January 1924.

Geo. Koshel, age 48, and a citizen for more than 20 yr., South Donora, says that on Sept. 30, about five thirty P. M., he was on his way home, on south McKean Ave., when he was arrested by a deputy sheriff and was ordered to come to jail. He protested that he was doing nothing, when superintendent —— of the A. S. & W. Co. came along in his auto and helped the deputies to push him in his car. He was then handcuffed and taken to jail. Late in the evening he was brought before the burgess and charged with refusing to move on, when ordered to do so. He claimed that he was walking and was never told to move on. The burgess then fined him $10 which he paid. Mr. Koshel, has a wife and six children depending upon him.

(signed) George Koshel.

Mike Sava, 623 Sixth St., Donora, and Joe Sava, 545 Castner Ave., Depose as follows:

On Oct. 9th about 7 A. M. Mike Sava was going to the barber shop on Thompson Ave., when he met his brother Joe on Sixth Street., who was going to his father-in-law's house on Sixth

Street; they started to talk for a few minutes when about six or seven deputies came over and asked them where they were going. They explained to them their business. Without further notice the deputies handcuffed them, searched them, and although found nothing placed them in an automobile which was owned by Mr. ——, paymaster of the American Steel & Wire Co., and a member of the Borough Council, and were brought before Burgess Harry A Cox, who is also master mechanic of the Donora Zinc Works. The Burgess noticed that Mike Sava was wearing a red neck tie and told him that he was a Bolshevik. Sava protested that he is a good Catholic, but to no avail. The two brothers were kept in jail for two days, when they were fined $5.00 each, which they duly paid, and were released.

(signed) Mike Sava.
Joe Sava.

Duquesne, Pa.

Mayor Crawford of Duquesne, who is also the president of the First National Bank in that city and a brother of the president of the McKeesport Tin Plate Company, in addition to his frank announcement that " Jesus Christ himself could not hold a meeting in Duquesne," is also charged with calling together in the early days of the strike the property-holders and merchants of the town and instructing them to make the employees of the steel company pay cash for all their purchases and to pay rent on the first of each month in advance, and to refuse them food and eject them from their homes if they stayed on strike. The strike leaders attempted to hold meetings several times in Duquesne upon a vacant lot which was rented for that purpose. The speakers were all arrested on violation of a City Ordinance forbidding street meetings which was passed in March, 1919, and most of them fined $100 and costs each.

Affidavits Nos. 73 and 77 are given.

DUQUESNE

Steve Bucky
Sam Kelencky
John Batursky   No. 132 Linden Avenue, Duquesne, Penna.
Aleksei Bilenock

The above named persons were all arrested at 5:30 P. M., September 22nd, while sitting on their porch by the Chief of Police of Duquesne. They were taken to the Duquesne jail and told to give bail. Mayor Crawford told them if they go back to work then they will be discharged. They had a hearing on September 23rd, at 8 P. M. Were fined $27.75 each.

Witnesses: Thomas Lasobek
    Nick Prejadoha
    Wasil Zayaz
    Fred Abdosenic
    132 Winden Ave.

DUQUESNE, PENNSYLVANIA.

I am married; age 33; and live at No. 138 Fair Alley, Duquesne, Pennsylvania. I was working at Rod Mill, Carnegie Steel Company, Duquesne, Pennsylvania.

I was arrested in Duquesne September 7th, 1919 and fined on September 8th, 1919, Ten ($10.00) Dollars and costs.

I got a transcript to take the case into Court. The case was to come up Tuesday, September 23rd, 1919. On September 23rd, 1919 at 6:20 A.M. I was arrested while walking on Linden Avenue, Duquesne, Pennsylvania, where I was going to the street car-stop in order to get a car to attend my case in Pittsburg. The police stopped me and asked me where I wanted to go, and I answered him I wanted to go to Pittsburg. He said you are not going to Pittsburg now you are going to another Pittsburg, and he called the patrol wagon and took me and my brother John to the Duquesne police station. I asked him what am I arrested for and he did not answer me. When I was at the police station I asked about bail and the Chief of Police told me there is no bail from you, and I was kept in jail until the next morning when I was fined Twenty-five ($25.00) Dollars and costs. I asked for a transcript and they told me " no transcript until Saturday."

(Signed) Joe Yuha.

Farrell, Pa.

No strike meetings were permitted by the authorities in Farrell. These were held, however, several times a week across the Ohio line, a few miles distant. Unlike other towns where men were mostly clubbed and fined, the policy of the Farrell authorities, it may fairly be inferred, was to "shoot to kill." Thus, in Farrell, two persons were killed outright,—one while on the steps of his own house,—several persons were wounded badly, among them a mother of six children. In spite of the fact that there are plenty of witnesses who saw these killings, no inquiry of any sort was made or attempted by the public officials and no one was held for court. The men who witnessed these shootings state that there was no riot at that time and that there was no provocation of any sort on the part of the strikers. The testimony is in Affidavits 80 to 83 inclusive. Nos. 80, 81 and 82 follow.

FARRELL

On Sept. 23, about 10:00 A.M., Dominic Gratichini of 108 French St., Farrell, was in his own house when he heard shots fired outside. His brother, Nick Gratichini was at that time near the smoke house in his yard fixing some tools while Dominic's four year old child was sitting on his knee. Dominic Gratichini then came out of his house to get his child and when he came out he saw State Troopers coming out from the gates of the Wire Mill of the American Steel and Wire Co., firing shots in all directions. As he approached his brother, he found his brother struck down with a bullet in his leg and lying on the ground. He grabbed his little girl and tried to take her into the house when he, too, was shot with a bullet in his leg. His brother then struggled to get inside the house and as he was half way in the door, he was shot again and killed instantly. Dominic Gratichini was taken to the Company hospital by William Maxwell, foreman of the plant and his wounds were dressed there by the company doctor. Before he was taken to the hospital, his house was searched, and the police would not allow him to attend to his dead brother.

Mr. Dominic Gratichini has seven children. His wife was about to give birth to a child.

Mr. Frank Weber, a U. S. citizen, of Spearmint Ave., Farrell, testifies that he had seen the State Troopers firing at the above men while they were in their yard.

(signed) Dominic Gratichini
X his mark
(signed) Frank Weber.

On Sept. 23d, about 7 P.M., John Bauzdak, of 2 French St., was standing on the corner of Greenfield and Stanton Sts., talking to a few friends. State Troopers were chasing up the streets at that time and were firing from their guns. Hearing the shots, Bauzdak turned his face to the street below to find out what it was. As he turned a bullet struck him in the eye and he fell dead instantly.

Jacob Notz of 610 Louisiana St., who stood near the dead man, testifies that he had seen the man standing peacefully on the corner and that he was not provoking any disorder whatsoever.

John Bauzdak left a wife and two small children.

(signed) Jacob Notz.

Helen Jesko, 1108 Darr Ave. On Sept. 23d, about seven P.M., Helen Jesko went out from her house to go to the butcher shop. When she returned with her purchase, she heard firing up the street. She was running into the yard of a neighbor when she was struck in the leg by a bullet, fired by a State trooper. She was then taken to the hospital in an ambulance and kept there for two days after which she was cared for by a doctor in the house. Mrs. Jesko has six children. The oldest 13 years, the youngest one seven months. During her mother's absence, the oldest child cared for the youngest.

(signed) Elli Jesko.

Homestead, Pa.

During the summer of 1919 meetings were held from time to time in Homestead, the first labor meetings in twenty-six years. The Burgess withheld written permits, but gave verbal ones on the condition that no foreign speakers be used. To this condition the organizers did not agree, but held themselves ready to act according to their own judgment. Once, toward the end of August, foreign speakers were used and thereafter no permits, even verbal ones, were given. The organizers waited one week and in the second attempted to hold a street meeting in front of the Sokol Hall. " Mother " Jones among others was a speaker. The meeting was stopped and J. L. Beaghan, the vice-president of the Allegheny County Federation of Labor; J. G. Brown, organizer for the Pittsburgh district; " Mother " Jones, and Mr. Riley, the district organizer, were arrested on the charge of holding a meeting without a permit. After several delays and postponements the first two were fined $1.00 and costs and Riley and " Mother " Jones were discharged. Another street meeting was held the following week with " Mother " Jones as the speaker. Acting Chief of Police Hood ordered her to stop, which she refused to do until she was through, five minutes later.

At this time the Amalgamated Association of Iron, Steel and Tin workers attempted to hold a local lodge meeting for the purpose of installing the local. The Burgess required that no foreign speakers be used as a condition of granting the permit. This the organizers refused to agree to and the permit was withheld. A writ of mandamus was taken out and the case pleaded before Judge Swearingen, of the County Court of Common Pleas. There Burgess McGuire informed the court that he had no legal authority to issue a permit. Meetings, both local and mass meetings, were held thereafter with foreign speakers until September 22, when the strike began.

Two meetings were held after that when Organizer Riley was notified to get permits from the Sheriff in Pittsburgh for future meetings. The Sheriff informed Riley that he would not prohibit meetings as long as the local authorities would allow them. The Burgess told Riley that inasmuch as the past meetings were peaceful he would not interfere, but that no foreign speakers be used. Riley refused to accept the condition, but did not use foreign speakers. At first he held as many as three meetings a week, but late in November was restricted to two. For every meeting the Sheriff, the local authorities and the state constabulary had to be notified and verbal permits obtained. At the meetings the strike was freely discussed, but not a word of criticism against local, county, state or national authorities was permitted. At practically every meeting speakers were warned or stopped by the deputy or the police who occupied seats of honor on the platform. Picketing was not even thought of.

Meetings were eventually stopped because one of the speakers criticized a public official. The president of the Borough Council of Homestead is chief of the mechanical department of the Carnegie works, and the Burgess of Munhall, an adjoining borough, where most of the strikers live, is a superintendent in the Homestead mills. The sworn testimony of the Homestead residents charges the State Police with not only breaking into peaceful and respectable strikers' homes, in the middle of the night, destroying their property without cause, and dragging men out of their beds half naked, and beating them while being taken to jail, but charges are also made of unwarranted attacks upon respected business men and non-strikers, while on the premises of their property. It is charged that men were held incommunicado in jail, refused medical assistance while in the cells suffering from wounds inflicted upon them by the arresting officers; men and even women it is claimed were beaten for no reasons whatsoever, and persons fined excessively, although no charges were lodged against them. From statement No. 99

it appears that the police power of the city was in the hands of the superintendent of the mill. Statement No. 85 charges that besides the arresting of men without provocation, frame-ups were also conducted by the mill guards in order to increase the number of arrests. Numerous affidavits charge that Burgess McGuire would first ask the prisoners whether they were on strike and why; and then fine them if they admitted they were not working.

In Homestead two Interchurch Commissioners, while driving slowly through the street watching the workers leave the mill at the change of shifts, were first closely inspected by two State troopers and finally stopped by one of the mounted officers. " Seeing that the car was a limousine, they allowed us to proceed," said one of the Commissioners when making a record of his observations in Homestead. " As an American, in contrast with the foreigner, you have the utmost freedom, provided you do not in any way identify yourself with the strikers, and are not clothed as a laborer. However, without apparent reason you may be stopped on the street, hurried on, or questioned and perhaps more closely inspected. So far as those not identified with the Corporation are concerned, not *known* to be ' against the strike,' the atmosphere is one of suspicion and terror. Homestead is not a ' free city ' under the terms of the Constitution of the United States."

Homestead affidavits are Nos. 84 to 113 inclusive, of which Nos. 85, 90, 92, 93, 94 and 99 are printed. Affidavits Nos. 106 to 113 were among those forwarded to Governor Sproul by J. H. Maurer. Other affidavits contained in the United States Senate Report, Part 2, pp. 621-22, charge that citizens in no way connected with the strike were the victims of attacks by the State Constabulary, and of arrests and fines, no charges being lodged.

Frank Lopashanki, 403 S. Second St., Duquesne. Lopashanki says that about 10:15 P.M., Saturday, October 25th, he was sitting on the porch of his house talking to a friend. Two fellow strangers came up and said they were very tired and asked to sit beside them. They said they had come from Youngstown, Ohio. Lopashanki asked how the strike was going there. The strangers replied that the mills were down tight. Lopashanki said "That's very good." The strangers asked "How are things here?" Lopashanki said "Two thousand have joined but some are going back." The strangers then said "It looks to me they be scabs," to which Lopashanki replied "That's the way it looks to me too." The stranger pointed to another man passing in the street and asked "Is he a scab?" Lopashanki said "Yes, he is a scab." The stranger turned back his coat, showing a deputy's badge and said, "Well, if he is a scab I am a scab too," and, Lopashanki says, "grabbed me same like dog," and took him inside the Carnegie Steel Mill, where he was met by several bosses, who asked him if he was a union man. Lopashanki replied, "Yes, I am." "All right we've got you, we've been looking after you two weeks." He was kept in the mill one hour and then taken to jail, where he remained two nights and a whole day until the hearing Monday morning. They refused to release him on bail Sunday. At the hearing before the Burgess, he was charged with "calling the man a scab." Witnesses were refused him to prove that he did not call him a scab. He was fined $27.75. Sunday night, three bosses of the Carnegie Steel Company came to the jail inside his cell, and told him to tear up his union card and go back to work. When he refused, one of them replied, "If you don't, you won't have your job anymore." Later in the evening, the Assistant Superintendent of the Carnegie Steel Co. and the company doctor, ——, came into his cell and argued with him to tear up his union card as "It was no use sitting in jail." To this Lopashanki replied, "Nothing doing." He is married, has two children, has taken out his first papers, and has lived two years in Duquesne.

(signed) Frank Lopashanki.

STATE OF PENNSYLVANIA, ⎫
                        ⎬ ss.
COUNTY OF ALLEGHENY,   ⎭

Before me, the undersigned authority, personally appeared Trachn Yenchenke, who being duly sworn according to law deposes and says that he resides at 327 Third Ave., Homestead, Pa. that on Sunday, Sept. 28, 1919, at about 1 P. M. when the said deponent was in his home and asleep, two State policemen made a forcible entry into the home of deponent at 327 Third Ave., Homestead, Pa. and came to the place where deponent was asleep, woke him up, kicked him and punched him, and handled him with extreme violence and took deponent without any explanation, without permitting deponent to dress, dragged him half naked from his home to a waiting automobile and conveyed him against his will to the Homestead Police Station; deponent was informed that the police were looking for some one who had shot at a certain Peter Luke, for the arrest of the persons being guilty, a reward of $1000, was offered by posters in prominent places by the Carnegie Steel Company. Deponent knows nothing about the matter and so informed the police; nevertheless, he was locked up in the Homestead Police Station, from Sunday afternoon, Sept. 28th, 1919 to Tuesday night 9 P. M. Sept. 30, 1919, after paying a fine to Burgess McGuire the presiding magistrate of $15.10.

Trachn Yechenke.

Sworn and subscribed before me
this 1st day of Oct. A. D. 1919.

    A. F. Kaufman,
    Notary Public.

My commission expires Feb. 24, 1923.

(SEAL)

STATE OF PENNSYLVANIA,   ⎫
COUNTY OF ALLEGHENY,   ⎬ SS.

Before me, the undersigned authority, personally appeared Steve Dudash, who being duly sworn according to law deposes and says that he resides at 541 E. 5th Avenue, Homestead, Pa.; that on Tuesday, Sept. 23, 1919, in the afternoon of said day, his wife, Mary Dudash, was severely scalded, burned and injured by reason of a sudden fright sustained when a State Policeman forced John Bodnar into the home of the deponent and his wife, Mary Dudash, that said Mary Dudash, the wife of the deponent, was in a very delicate condition at the time of the fright and injury complained of, caused by the State Police and that on Sunday, Sept. 28, 1919, following the date in question, namely the 23d, the said Mary Dudash, wife of deponent, gave birth to a child; that on account of the action of the State Police in forcing John Bodnar with terror into the home of deponent and his wife, Mary Dudash, she, the said Mary Dudash, wife of deponent, has been rendered very sick and has suffered a nervous collapse and is still suffering from the nervous shock sustained, on account of the action of the State Police, above referred to.

Steve Dudash (X his mark).

Sworn to and subscribed before me this
first day of October, A. D. 1919.

    A. F. Kaufman
    Notary Public.
My commission expires February 24, 1923.
(SEAL)

STATE OF PENNSYLVANIA,⎫
COUNTY OF ALLEGHENY, ⎬ss.
    ⎭

Before me, the undersigned authority, personally appeared Wasil Bodrick, who being duly sworn according to law deposes and says: that he lives at 216 McClure St. Homestead, Pa. He says that on Friday, Sept. 26, 1919, at about 4 P.M. four State Police and two Borough Policemen entered his home at 216 McClure St. without the consent or permission of the deponent, and then and there demanded of the Boarding Boss on the premises, a hatchet, and when refused the demand, the State Police threatened the occupants of deponent's house and eventually found a hatchet and proceeded upstairs to the second floor, and did then and there without cause, without permission and without justification, and without warrants, or process of any kind, proceed to destroy four trunks on said premises and after smashing same up scattered the contents consisting of clothing all over the floor; said police found no weapons of any kind or character whatsoever, but on the contrary, found nothing but clothing, which was thrown upon the floor. No offer was ever, at any time made to compensate the owners of the trunks for the damage committed by the State Police as complained above, nor does deponent ever expect that any compensation or damages will at any time be paid by the said State Police who are here in Homestead only temporarily. Deponent was not informed, does not know, and is at a loss to understand why his home was entered by the Police against his will and does not understand by what right or for what reason the trunks and property on his premises was destroyed as above stated. The owners of the said trunks destroyed as above stated are all quiet, respectable and peaceable people and deponent avers and says that there was no cause or justification for the violence and unlawful acts of the State Police. Deponent further avers and says that the said acts of the State Police caused great terror to the occupants of the premises.

Wasil Bodrick (X his sign).

(SEAL)

Sworn to and subscribed before me
this 1st day of Oct. A. D. 1919.

A. F. Kaufman
　　　　Notary Public　　My commission expires February 24, 1923.

———

George Kuretka, 1313 Margaret St., Homestead. On Sept. 28th, between 6 and 7 in the evening, as he was walking home, he was handed a bulletin distributed by the union. He walked on reading it, till he reached Library St., where he handed it on to a young man who passed him, and then continued on his journey. The young man then called after him, saying that there was a man who wanted to see him. Kuretka replied that the man should come himself. The young man replied that the man is too busy. As Kuretka walked up, Supt. —— of the Carnegie Steel Co. ran towards him and said, "Is this the fellow?" The young man said, "Yes." The Superintendent then grabbed Kuretka and called for a policeman. Supt. —— told the policeman to take and keep the man in jail over night and he would appear in the morning. The policeman then took him to the police station and told policeman Stevenson, on duty at that time, that —— has asked him to have Kuretka kept all night. Kuretka asked permission to pay bail but this was not allowed. Later he was allowed out on bail and the next day was given a hearing by Burgess Lincoln. He was charged with "throwing bills on the streets" and was fined $13.60. Mr. Kuretka has been a citizen since 1894 and has lived ever since at his present address. He is a member of the Munhall Borough Citizens' Club. He is married and has six children. Kuretka has worked for 36 years for the Carnegie Steel Co.

(signed) George Kuretka.

Johnstown, Pa.

Unlike other towns in Western Pennsylvania, no attempt was made to prohibit meetings of strikers in Johnstown. Meetings were held daily and no difficulties resulted. From September 22, the beginning of the strike, till November 7, while the mills of the Cambria Steel Company were shut tight, there were no disturbances in Johnstown. Picket lines were permitted and maintained without any trouble occurring. On November 7 a Citizens' Committee headed by W. R. Lunk, the secretary of the Y.M.C.A. of Johnstown, as well as a number of other prominent citizens and business men, took it upon themselves to order the organizers of the American Federation of Labor who were conducting the strike—namely, T. J. Conboy, Domenick Gellotte and Frank Kerowski—out of Johnstown. On the same day W. Z. Foster, who arrived there to address a mass meeting of strikers, was forced out of town by a crowd of armed men. The next day Gellotte and Kerowsky were arrested on the streets by the city police and held as " suspicious " persons, and the latter was ordered out of town two days afterwards.

During the first eight weeks of the strike there were no State Constabulary in Johnstown. According to the Mayor and Sheriff of Johnstown, the state police did not come at their request, but at the request of the officials of the Cambria Steel Company. Since the arrival of the State Police in Johnstown, there were many arrests and other forms of intimidation common in steel communities in Western Pennsylvania. Johnstown cases are in affidavits and statements Nos. 128 to 136, of which the following is printed.

Frank Kerowski of Scranton, Penna. an organizer of the American Federation of Labor, came to Johnstown in May, 1919 to help organize the steel workers. On November 9th about 3 P.M., as he was going down to the office, he was arrested by a city policeman who took him to the police station, saying: " The government wants you." When he was brought to the police station he inquired as to the reason of his arrest and was told: " We don't know, we have orders to do so." He was refused bail and kept in jail for about 45 hours when he was ordered to go out of town, by the Mayor. He asked for permission to at least give him time to arrange his affairs in the city, but the Mayor said: " No, you must go right away for your own protection." They then told him that he was charged as a " suspicious character," and that they were protecting his life. The Mayor first ordered him to go back to Scranton, but he protested that as a citizen he at least had a right to choose where to go. He was then finally taken to the station and placed on board a train for Pittsburgh. Mr. Kerowski states that there were at least about a dozen men of the " Citizen's Committee " who followed him to Pittsburgh, in order to watch that he did not return. Mr. Kerowski has been a citizen for the past 20 years and is the father of 10 children.

(signed) Frank Kerowski.

McKeesport, Pa.

Prior to the strike call McKeesport figured prominently in the public press by the persistent refusal of Mayor Lysle to permit steel workers to meet, whether indoors or outdoors. This policy of the Mayor was maintained after the formal request of Samuel Gompers, president of the American Federation of Labor, for the permission of such meetings and a protest from Governor Wm. C. Sproul.

There had been no attempt to suppress meetings in McKeesport prior to the spring of 1918. After that the Mayor prevented the holding of meetings. No meetings were held until the summer of 1919, when through the efforts of City Councilman Thomas H. Howe, three or four street meetings were held in spite of the Mayor's refusal. After the fourth of these meetings the Mayor agreed to allow indoor meetings, and a few of these were held. According to Mr. Howe the Mayor of McKeesport for the last year and a half had not permitted meetings of steel workers. Other meetings of all sorts were regularly permitted. No disorder had preceded the Mayor's refusal. During the Mayor's vacation in August, Howe by virtue of his position had become acting mayor. He granted permits for meetings and there was no disorder. A meeting had been announced for Labor Day, September 1. Mr. A. W. Crawford, president of the McKeesport Tin Plate Co., requested Mr. Howe to stop the meeting. The latter refused. The Mayor then unexpectedly returned from his vacation and canceled the permit for the meeting. Mr. Foster and Mr. Beaghan were present to speak. They requested permission to tell the crowd in front of the locked doors of the hall that the meeting was called off. Permission was declined. Mr. Foster, however, stood up and said, "Boys, the meeting's off," whereupon he and Mr. Beaghan were arrested; after that there was some disorder.

When the strike became imminent the Mayor, it is reported, swore in between 2,000 and 3,000 men to act as deputy police. These were largely recruited from the mill employees, merchants, etc. The policy of suppression went so far as to forbid the meetings of regularly chartered unions at their own meeting halls. After the beginning of the strike the police did not permit the congregation of more than a half-dozen strikers even in their own offices and headquarters. On the first day of the strike men who attended an attempted meeting outside the borough limits were clubbed, arrested and heavily fined. On October 1, 1919, when an attorney and his stenographer attempted to take down affidavits of men who were thus beaten and arrested, the police broke into the hall, arrested the men there, took the attorney and his stenographer under guard to the police station and compelled them to leave town immediately. Affidavit No. 117 is printed here:

State of Pennsylvania, } ss.
County of Allegheny,

Before me, the undersigned authority in and for said County and State, personally appeared Harry Bastow, who, being duly sworn according to law, testified as follows:

I am a shorthand reporter practicing in and out of court, with headquarters at 429 Union Arcade, Pittsburgh, Pa. where I have been located for two years past. On Wednesday, October 1, 1919, by prior arrangement, I went to McKeesport, Pa. to the office of Alderman A. C. Markus on Walnut Street, and reported a hearing in re Commonwealth vs Frank Kiss et al, for Attorney Jacob Roe of Pittsburgh, Pa., who represented the defendants. I also reported the hearing in Commonwealth vs Mike Nagy, immediately following the first hearing.

I then went with Mr. Roe to the meeting place of the workers whom Mr. Roe represented at 416 Market Street, McKeesport, Pa., for the purpose of taking affidavits by several of his clients. I had made shorthand notes of the affidavits of Albert Fillippino, Mike Stefan, Joe Kornak, Peter George, Alex Gamyu, Andy Balog, Steve Barkner, Landor Nagy, Steve Besch and Paul Popovich, transcripts of which are attached hereto, and had commenced taking the affidavit of Frank Kaminski, when the proceedings were interrupted by the announcement from a man at the door that all were under arrest. The room was cleared of men, of whom about thirty-five were present, and the officers approached Mr. Murphy, the district organizer, Mr. Roe and myself and required us to accompany them out of the hall and to the Police Station, where we were taken before Chief of Police Reddington.

Chief Reddington told Mr. Murphy that he thought he (Murphy) had been told to keep the hall closed. Mr. Murphy replied that he knew nothing of such an order, and the Chief stated that the trustees of the hall had been notified and had said that they would see that the hall was kept closed. He required Mr. Murphy to go and see Mayor Lysle, and informed Mr. Roe and myself in response to Mr. Roe's question, that we were not under arrest.

It being impossible to continue the work of taking affidavits, Mr. Roe and myself left McKeesport for Pittsburgh on the first street car we could get.

We had been taken from the hall by one policeman in uniform

and two men in plain clothes, and through the crowded streets. This occurred about four o'clock in the afternoon.

Harry Bastow.

Sworn to and subscribed before
me this 3rd day of October, 1919.

Anna L. Allen

Notary Public

My commission expires at
end of next session of Senate.

(SEAL)

(This evidence is borne out by transcripts of the affidavits referred to, describing the arrests of strikers for attending a public meeting, and by the testimony of Frank Roe, in the report of the United States Senate Committee, Part 2, pp. 597-98.)

Monessen, Pa.

In Monessen neither mass meetings nor lodge meetings on the part of steel strikers were allowed. At the beginning of the strike the Mayor posted the proclamation forbidding meetings of all sorts and closing all " clubs and other places where men gather." This proclamation, while strictly enforced against the strikers, was not enforced in other cases, as certain workers were permitted to meet for the purpose of discussing a petition to return to work, and large meetings in behalf of the League of Nations, as well as other causes, were not forbidden by the authorities.

Monessen affidavits, as well as the testimony before the United States Senate Committee, which was given under oath, again charge the state police with unwarranted assaults upon innocent men and women. Affidavit No. 118 recites that a pregnant woman was beaten and abused by the state police; other affidavits state that men and women were clubbed, arrested and fined, although they state they had done nothing to provoke these assaults. Men tell how they were driven inside the company plants, locked in a cellar and threatened to be hung in the morning if they did not go to work. At least one man will probably be crippled for life through an assault upon him by negro deputies while he was on his own premises. Monessen incidents are given in eight affidavits, of which the following are printed.

MONESSEN

STATE OF PENNSYLVANIA, }ss.
COUNTY OF WESTMORELAND, }

Before me, Henry Fusarini, a notary public in and for said County and State, personally came Concetta Scudieri Cocchiara who, being sworn in accordance to law, doth depose and say, that she is twenty-five years of age and has resided in Monessen for the past seven years and always conducted herself in a peaceable manner and been regarded by her neighbors and acquaintances as a law-abiding citizen:

That she is a married woman (wife of Samuele Cocchiara) and resides at 1008 Morgan Avenue, Monessen, Penna., and, at the present time, she is in an advanced state of pregnancy (8 months) and unable to stand the strain of undue excitement or abuse:

That on Tuesday, the 7th day of October, 1919, on or about 11:30 A.M. as she left the grocery store, on Morgan Avenue, at which she had been shopping with her sister, she stopped a moment in the doorway to see what was being done by the State Police, and two State Policemen stepped up and told her to go home:

She replied to them that she was not hurting anyone, and the policeman then made an attempt to force their horses on them:

That one of the policeman alleged that she had called him a son of a ———, which affiant says is untrue, and that neither to him nor to any other person did she use any language of a vile or opprobrious character or nature; and further she at once, when told, proceeded on her way home; that the policeman followed her and forced himself into the house and struck affiant with a stick on the head and grabbed her by the hair and pulled her from the kitchen to the outside and forced her into the patrol wagon taking her to the Borough Jail.

That at the same time her sister was also struck;

That the committing magistrate gave her no opportunity to call witnesses in her behalf, and, solely on the evidence of the policeman, affiant was pronounced " guilty " and sentenced to a fine and costs amounting to $9.80;

That the statements herein made are true and correct as she believes.

(signed) Concetta Scudieri Cocchiara.

Subscribed and sworn to this
11th day of October, 1919.

(SEAL)

Henry Fusarini
Notary Public

(SEAL)

My commission expires Jan. 20, 1923.

John Komer, 265 Schoonmaker Ave., aged 42, citizen for 24 years and father of two children. On Sunday, Nov. 10th, about 8 P.M., he was sitting at his table when he heard shots fired near his house. He went out to learn what the trouble was and started to talk to his neighbor Krucik who came out for the same reason. He stood there only for a few minutes when two negro deputies came to the steps of his home. Without saying a word, the deputy struck Komer with a gun, hitting his face and eye. Mr. Komer fell against the door. His eye was nearly coming out and he tried to get back in his house when city policeman, Haskell, grabbed him and started to pull him. Mrs. Komer, seeing the blood on her husband and the condition he was in, tried to get him into the house. Haskell then struck and kicked Mrs. Komer. With the aid of negro deputies he twisted her arms and succeeded in taking Mr. Komer away from her. Although Mr. K. was bleeding profusely, he was dragged to the police station. He called for a doctor or to be taken to the hospital. About fifteen minutes later, he finally succeeded in getting some medical assistance. Dr. Israel had to make five or six stitches on his forehead and head. A little later, Mrs. K. was also brought to the police station and Mr. Komer was locked up in the cell and finally released on $25.00 bail.

At the hearing next morning before Burgess Stewart, no charges were made against him. The Burgess asked him why he was not working. He answered he was not working since strike was on. He then fined him $10. Also one of the negro deputies who hit Komer was fined $10 while the other one was discharged. The guns were returned to both negroes after the hearing.

Mr. Komer is laid up in bed under strict medical care. His head is bandaged and there is danger that he might lose his eye.

(signed) John Komer.

On Sunday November 9th, about 8:30 P.M., Mr. George Krucik of 265 Schoonmaker St., Monessen, was sitting in his own house when he heard some shooting outside. He came out to see what was happening. He could not see clearly because it was dark. He then inquired of his neighbor, Mr. Komer, who also came out to discover what was taking place, as to the reason of the shooting. While he was talking with him, a negro deputy who lives nearby, came over with a gun in his hand, grabbed him by his shirt and struck him in the jaw. The negro tore Krucik's shirt off him and Mrs. Krucik who just appeared at that time, pulled him into the house and locked the doors. In about a half hour, a number of policemen came over and placed him under arrest. They took Mr. Krucik to the police station and he was charged with "throwing bricks" on the testimony of the wife of the neighboring negro. He was kept in jail over night and was fined next day $13. Mr. Krucik stated that he was not out of the house that evening until he heard the shooting and did not throw any bricks. Mr. Krucik is 55 years of age and a father of two children.

(signed) George Krucik his (X) mark.

Note: The above two witnesses also interviewed by Commissioner Coleman.

————————

Mr. Paul Yagodisch, 16 Bridge St., Wiretown, Oct. 21st. About 11 P.M., he was coming from Pittsburgh and stopped on Aberdeen Ave. to talk to three of his friends whom he met on the street. Three deputies then approached them and started to arrest his friends. As he was standing watching, two deputies came over and placed him under arrest. As they grabbed him to take him to the police station, he refused to go, claiming that they had no right to arrest him as he had done nothing. He was then kicked and thrown on the ground while a third deputy, who came over, hit him first across the shoulders with a piece of iron pipe and later took a knife out and deliberately cut his head open. While he was bleeding terribly, they took him to jail. Later a doctor was called to stitch up his head. He was kept there over night and next day, later in the afternoon, he was given a hearing. Mr. Yagodisch was charged with insulting colored men on their return from work and resisting arrest. He was fined $12.48 on the first charge and held for court on $500 bail on the second charge. Mr. Yagodisch paid a doctor bill of $7.00. (Doctor's certificate attached).

(signed) Paul Yagodisch.

Doctor's Certificate.

Monessen, Pa.
Oct. 22, 1919.

This is to certify that I attended Paul Yagodisch on Oct. 21, 1919, due to injury to head and face. Sewed cut in head and dressed bruises on face and forehead.

Respectfully,
(signed) James F. Kelly, M.D.
Address 539 Donner Ave., Monessen, Pa.

George Wokaly, 1217 Highland Ave., Monessen.

On Oct. 17th 1919, he was driven into the Tube Mill by State troopers. He was asked if he would sign for work, and if so would be freed. He refused and was locked up. He was finally released on $500 bail.

(signed) George Wokaly.

New Castle, Pa.

On the first day of the strike New Castle witnessed the wounding of a number of men and a child of seven years of age, as well as the killing of a woman, Mrs. Johnson, twenty-five years old, and a mother of two children. Unlike the other towns in western Pennsylvania, the terrorization here was done entirely by the hired guards of the companies, while the state police behaved with fairness and, according to report, arrested a number of deputies. The number of people deputized varies from the strikers' estimate of 1,200 to the admission of Sheriff Boyd, of Lawrence County, that he had deputized over 500 men, " 265 members of the Board of Trade, and the rest ex-soldiers," in addition to the police sworn in under the " coal and iron police " law. At the end of the first week of the strike the Chief of Police of New Castle said that they " had made 100 arrests of strikers during the week," that these were charged with " carrying concealed weapons, disorderly conduct, and suspicion." He said that bail was fixed at from $1,000 to $1,500 and those held on suspicion could not obtain bail. He further stated that of the 100 arrests made, 40 were charged with '' suspicion.'' He said hearings were not being held nor would they be for some time, as " it takes time to arrange cases." He said that those held on " suspicion " would be held ten days at least or for the entire period of the strike, even if he " had to build a new jail to house them."

During the first two months of the strike there were at least three hundred strikers or strikers' wives arrested by the deputies. Affidavit No. 143 charges that Sheriff Boyd deputized men only after they had been inspected by the mill superintendent, and that on several occasions he promised the men in jail to release them immediately if they would return to work. The special deputies are charged with assaulting men and women, with breaking into their homes without provocation, and with arrest of a mother of five little children, without cause. She was kept in jail for several days. Other charges of deputies robbing citizens, of holding men for long periods in jail without cause, and of excessive fines are also included in affidavits and signed testimony. Four of these affidavits were among those forwarded to Governor Sproul by J. H. Maurer.

STATE OF PENNSYLVANIA, }
COUNTY OF LAWRENCE,   } ss.

Before me personally appeared Mr. H. J. Phillips, 630 Superior St., New Castle. Age 35, born in Lawrence County, Pa., who being duly sworn deposes and says as follows:

While standing on the corner of Mill and Washington Streets, and conversing with Harry Dorer and Carl Smith, both of New Castle, about 6 o'clock, on Monday, September 22, saw Sheriff Boyd approach two men who were also standing on the corner, and asked them where they were working. They stated that they were working in the tin mill. Sheriff Boyd then said, " Boys, come along with me down to Mr. Pyle, Manager of the Shenango Tin Mill, and if you pass his inspection we will deputize you into special deputies!"

The men together with Sheriff Boyd then headed towards the mill. The Shenango Tin Mill is a subsidiary of the United States Steel Corporation.

(signed) H. J. Phillips.

Attest:

    J. H. Norrington (signed)
Sworn to and subscribed before me
this 9th day of October, 1919.

    J. Roy Mercer,
    Notary Public.
My commission expires Jan. 29, 1921.
(SEAL)

STATE OF PENNSYLVANIA, }
COUNTY OF LAWRENCE,   } ss.

Before me personally appeared Andy Sabados, Andy Sczmak and Andy Bellock, who being duly sworn depose and say as follows:

On Tuesday the 23d of September about 1:30 P.M. Andy Sabados 12 Balph Ave., Andy Sczmak, 1512 So. Jefferson St., J. Matonak, 123½ W. Terrace St., and Andy Bellock of 1615 Moravia

St., New Castle, were sitting together on the porch of the latter address.   Seven special deputies in the uniforms of the United States soldiers approached them and inquired " What are you hunkeys doing around here, ———— You ————." The men told them that they were boarding there and one of them protested that they had a right to stay on the porch as it was their property.   One of the soldier deputies said, " I'll show you ———— what business I got here" and promptly shot twice into the air.

Andy Bellock frightened ran into the house whither a soldier followed him and struck him twice with his gun on his head.   He then grabbed him by his shoulders and started to hit him with the bayonet on his back.   With his face bleeding terrifically they then took Bellock, Sabados and Matonak to an awaiting automobile and after taking them first to the lockup at the mayor's office they finally brought them to the county jail.   At that time there were about 115 more strikers herded together in the corridor of the jail.   In the evening Sheriff Boyd came to the jail and addressed all the prisoners by saying, " Who wants to go back to work ? " and adding that he will see to it that those that want to go back will be released immediately.   No one in the crowd wanted to go back and more than a 100 of the men were compelled to sleep on the stone floor without any covers or pillows whatsoever.

Next morning the sheriff came again and after asking the same questions told them that they better go to work as the strike was about over and all the men are going back to work. The men could learn nothing about the strike as all the efforts of the local union organizers to secure their release were of no avail, for they have found after calling on about 14 attorneys in the city they had all been deputized by the county sheriff, and could not take up the cases.   Only one attorney in the city was discovered after much efforts to be willing to take up the cases of the strikers.

When Mr. Sczmak, went to see his friends in jail and when he went to the court house to try to find out what had happened with his friends a soldier deputy in the corridor of the court house told him " You can't see the men, and you better get out quick before I'll land you in jail too." After much effort and with the help of an attorney he secured the release of Mr. Bellock, on $500 bail after he had spent about a week in that place, while Mr. Sabados, was released on $500 bail after he had spent ten days in jail.

The scars on Mr. Bellock's head were still visible at the date of testimony more than two weeks afterwards.

his
Andy (X) Sabados
mark

Attest: (signed) Andrew Bellock

Jas. A. Norrington

(signed)   (signed) Andy Sczmak

Sworn to and subscribed before me

this 9th. of October, 1919

J. Roy Mercer (signed)

Notary Public

My commission expires Jan. 29, 1921.

(SEAL)

Statement of James A. Norrington, Hotel Henry, New Castle, Pa.

On September 24, 1919 there was a meeting at the Eagles Club, New Castle, for Americans who were not working. The purpose of the meeting was to vote on a proposition of going back to work. I was invited to talk to the men and explain to them the issues involved in the strike.

When I left the hall, and was on my way to the office while crossing Mill Street at Washington a Deputy ran up behind me and ordered " Hands up," and pushing a gun into my ribs. Almost immediately six or eight deputies in soldier uniforms and one in civilian clothes were around me. One of the soldiers went through all my pockets pulling out my memo books and papers, while another holding a gun in front of my face, said " You ————— of a ————— You're one of these G—— D—— Bolsheviks and we are going to put you where the dogs won't bite you."

They then took me across Washington Street and put me in an automobile, with one Deputy on each running board and one in the front seat and one in the back, and each holding a gun. They brought me to the city lock-up and took me before the police sergeant and asked him if he knew me. The sergeant recognized me and let me go. I then asked the sergeant for protection so that I could get to the office and he sent one of the Deputies along with me. This was a boy not much over 18 years of age, who was dressed in a sailor uniform.

A man named William Bryan, who asked me to speak at the above meeting, was afterwards picked up by a Deputy on Moravia

Street while he was on his way home, and placed under arrest on a charge of sedition and is now held on $1500 bond.

James A. Norrington.

STATE OF PENNSYLVANIA, } ss.
COUNTY OF LAWRENCE,

Before me personally appeared Gabriel Boron, who being duly sworn deposes and says as follows:

Mrs. Antonio Boron, wife of Gabriel Boron, 1611 Hanna Street, financial secretary of New Castle Local Amalgamated Iron Workers; was walking down to the grocery store on the 23rd of September, about 2 o'clock in the afternoon when she heard some shooting in the neighborhood. She stopped, while two deputies dressed in soldier's uniforms, came over, pushed her by the arm and told her to go back home. She protested that she was going to the grocery store and that she had a right to do so. They then grabbed her, shoved her in an automobile, which was waiting. Another woman by the name of Demazo watching this said "We should not let this woman to be taken in jail." The deputies then grabbed her too. After many difficulties in procuring an attorney and approaching the jail authorities, they were released on $1500 bail each, on the 3rd day.

Meanwhile Mr. Boron, while his wife was in jail, was notified that a deputy was over at his home with a warrant to serve upon him. A neighbor woman by the name of Litvinovitz asked the deputies as to what the cause of the warrant was. She was told that Mr. Boron was charged with sedition and that they would shoot him when they get him. When pressed for details they said that once while at work in the shop he threw a couple of gloves at an American Flag, which was near by. Mr. Boron was advised by his friends not to go to his home and after seeing Mr. Cunnegn, his attorney, he was advised to put up $1000 in bonds, although the warrant was never served upon him. A hearing on this case is to be held next week.

(signed) Gabryel Boron

Attest: J. A. Norrington (signed)
Sworn to and subscribed before me
this 9th day of October 1919.

J. Roy Mercer (signed)
Notary Public
My commission expires Jan. 29, 1921.
(SEAL)

Frank Didiana, 701 S. Mill St., New Castle. On Nov. 15, 1919, about 5:30 P.M., he was walking down the street to the grocery store by himself. As he was walking peacefully along, he was struck by a bullet through his neck and shoulders, the bullet going down his back. The shots were fired from inside the gates of the Carnegie Steel Plant. A friend helped him to the Municipal Hospital where he stayed for one week. He is still disabled that he cannot work. The police never made an inquiry regarding this shooting. Mr. Didiana paid $20.00 for an X Ray examination, $50.00 to the doctor and $12.00 for hospital service. He states that at the time he was shot, he was walking by himself and was causing no disturbance whatsoever and saw no disturbance upon the street. He is married.

(signed) Frank Didiana.

On September 23, Mary Pastorak was in her kitchen washing clothes, while her three children were playing about her. About 2:30 in the afternoon, her cousins dropped in to see her, but as Mary was busy washing, they went out to the porch to talk. These men cousins knew that Mary's "man" was away and that she was at home alone with her five children. They, therefore, wanted to look out for her.

As they were seated on the porch, two State Troopers came up. "Do you belong here?" one of the Troopers asked. "sh—Shut up . . ." warned one cousin to the other, thinking it was best not to give unnecessary information.

The Trooper thought that the words "shut up" were meant for him. Mary heard the noise and ran out, (with her baby in her arms) on the porch to find out the trouble. She saw her cousin being beaten up and shots being fired inside the front room. "Why you want to shoot up my place?" she asked. The Trooper disregarded the presence of the mother and child. They entered the house to search. They tore down curtains and broke the flower pots and overturned the chairs. They searched but found nothing.

When they left a bullet was found on the stone hearth under the mantel piece.

Because of the terrorization the children didn't sleep that night. Her smallest boy kept jumping out of bed and crying: "Mother, soldiers come shoot me."

Mrs. Pastorak had bought $500 worth of Liberty Bonds; had given money to the Red Cross as well as to other organizations.

(signed) Mary Pastorak.

Zyzmont Pafuncki, Ellwood City. On Sept. 27th, 1919, he was coming from Ellwood City to New Castle and was walking from Harmony Street car office, going south on Jefferson St. This was about 2 P.M., and as he reached the bridge, three deputy soldiers and another deputy approached him and pointing guns to him, searched him. He had $30.00 in his pockets which they took from him and ordered him to proceed ahead and not look back.

(signed) Zyzmont Pafuncki.

New Kensington and Natrona, Pa.

A meeting at Natrona, held after the strike was called, was suddenly broken up without any warning by deputy sheriffs. The men in the audience were roughly handled and the speakers who tried to quiet the crowd were abused and dragged toward the door. Since then no meetings were allowed in that district by the sheriff. East Vandergrift is the only town in the region of the Allegheny River where meetings have been held. This is due to the fact that this Borough is entirely inhabited by Polish people who work in the mills and where the Burgess, Chief of Police, and town policemen are all on strike.

New Kensington and Natrona and the adjoining towns repeat the characteristics of other Northern Pennsylvania cities. The affidavits charge that a citizen was beaten up by a Slavish State Trooper "just to scare him a little." Homes were broken into in the middle of the night and searched without warrants. Affidavit No. 163 is interesting as throwing light upon the attitude of Sheriff Haddock of Allegheny County, as well as upon the newspapers, who had been featuring stories of plots and explosions. Affidavits Nos. 160, 161 and 163 are here printed.

NEW KENSINGTON

Julian Wisniewski, No. 636 Second Ave., on November 11, 1919, he went to the store on Third Avenue. Was going along peacefully towards the store when he was grabbed by the neck by a State Trooper who asked him what he was doing. He said he was going to the store. Another man in civilian clothes approached and said: "Arrest the son of a ————." As he was grabbed by the neck and almost choked, he protested and said that if he wants to arrest him he would go with him. In reply to this, the Trooper —— only started to twist his hands. When he yelled for help, the other man said to ——: "Make him shut up." He again protested saying that he was willing to go to jail if they wanted to arrest him—that they didn't need to hurt him. He also told them that they could search him. State Trooper —— shoved him back and ordered Mr. Wisniewski to move. Mr. Wisniewski was so frightened and pained that he couldn't move and asked —— to feel his heart. —— did so and said: "Oh, we just tried to scare you a little," and left him. Mr. Wisniewski is a citizen of the United States. He has seven children; has lived in New Kensington for 14 years and is well known in that city.

(signed) Julian Wisniewski.

John Kashmarchik, No. 655 Second Ave., New Kensington, Penna., who is not a steel worker and not a striker, was suddenly awakened about 2 A.M. Monday, October 28th, while he and his wife were in bed. Two State Troopers broke the door after having knocked once, and not waiting for the people to get out of bed to open the door. They had flashlights in one hand and pointing a gun in the other, at the man and wife, began to search the house without a warrant of any kind, and without telling them any reason for their entrance. They found nothing and then left to search other houses.

Mr. Kashmarchik has five children, the youngest is 21 months old. During the raid the children were frightened, one of them, the oldest, hasn't recovered as yet and can't fall asleep because of her fear. Mr. Kashmarchik lived in New Kensington 8 years. Mr. ————, Superintendent of the American Sheet & Tin Mill Co., was in charge of the raiders. He was outside the house while the troopers were searching in the house.

(signed) Elizabeth Kashmarchik.
her (X) mark

Natrona

Mr. Henry McNeely, organizer for the Amalgamated Iron, Steel
& Tin Workers, states that about the 8th of October, two Greek
strike breakers approached him and proposed to him that he give
them some money and that they would blow up the Allegheny
Steel Plant at Natrona. Mr. McNeely called in Mr. Clifford
Wheeler, a prominent citizen of Breckenridge. They told him
the same story and Mr. McNeely told the Greeks that he will take
it up and immediately went to Policeman Ed. Hilleman and told
him this story. The same evening the Greeks were arrested. Mc-
Neely and Wheeler were put under survey to appear at Pittsburgh,
before Sheriff Haddock. After they had given the testimony the
sheriff said that the Greeks would be held for conspiracy. The
following morning McNeely saw the two Greeks walking freely
on the streets of New Kensington. They have never been called
again regarding this case. Not a word leaked out to the newspapers.

(signed) Henry McNeely.

Pittsburgh

At the beginning of the strike meetings were allowed in
several places in Pittsburgh. The authorities finally refused
permits for the strikers' meetings, except in one place—the
Labor Temple.

Charges against the police and public officials were made
by witnesses who testified before the United States Senate
Committee.[1] It was charged that men were clubbed, arrested and fined without due cause. It was also charged that
witnesses for strikers were not permitted to testify by magistrates. Attorneys for the strikers testified before the Senate
Committee that they were not permitted to consult with their
clients; that they were refused transcripts of the proceedings;
that magistrates discharged men who promised to go to work
and fined others who insisted on remaining on strike, and
further stated that very often the evidence on the magistrate's

[1] See U. S. Senate Committee testimony (Vol. II).

transcript differs materially from that produced at the hearing.

Woodlawn, Pa.

Woodlawn is what is known as a company town.   One of the largest plants of the Jones and Laughlin Company is located there.   During the early days of the strike it is charged that American citizens, whether strikers or not, were stopped at the railroad station by special deputies of the company, were searched, beaten, placed under arrest and then fined excessively without any provocation or cause whatsoever.   The only offense of these affiants apparently was the fact that they got off the train at Woodlawn.   Affidavit No. 167 tells the story:

WOODLAWN

STATE OF PENNSYLVANIA, } ss.
COUNTY OF ALLEGHENY,

Victor Thomas, residing at Park Avenue Hotel, Clairton, Pa., and Daniel Colangelo residing at 301 St. Clair Ave., Clairton, Pa., who, having been duly sworn according to law depose and say:

On the 26th of September 1919 Victor Thomas went to visit a cousin of his by the name of Frank Colangelo, at Woodlawn. As soon as he left the train and while on the station he was approached by a special deputy who asked, " Where are you going? " He said he was going to visit his cousin, to which the deputy replied, " You can't go, as we don't allow any foreigners in this town." Mr. Thomas has been in the country eighteen years and has been a citizen for the past seven years. He then took him to the improvised police station at the Jones & Laughlin plant and brought before a captain who had a cap wearing the badge of Jones & Laughlin Co. He was then searched thoroughly and his union card found in his possession was taken from him. When he asked for it, they told him " you don't need the card." He was again told that he can't go to Woodlawn to visit his cousin and was held there under guard for several hours until the next train left for Pittsburgh. Two deputies took him down to the train and while boarding the train told him " We'll let you go back to Pittsburgh, but don't you ever come back, if you do we will lock you up."

On the 7th of October, Mr. Thomas and two friends of his, Daniel Colangelo, and Fred Nero, both of 301 St. Clair Ave., Clairton, went again to Woodlawn to visit their cousin and friend Frank Colangelo. The party got to Woodlawn about 10:30 P.M.

As soon as they left the train special deputy no. 9 approached the party and ordered them to stop. When they stopped he inquired as to where they were going. They told him they were going to visit Mr. Colangelo, at the same time about eight or nine more deputies came to the platform and surrounded the parties. They took the three men to the improvised police station at the Jones & Laughlin plant. When they brought them there they took each one separately and searched him in another room and while doing so, they kept on beating them and using the most violent language. Mr. Thomas was grabbed by the throat and struck in the face while the deputy kept on shouting, " Why in hell do you come back here again?" The other two men were beaten up and kicked by four or five deputies who surrounded them when they were searched. When they brought them out again blood was streaming down Mr. Thomas' lips and Mr. Colangelo asked him what happened, while his own clothing was all dirty and bore the distinct marks of the deputies' boots where he was kicked. Mr. Thomas responded by saying, " Did they beat you too?" When the deputy heard them conversing he ran over and struck Mr. Thomas again in the face in front of all present. They did not find anything on any of the men except a small looking glass upon Mr. Colangelo. They took it and threw it away saying. " You were going to kill people with this, eh. . . . They were then ordered to shut up and not to talk to each other. After a while a deputy after having his dinner with his belly stuck out approached them and pointing to his stomach said, " I can lick the whole ———— out of you." When the next train came the deputies, about two hours later, shipped Nero away to Pittsburgh and told him not to come back any more. Mr. Thomas and Mr. Colangelo were then held until 7 o'clock in the evening when they were taken in an automobile to the Squire. The police deputies told the squire that they were union men, as the union card of one of them was taken up long ago and that they arrested them as suspicious persons. Mr. Thomas and Mr. Colangelo explained to the squire the reasons for their coming and protested at their arrest. The squire told them,

"Weren't you told before not to come here anymore. You can't come here while the strike is on. You will be able to come, perhaps when the strike is over. You come from Clairton and that is where all the bad bunch of people come from." He then fined each one of them $13.60 and when he was asked for a receipt he refused to give it to them. When they left the squire's office and thinking they were free, Mr. Colangelo went down to a grocery store across the street while Mr. Thomas was waiting in front of the store. Two deputies again approached them, put them on the same automobile and after circling through all the alleys so that no one could see them, brought them back to the police station at the Jones & Laughlin plant and held them there for the next train to Pittsburgh. While there a deputy took his revolver out and pointing to the men said, "If you fellows try to run from us you will see what will happen." When the 10:46 train came two deputies took both men down to the station and they boarded the train, told them, "Don't you ever dare to come back again, you ———."

Victor Thomas   (signed)
Daniel Colangelo   (signed)
Sworn to and subscribed before
me this 8th day of October, 1919.
Myrtle B. Henderson (signed)
Notary Public
My commission expires January 21, 1921. (SEAL)

The Blanket of Silence

Numerous efforts were made by individuals during the strike to make it publicly known that such happenings were being charged by very many people in the steel towns.

These efforts at publicity and urgings for investigation of the charges were quite unsuccessful.

Local newspapers suppressed what they knew and for the most part did not try to find out " what was happening to hunkie strikers." Correspondents of out-of-town newspapers signally failed to investigate. The " steel strike number " (November, 1919) of *The Survey* of New York contained more of the facts than most of the newspapers *in toto*.[1]

How the blanket of silence was held down tight in Pittsburgh is shown in the following statement concerning not a " hunkie strikers' meeting," but *the one public meeting held in Pittsburgh during the strike* (outside the labor temple). This is the statement (condensed) made by Sidney A. Teller, Resident Director of the Irene Kaufmann Settlement, before the Commission of Inquiry in November, 1919.

The Irene Kaufmann Settlement maintains an open forum. The position I took was that so long as both sides were represented, there was no objection to discussing the steel strike. The Forum committee went down to the strike headquarters, asking that a speaker be assigned for the following Sunday. They were assigned William Z. Foster, on the condition that he was not needed at any other place to address a group of strikers.

[1] Labor men in December took copies of the affidavits gathered by the Pennsylvania State Federation of Labor to out-of-town newspapers which refused to publish or investigate.—H. B.

I have had no objection to Mr. Foster, irrespective of the way newspapers talked about him, because Dr. Tyson and I heard him at the Social Workers Club. I am president of the Social Workers Club at this moment, and Mr. Brown and Mr. Foster were given a hearing before the Club last year, when we heard the right of free speech and assemblage was denied them. We felt they were the representatives of the American Federation of Labor, coming down here as their official representatives to discuss questions of organization. . . .

So I had no objection to Mr. Foster. The notices went out for the Forum meeting, and they delayed it to the very last minute trying to get a speaker on the other side. For the first time in the history of my being at the settlement, the Board of Trustees requested that the meeting be called off. Their arguments were twofold. They said it was not wise to discuss the steel strike because of the great excitement in the city. And then they believed what they had read about Foster, and said the platform of the Settlement should not be given to him. I said he was chosen by the steel workers as their representative, and we weren't discussing individuals, we were discussing issues.

The President, acting for the Board of Trustees, requested that no meeting be held until the Board met and acted on the matter.

The President of the Settlement Board then called a meeting to bring up for discussion the future of The Forum in the settlement. Fourteen members of the Board of Trustees were present, and after an hour and a half of discussion they voted by a vote of 12 to 2 to uphold the principle of the Forum.

The meeting was about to adjourn, when I arose and said I wanted them to know before they left the room that I had received a request from the Civic Open Forum that the postponed meeting of October 12th, in reference to the discussion of the steel strike be held on October 19th. Well, that reopened the whole thing.

Meanwhile it is important to remember that the Sheriff of the County had issued an order that there would be no meetings held for the discussion of the steel strike, and the Mayor of the city had prohibited a meeting of the strikers, or a meeting to discuss the strike anywhere in Pittsburgh except in the Labor Temple.

The Directors wanted to know whether I would go contrary to the established law and order of the community, and the orders of the Sheriff and Mayor. I said I was not interested either in the workers' side of the situation or in the steel corporation's side, but that civil liberties were being abrogated.

I was making a fight on the principles of American citizenship —the right of free assemblage to discuss a legitimate question, and I took the stand that the Mayor was beyond his jurisdiction and authority, as well as the sheriff. . . .

That same day the Mayor had restated his position, under pressure. The machinists had asked to be allowed to hold a meeting to discuss the steel strike, and he prohibited it saying in his proclamation, " No meeting should be held in the strike zone."

I interpreted the words " strike zone " to mean the district around the mills, and the Irene Kaufmann Settlement was not in the " strike zone." After an hour and a half of debate, the directors said: " Mr. Teller, the responsibility of what is said, the speakers and the audiences of the forum, is on your shoulders." And the meeting closed with that.

So I went back to the settlement, and found that Mr. J. G. Brown was assigned to us by the strikers committee to represent the workers. The meeting was held, and Mr. Brown discussed the steel strike from his point of view. We tried to get some one on the other side, but everybody we went to said they had no authority, or Mr. Gary had spoken for them, or they didn't know the facts well enough, or if they spoke they'd lose their position with the Company. Not one person directly connected with the steel companies here could we get. The only person we could secure was Mr. I. W. Frank, a member of my board, of the United Engineering Company, who said he would speak not for the steel corporation or his own concern, but from his own personal experience in the foundry business. That is the nearest we came to discussing the other side. That meeting was held under the same conditions and auspices as the other.

I want to add that to my knowledge I do not know of another public discussion in Pittsburgh connected with the steel strike. We sent notices of the meeting which Mr. Brown addressed to the newspapers. Two reporters were there expecting trouble, but there was not even a line in the papers the next day on what he said.

Next week notices went out on the meeting to be addressed by Mr. Frank. That was given publicity.

Note:—The Steel Report gives (p. 18) the recommendation of the Commission that two reports for the government on Pennsylvania conditions be made public: one, Mr. Ethelbert Stewart's report on civil liberties, made to the Secretary of Labor (1919); the other Mr. George P. West's report made to the War Labor Board. Inquirers have always been denied access to these reports.

IV

THE MIND OF IMMIGRANT COMMUNITIES IN THE PITTSBURGH DISTRICT

BY DAVID G. SAPOSS

CONTENTS

Foreword.—European Background of Strikers.—Sources of Immigrant Information and Leadership.—Church and Pastors.—Solidarity of Rank and File.—Psychology of Immigrant Rebellion.—Psychology of Disillusionment.

FOREWORD

A CHARACTERISTIC of the steel strike in and around Pittsburgh was the average " American " citizen's panicky fear of the " foreigners," the " hunkies." The real basis of the fear was ignorance.

Like most cities having large communities of immigrant workers, " American " Pittsburgh had and has no real knowledge of the dominant thoughts or " public opinion " within those communities. Physically, linguistically and mentally segregated, the masses of steel workers live in worlds of their own. " What influences move those worlds is an unanswered question to most good ' Americans ' and for the most part an unasked question." [1]

The author of the following study, Mr. Saposs, spent two months of the strike ceaselessly questioning hundreds of strikers and non-strikers, conversing with their community leaders, examining their newspapers, etc. He had the background of three months spent in the same communities in the spring of 1919 while at work on the Carnegie Corpo-

[1] " The Steel Strike of 1919," p. 30.

ration's Americanization study, as well as of many years' special study of immigrants.

Here are the facts, for the lack of which the English-speaking citizens let themselves believe wild rumors about their foreign-speaking fellow citizens.

—H. B.

THE MIND OF IMMIGRANT COMMUNITIES

European Background of Strikers

THE bulk of the strikers are of the "new immigration" and chiefly Slavs. The principal Jugo-Slav workers are Serbs and Croatians. Slovaks, from what is now the Czechoslovakian Republic, make up a large percentage in many mills. Russian and Austrian Poles, as they called themselves when they emigrated, form the largest single racial blocks in other mills. Hungarians, Roumanians, Italians, Greeks and Lithuanians comprise smaller or larger percentages in certain mills, one race tending to crowd others out and to monopolize a plant or at least a department. A dozen other nationalities of the " new immigration " are represented, from Ukrainians (Little Russians) to Horvaths (Jugo-Slavs), from Great Russians to Turks, from Finns and Jews to Syrians and Armenians. The " new immigration " of course is predominantly Balkan or Southeastern European.

Very few of these immigrant workers in the steel mills are from industrial communities. Outside of Hungary and Italy, the regions from which the steel workers come are almost wholly agricultural. This horde of immigrants reached America entirely unacquainted with modern industry and practically ignorant of the existence of labor organizations. Whatever schooling they have is of a primary and rudimentary nature, acquired chiefly as a part of religious training. Their only previous experience as workers was as agriculturists and most of their life in the old country was spent in small farming villages.

The Hungarians are the principal exception, in that a good portion of them come from industrial centers and mining communities. These naturally have a working acquaintance, at least, with labor organizations and labor conceptions. Most of them are socialists, since Hungarian labor organizations are politically socialist by tradition. The few Finns in the industry are strongly socialist and very clannish. Italians who come from North Italian industrial centers also are acquainted with labor organization ideas and often with socialist principles. Most of the Italian steel workers, however, come from Sicily or from other backward communities. For the most part the steel workers were previously wholly unacquainted with modern industry and labor organizations.

Sources of Immigrant Information and Leadership

Transplanted into a highly developed and complex industrial country, totally different from their former home, they seek guidance and leadership principally for the purpose of adapting themselves to their new surroundings. Their immediate sources of information and guidance are the local club or individual relatives or other fellow countrymen. It is the immigrant of a few years' experience here who guides them to jobs, familiarizes them with routine and procedure in the plant, enables them to find homes and to furnish them if they have families. At the club, they meet fellow countrymen who gladly give them their conception of America. If they can read, they also find here newspapers in their own language which keep them informed of developments at home as well as of news in this country. In church they are enabled to maintain the habits and traditions of their old country. Quite generally, their priest also is a counselor and a guide.

But these local sources of information naturally look for guidance to higher and better informed channels, since they themselves are practically isolated or too steadily at their work to seek this information independently. Even the priest must have a higher and an outside source for his knowledge of developments in America. Quite often he too has been transplanted from an agricultural to an industrial country.

In the final analysis, the immigrant workers look for guidance and for interpretation of America to leaders of their own nationality, who are generally associated with a benefit society or are editors of a newspaper. Almost every benefit society has a weekly paper of its own, and there are some independent papers with influence among the immigrant workers.

The national leaders themselves are not workingmen, and, with a few minor exceptions, were not workingmen in the old country. They come from middle-class families and are imbued with middle-class notions. In this country, while their entire constituency and following are made up of workingmen, the leaders live among and associate with middle-class people and read the usual papers in English.

In their desire to be of service to their fellow countrymen, or to develop a clientele off whom to make a living, the leaders naturally try to devise societies or other agencies to serve their countrymen. In doing this they overlook the principal problem confronting the immigrant as a worker. For a professional man ordinarily does not need the kind of organization to protect his economic interests which a workingman needs. He is fairly conversant with the business or the profession that he is in; he has a certain amount of initiative and bargaining ability so that he can protect himself as an individual. What he needs is protection against exigencies beyond his control such as sickness insurance, death losses, etc. He also wants a club for social intercourse.

All immigrant leaders from their own experience also realize the difficulties of adaptation for those who are unacquainted with the language. They remember how they were imposed upon and how perhaps they were persecuted by the police or other civil authorities.   Hence, guiding themselves by their own experience and not seriously studying the conditions and the needs of the immigrant workers, these leaders provide protection for their fellow countrymen as if they were business or professional men, not immigrants and workers.   So it happens that these immigrant nationalities have highly developed benefit societies and social clubs in every community, but almost no organizations to protect their economic interests as workers.

The only exceptions of importance are the Hungarians. Since a large number of these workers come from industrial and mining centers, acquainted with protective economic organization, their leaders are of a different type.   Many of them were workingmen or otherwise connected with the labor movement in Hungary and know what workingmen need. Consequently, while they realize that their fellow countrymen (as strangers in a new country) need benefit societies and protection against persecution and imposition, they also seek economic protective organizations as wage workers. Hence, we have in this country the Hungarian workmen's benefit societies based upon a philosophy and preaching ideals entirely different from the societies of the other immigrant workers.   This is also true to some extent among the Italians.   But while both Italians and Hungarians educate their fellows as workers, they rarely develop labor organizations of their own.

Among the other nationalities a few leaders have recently organized radical and socialist papers and societies.   They are a very small percentage and so far have not succeeded in counteracting the influence of the middle-class immigrant leaders, who got in on the ground floor.

It is interesting to contrast the run of immigrants in the steel mills with such nationalities as the Finns and the Jews, both of whom have but few representatives in the steel industry. The immigrants from these two races are largely from Russian industrial and commercial centers. Owing to the persecution of the Czar, they developed a definite working-class philosophy. Hence, while their leaders also come from the middle class, they have a distinct knowledge of and adherence to workingmen's notions. They educate their fellow countrymen in working-class concepts, founding organizations based fundamentally on working-class needs. They have benefit societies, they have clubs, but the underlying doctrines of these are working class rather than middle class. Naturally, the newspapers which they publish reflect working-class philosophy. The chief Jewish working-class paper has a circulation of 300,000. They have numerous magazines and extensive workingmen's educational societies. This is true of the Finns likewise, although they are very few in number. They have four workingmen's daily papers, one monthly magazine and one quarterly, edited as working-class periodicals. Naturally, these races have also developed independent labor unions and labor leaders, although they generally work in harmony with the " American " labor movement.

The difference between the leaders of the vast majority of workers in the steel industry and the leaders of the Jewish and Finnish workers can be stated as follows: *The leaders of the immigrant workers in the steel industry might be termed clansmen.* A clansman in this sense would be a person accustomed to profit from the helplessness of his fellow countrymen. He generally has qualities of leadership, is somewhat better educated than his fellows, has a little more initiative and is more adaptable to a new environment. He comes from a family which even in the old country has been accustomed to profit by the helplessness of fellow countrymen.

He is seldom one of the working masses in upbringing or

in intellectual outlook.   He generally has a highly developed
business instinct.   With business motives, he assumes leadership because it is financially profitable.   Whether honest
or dishonest, he is bound to lead them in accordance with his
business ideals and his conception of a business society.

The leaders of Jewish and Finnish workers, on the other
hand, might be termed intellectuals.   They are generally
students and idealists, men who not only sympathize with
the political oppression of their fellow countrymen, as do
the leaders of the immigrant workers in the steel mills, but
who also have studied the economic life of their fellow immigrants and have a thorough knowledge of their economic
problems.   They have developed primarily into crusaders
and evangelists who see more clearly the economic condition
under which their people labor.   They undertake leadership
from idealistic motives rather than for business ends.

Church and Pastors

The priest and preacher of the immigrant workers in steel
communities as a rule gets his philosophy from the nationalistic leaders and foreign language press of the business
stamp.   His industrial conceptions are those of the secular
leaders.   He is often unacquainted with the labor movement, except as he has indirectly heard or read about it.
He is generally on good terms with the management of the
plants where his parishioners work.   The management usually makes an effort to cultivate the friendship of the priest
and contributes to his church.   He, therefore, would be inclined to act as an interpreter of America and its industrial
problems from the viewpoint of the employer.

Amalgamation, Industrial and Economic

By organizing their fellow countrymen into benefit societies
and clubs on nationalistic lines, the leaders naturally empha-

size segregation. It is charged that this explains why employers have fostered these societies and cultivated the friendship of the priest and financed his church. There are, however, deeper forces working underground which are breaking up these nationalistic segregations and which develop a spirit of fellow-feeling and solidarity among the immigrant workers in the iron and steel industry. Forces leading to economic and industrial amalgamation, although often poorly guided, are overcoming the stimulated forces that make for nationalism and segregation.

In the mill, immigrant workers of various nationalities work side by side. They learn to know each other, they learn to work in harmony with each other, but, above all, because of the discrimination against all of them as " hunkies " and foreigners, they develop a feeling of fellowship which cuts across racial and nationalistic animosities. This is an inevitable, natural and unforced development based on common experience and common grievances. At the same time it intensifies rather than overcomes the cleavage with the English-speaking worker.

Labor organizations, out of self-protection, undertake to develop conscious industrial and economic amalgamation by organizing all the workers on an equality. Among the Jews and the Finns, where their own national leaders are cognizant of this need, the old American trade unions do not need to develop foreign language organizers. All that is necessary is to cooperate with the labor leaders of those nationalities.

Among the great majority of immigrant workers in the steel industry, just as in the coal and metalliferous mines, and later in the packing industry where their nationalistic leaders had neglected the economic interests of their fellow countrymen, the American trade unions began to develop a new type of leader who could organize the immigrant workers.[1] This marks the advent, then, of what is known as the foreign language organizer in A. F. of L. unions. These are young fellows with initiative and more than the usual amount of intelligence, who possibly have some knowledge of trade unions in Europe, but who learned their unionism chiefly in this country through the guidance and tutoring of native-born trade unionists. These become the economic leaders of their fellow countrymen. They are mainly responsible for organization among immigrant workers in this country.

The I.W.W. has followed a similar policy, generally more aggressively than the A. F. of L., and almost always more democratically, which explains some of its successes in initiating organization among immigrant workers.

The first A. F. of L. union to try this policy with great success was the United Mine Workers (coal). The old Western Federation of Miners (metalliferous mines), now known as the Mine, Mill and Smelter Workers, also uses the method with great effect. Mr. Fitzpatrick and Mr. Foster followed this policy in the packing industry and applied it in the iron and steel industry.

With a little information on trade unionism and on their immediate needs as wage earners, the immigrant workers in organized industries begin to assert themselves, and, while not challenging their old leaders, proceed to impress their own point of view upon their benefit societies and newspapers.

Since these benefit societies are democratically controlled, they often amend their constitutions by committing the societies to trade unionism, urging the members to join unions, and providing for the expulsion of members who break strikes.

From their newspapers, they begin to demand labor news and discussions of industrial problems. They force the dis-

[1] See "The Steel Strike of 1919": Organizing, p. 162.

cussion of specific strikes through communications to the newspapers. Thus the workers in unorganized industries first learn of trade unions and of what their members claim for unions.

(It is interesting to note that not only have the nationalistic leaders or clansmen been ignorant of the desires of their fellow countrymen, but that organizations like the Inter-Racial Council make the same error. Editors of foreign language papers in Pittsburgh refused to subscribe to the Inter-Racial Council's advertising and news because they said that their readers were not interested in the news matter which the council supplied. They want news on industry and labor, not on political happenings in Washington, which seem to them remote.)

Those of the workers who cannot read, hear labor problems discussed at their clubs. In the course of their migrations, workers from unionized industries bring news of the doings of the union and its results. Other workers read newspapers aloud, giving the news of conditions in other places and in other industries. If the information which comes to their attention stands out in contrast to conditions in unorganized territories where the management is arbitrary and working conditions and wages not as favorable, they note it. The workers of the various nationalities, although living apart, worshiping at separate churches, and attending separate clubs, readily begin to feel common interests based on common grievances.

Thus conditions ripen for labor organization. Workers begin to look for the union to come to organize them. This explains why in many towns little exhortation was necessary in organizing the iron and steel workers. In dozens of towns single mass meetings resulted immediately in thousands of applications for union membership. The Fitzpatrick-Foster committee had very loose and unsystematic methods, but the immigrant workers joined readily and placed large confidence in this mushroom organization; many who were not members responded to its strike call.[1]

Alignment of Forces in Steel Strike

Within the effective strike areas, immigrants walked out practically as units. Those who remained at work were of two classes. First there were those who expected to return to the old country in the following spring or summer. Contrary to the impression conveyed by the American press, the immigrants who worked during the strike were the ones least interested in the welfare of this country; *those who struck were the ones who have their homes and families here and who intend to remain and make this their permanent home.*

A second element among immigrants who did not strike was from races with few representatives in this country or with so few workers in the iron and steel industry that it was either financially or otherwise impossible to secure organizers who spoke their language. Such nationalities have very few papers in their own language and no previous knowledge of trade unionism.

When the dominant institutions of the community, controlled by native-born Americans, opposed the strike and raised the race issue through ministers, newspapers, civil authorities, etc., the immigrant strikers were not entirely surprised. It was the customary practice in steel towns and they were used to it, except that the " alien " cry was more violent during the strike.

In general, the immigrant strikers' own priests and clansmen leaders, as well as their newspapers, did not support the strike. This also did not surprise the strikers. Guided by commercial philosophy, surrounded by Americans whose

[1] See " Steel Strike of 1919 ": Organizing, p. 153.

respect they value highly, it is natural that the clan leaders quailed before epithets and charges of "bolshevism." The friendship of many of these leaders was cultivated by the large steel corporations; they were placed under obligations to the corporations or overwhelmed by unexpected friend-liness. One Pittsburgh leader said that he and his col-leagues were greatly embarrassed by the steel strike, since the Steel Corporation had contributed a "large" sum of money, the exact amount of which he refused to divulge, to the Red Cross of his nationality. He considered the strike of his fellow countrymen as "base ingratitude." In another case, strikers charged that the editor of a foreign language paper was bought by the steel interests. He ran nine articles in his weekly against the strike; he told an in-vestigator that he had them translated into English at the rate of fifteen dollars per article, but he was not in a posi-tion to supply the copy as he had turned it over to a certain person. When asked for the name of the person so that the translated copy might be inspected, he said that the person had sent it to "some one in New York." When told that the investigator intended going to New York and would like to ask permission to see these articles, the editor refused to give the name of the person in New York.

For the most part these leaders seemed honest in their opposition to the strike. There were two reasons for this: The national leaders are frequently more interested in the future of their newly emancipated European fatherlands than in this country. Some of the leaders interviewed told the investigator that they considered it inadvisable for their compatriots to embark upon a long strike and spend all their savings when they should be making preparations to return to their own country next spring or summer. By spending their savings, they would be penniless and would either re-main here or visit the old country as poor people. They felt that their fellow countrymen should bear the bad conditions for one winter longer and save up money to take back to the old country. They explained that the immigrants who worked during the strike had definitely decided to return to the old country.

The other outstanding reason is probably as " un-American " and is to some extent copied from the English-speaking public and press. The latter constantly pointed out to the American workmen that this was a strike of foreigners and incidentally asserted that these foreigners or aliens were essentially Bolshevists and enemies of law and order. The immigrant leaders opposed the strike by arguing that American labor unions never cared for the immigrant, that they were using the immigrant as a cat's-paw to strike to improve conditions " for the American workers who did not even go on strike." [1] The editor-leaders in the same pronouncements pointed out that the chief labor leaders were Americans and declared that Americans called out the immigrant workers and double-crossed them by letting the Americans stay at work.

Another argument which the editor-leaders used effectively was that the A. F. of L. " had always been against immigrant workers "; also that this was not the first strike which Americans had called and then remained at work. Thus, just as the English press and public were raising anti-foreign prejudice, so the immigrant press and leaders tried to raise anti-American prejudice.

Solidarity of Rank and File

Notwithstanding that the immigrant leaders and their newspapers almost wholly opposed the steel strike, few dared make the opposition very open and blunt. In private the editors explained that the workers were leaning to unionism

[1] See " Steel Strike of 1919 ": Organizing, p. 179.

in general and they did not dare oppose the strike too openly for that reason. One editor explained that a competitor of his in Chicago had openly opposed the strike and had lost almost all his subscribers and was on the verge of bankruptcy. He said that he was more " foxy " and instead of openly opposing the strike he published nothing in favor of it; in fact, he refrained from discussing it entirely and indirectly " warned his fellow countrymen to be law-abiding," not to listen to " agitators," and above all things not to be " ungrateful to this country which had done so much in emancipating their fatherlands." He said he followed the policy of the English papers by intimating that instead of a strike against the Steel Corporation it was a revolution against the government.

Of the nine foreign-language papers whose editors were visited in Pittsburgh, only two were openly for the strike, one a Hungarian weekly with only 2,000 circulation, the editor really making most of his income from job printing, and the other a Russo-Carpathian paper with a circulation of 4,500, which favored the strike because its immediate rival openly opposed it. Another paper supplied fair information on the strike. The editor is a conscientious and scholarly man who, despite his business and professional associations, seem to be more in touch with his fellow countrymen. Two papers openly opposed the strike, one a weekly of 6,000 circulation, which printed the nine articles against the strike already referred to. The other paper is published in Homestead and has a large circulation. The remaining four papers did not come out openly against the strike, although their editors were distinctly opposed to it. These editors said that the societies of which the papers are the official organs, are composed almost wholly of workers in the iron and steel and mining industries and that they did not dare openly to oppose labor organizations or strike.

The determination of the immigrant workers, with their firm conviction that they had grievances, was curiously attested by their attitude to their old-time leaders.   In instances where newspapers opposed the strike, the workers repudiated them and registered vigorous protests.   For almost the first time the immigrant workers dared to defy the dominant elements, their old leaders and newspapers, and followed the National Committee for Organizing the Iron and Steel Industry.   Apparently this was because only the latter recognized their grievances.   Immigrants who differed in language and had their traditional nationalistic animosities accentuated during the war, cast away their race prejudices and struck together.   This was further evidence that the strike was a strike of rank and file where leadership was secondary.

Immigrant Rebellion

The determination of the immigrant worker to assert himself in spite of all the opposition of dominant opinion in his own community, was the chief reason why the foreign and the English press, and especially the " American " elements of society, considered the strike as having deeper motives than mere demands of ordinary trade unionism.   Not only the mill managers, but all the governing classes in steel towns were accustomed to seeing the immigrant docile and submissive; to them any strike was indeed a revolution.   Formerly the immigrant obeyed orders without questioning.   He did the unpleasant work, the heavy and exhausting work, and never asked the reason why.

He had submitted for years to militaristic mill discipline.[1] In the community he had acted in the same way.   He had lived his life away from the others, at first purposely keeping

[1] See " The Steel Strike of 1919 ": Grievances, p. 178.

out of their way. Then as he became " Americanized," he
began in recent years to assert himself as a member of the
community. As one " American " minister explained it,
" The foreigner wants too much; he owns the largest churches
in the community, is buying up the property, and is now
even running his own candidates for political office."

While it was natural that the immigrant should arrive
at this state of mind in the course of adapting himself
to his new surroundings and gradually becoming accli-
mated—that is Americanized—this assertive state of mind
seems recently to have concentrated on economic problems
and conditions. At his clubs and by fellow countrymen who
had worked elsewhere, he was being told that better conditions existed in unionized industries, particularly that there
was no twelve-hour day where there were unions. Also he
began to believe that these betterments could be acquired
through united action under the leadership of labor organizations.

Most important, the immigrant in the steel mills had tasted
better conditions during the war. He had had an opportunity
to earn more by working on the better paying jobs, for the
first time he had been treated considerately by the foreman,
etc. In the community, he had also been looked upon dif-
ferently, that is, either as an " American " or as a worthy
ally. At " home," his fellow countrymen were becoming free
citizens in nations rid of autocrats.[1]

The immigrant worker took these new developments seriously and was very much disillusioned after the signing of
the armistice when the employers and the dominant elements
in the community took the attitude that, now the war was
over, it was time to return to all the old conditions. The
immigrant was again a " hunkie." This was the last straw.

[1] See " The Steel Strike of 1919 ": Organizing, p. 148.

Thereafter he waited for anybody to lead him into the promised land.[1]

Thus the strike was also an outburst of the inhibited instincts for self-expression. If the immigrant worker had not tasted the satisfactions of recognized self-expression during the war, it would have required a more intensive and systematic campaign to organize him. It might also have been very difficult to get him to strike in the face of approaching winter. It was because the immigrant's deepest emotions and instincts were stirred that this huge and unprecedented strike was possible. The immigrant wanted not only better wages and shorter hours. He resented being treated as a chattel or a "hunkie." He was no longer content with being ridiculed and scorned and considered only good enough for the dirty work. He had caught the rivalry of the steel industry—that if any one is worth anything he is promoted from one job to another with the prospect of ultimately being a roller. This incentive had before the war existed only for the "American": it was felt that the "hunkie" needed no incentive. Therefore, steel officials as well as the highly skilled American workers and others in the community were frightened when the immigrant worker asserted himself as if he were on an equal footing with them.

Disillusionment

Many of the strikers said that if the strike was lost they would never return to the mill. Even those who had been born in this country but were sons of immigrant workers on strike, said they would return to their fathers' countries, which were become independent and free nations, rather than remain in the mills under old conditions. Most of the

[1] *Ibid.*, p. 138-39.

immigrant leaders interviewed held the opinion that if the strike was lost the immigrants in great numbers would return to the old country.   In previous years, when there was not this alternative, immigrant workers who were defeated in strikes in other industries would sullenly return to work. In such cases their efficiency was impaired and they were fertile ground for I.W.W. and other revolutionary seed.   A cause of I.W.W.-ism is despondency; hence, the strength of I.W.W. belief in sabotage.   A self-respecting workman, strong enough to meet any opponent on an equal footing, hardly ever resorts to underhand ways.   He will when he thinks he has been downed unfairly.   Thus sabotage commonly follows lost strikes among " American " workmen as well as among " foreigners."   As a result, the whole moral fiber of the worker is affected.   He loses faith in the worthwhileness of work, he loses faith in orderly methods of changing the conditions of work.

V

THE UNITED STATES STEEL CORPORATION'S WELFARE WORK

By George Soule

CONTENTS

I. Welfare Work, Pensions, etc.: A. Stock Subscriptions; B. Pensions and Accident Compensation; C. Company Housing; D. Safety and Sanitation.—Summary.

The features of the labor policy of the Steel Corporation which it has communicated to the public in detail consist of the welfare work, pensions, housing, stock participation, bonuses, recreation and sanitation facilities, and safety provision—in bulk calling for great expenditures. Detailed accounts of all welfare and allied activities fill many volumes in the corporation's offices. Lists of totals supplied by Mr. Gary to the Senate Committee include:

U. S. STEEL CORPORATION EXPENDITURES FOR PURPOSES LISTED BELOW

	1917	1918	First 6 months, 1919	Totals since 1912
Welfare	$1,652,956.42	$3,142,899.00	$1,493.341.84	$10,721,247.42
Sanitation ..	2,406,951.68	3,145,174.89	1,538,507.31	10,062,455.59
Accident prevention ...	998,806.94	1,110,064.00	574,446.19	5,961,618.09
Relief for injured men and the families of men killed	3,171,994.88	3,336,559.38	1,969,100.57	20,915,322.80
The employees' stock subscription plan (approximate) .	1,175,000.00	1,300,000.00	700,000.00	8,460,000.00
For pension fund payments in excess of income provided by permanent fund	339,093.52	136,644.39	66,525.33	1,748,063.19

243

Total pension payments to employees ..	712,506.65	709,059.82	366,525.33	4,452,175.51
For additional benefit payments and administration cost ..	30,763.69	31,424.58	15,484.71	277,599.74
For the creation of a permanent fund	500,000.00	5,000,000.00	....	8,000.000.00
Total....	$10,244.803.44	$17,171,241.66	$6,341,921.24	$65,868,707.09

Number of dwellings and boarding houses constructed
    and leased to employees at low rental rates [1] 25,965
Churches 23
Schools 43
Clubs 17
Restaurants and lunch rooms 53
Rest and waiting rooms 171
Playgrounds 131
Swimming pools 11
Athletic fields 86
Tennis courts 88
Band stands 16
Practical housekeeping centers 16
Piped systems for drinking water 355
Sanitary drinking fountains 2,835
Wells and springs protected against pollution 597
Comfort stations (complete units), either bath or dry
    houses, closets, wash or locker rooms, in separate
    buildings or within enclosures in the buildings...... 1,390
Water closet bowls 6,837
Urinals 2,329
Washing faucets or basins 16,479
Showers 2,446
Clothes lockers 110,759
Base hospitals 25
Emergency stations 279
Training stations (first aid and rescue) 64
Company surgeons, physicians, and internes 156
Outside surgeons serving on salary 106
Nurses (including nurses in training) 154
Orderlies and other attendants 98
Visiting nurses 62

[1] Over 15,000 of these houses are for workmen outside of the steel areas.—Ed.

Teachers and instructors 209
Sanitary inspectors 25
Safety inspectors (spending entire time on work) 106
Employees who have served on safety committees 22,000
Employees now serving on safety committees 5,426
Employees who have been trained in first aid and rescue
    work 16,637
Employees now training 676

Description of some of these activities is contained in Bulletin No. 7 of the Bureau of Safety, Sanitation and Welfare of the United States Steel Corporation (December, ⁽⁾1918).

First Aid and Rescue

In all our mining companies and in many of our manufacturing companies there are First Aid and Rescue crews, each composed of four to six men whose services are voluntary. Before entering a training class each employee must obtain a written statement from his physician certifying to his physical fitness for the work and the duties incidental thereto. The men are trained under the direct supervision of the Company doctors. The course comprises twelve lessons, covering lectures, drills and demonstrations; and upon completing the course a certificate is given to each employee.

There are at the present time 67 training stations throughout the operations of the Subsidiary Companies; and since the inauguration of this work, approximately 18,000 men have received instruction.

The excellent work of these First Aid Crews has had its effect in reducing the number of infected cases to a minimum. When we consider that infected cases require three and one-half times as long for recovery as non-infected cases, there can be no doubt that the work of these crews is of the greatest value to the workmen and to the employers.

Restaurants

When laboring overtime on break-down or emergency work the employee can secure a full meal at his usual dinner hour.

Workers in exposed situations during severe weather can be refreshed by a portion of hot soup or coffee.

When exhausted by heat and physical exertion in warm weather, a refreshing draught obtained when most needed frequently enables an employee to return to work with renewed vigor when otherwise he would be incapable of useful exertion for a considerable time. The aromatic bottled drinks furnished at practically all our restaurants seem to supply the necessary stimulation to overcome abdominal cramp among workers laboring in heated positions, the cramp being frequently superinduced by injudicious drinking of water when one is suffering from stomach derangement or careless exposure of the person to strong currents of air.

The burden of the housewife in the daily preparation of the dinner bucket, following the serving of an early morning meal, is eliminated. Where father and son have both to be provided for, as is often the case, the burden is by no means a light one.

When the wife is ailing or away from home, or sickness occurs among the little ones, the breadwinner may have to undertake the unfamiliar rôle of household cook—sometimes with disastrous results to his own internal well-being, not to mention that of his family. Where a mill restaurant is available, a half-hour earlier start from the house secures him an inviting breakfast at a moderate cost.

Visiting Nurses

The assistance rendered by these nurses is of both professional and practical value. The object of this service is to improve the general health and increase the happiness of the employees and their families. The principal duty of the nurse is to give instructions in those things which will enable the employees to better their condition mentally, physically and materially. Her services are offered free by the Company to the employees and their families, but are not forced upon them; she is not permitted to visit the homes of the employees upon any occasion unless requested to do so by a member of the family. But opportunities of giving instruction and advice in matters of household sanitation, economical purchasing of household necessaries, care of children, especially in infancy, and the numerous and perplexing problems confronting the mother are presented through her ability and willingness to help in cases of sickness. Therefore, the nurse must be skilled in her profession, and must also be tactful and of a pleasing personality, so that she will be a welcome visitor in the homes in whatever capacity her presence may be required. Her genuine interest and desire to be of assistance in time of trouble win the confidence of the people and she becomes the counsellor, helper and friend from whom they seek aid and advice, knowing that any problem submitted to her will be given careful consideration.

The work of these visiting nurses may be briefly outlined as follows:

1. Attending the sick.
2. Giving instruction in personal and domestic hygiene and in domestic science.
3. Helping the families to deal with financial, physical, marital and other domestic troubles.

Practical Housekeeping Centers

The following are some of the activities carried on at these Practical Housekeeping Centers:

1. Classes for children in sewing, cooking and housekeeping.
2. Meetings for the women of the community for instruction in infant welfare, cooking, sewing, housekeeping, public health and hygiene.
3. A club for the small girls of the community under the direction of the nurse. These clubs are self-governing, with constitution, by-laws and officers.
4. A club for the boys of the community under leadership of a young man, with definite rules covering the conduct, activities and qualifications of the boys for membership. The boys help to formulate these rules and therefore feel themselves bound to enforce them.
5. A club or association, under the direction of the nurse, for women employees of the Company, to afford those women employed in domestic service or similar isolated duties opportunities to mingle socially with other members of the community.

The corporation offices house uncounted thousands of photographs of company towns, company hospitals, clubs, churches, playgrounds, houses, pensioners, etc. Volumes have been written on corporation town planning, relief administration, etc.; similar volumes on welfare activities, which antedate the Steel Corporation's practice and are on a similar scale, were to be found before the war in the offices of various corporations in Great Britain, Germany and Russia.

The whole matter must be considered here from the standpoint of its relation to the issues of the strike.[1]

A—*Stock Subscriptions*

The Corporation offers to officers and employees annual opportunities to subscribe for shares of common stock, approximately at the current market price.

On December 31, 1911, 24,588 employees were stockholders, and owned 102,245 shares. On December 31, 1918, the number of stockholders had increased to 36,646, and the aggregate holdings to 143,528. In December, 1918, there were about 260,000 employees of the Corporation, the number of employee-stockholders thus being about 13 per cent. of the total. An index to the classes of employees who avail themselves of this opportunity (not merely of those who receive the extra payments) is obtained from the Corporation's statement of subscribers for 1912, 1916 and 1919, classified according to their annual earnings.

Employees Receiving	1912		1916		1919	
	No. Sub-scribing	No. Shares to Sept. 1	No. Sub-scribing	No. Shares to Sept. 1	No. Sub-scribing	No. Shares to Sept. 1
Less than $800 per year	15,349	17,233	7,288	8,961	1,473	2,148
$800-2,500 per year	20,096	35,255	16,272	31,952	46,676	101,764
Over $2,500 per year	1,501	8,866	1,583	9,356	13,175	54,149

[1] The account gives the statistics available at the time of making the report—December, 1919. They are the ones relevant to the conditions prevailing at the time of the strike.—p. 8.

The rise in wage-levels from 1912 to 1919 would in part account for the simultaneous and marked decrease in subscribers receiving under $800 a year, and the increase in those receiving over $800. The difference between those receiving under $2,500 and those receiving over $2,500, however, reveals the class of workmen most interested by the plan. No unskilled or semi-skilled workman received above $2,500 in 1919. Those above $2,500 are almost without exception the highly skilled and the managerial forces. If we roughly classify those receiving under $2,500 as the unskilled and semi-skilled, and those receiving over $2,500 as the highly skilled and managing forces, we find the following percentages:

	Unskilled and semi-skilled	Highly skilled and management
Increase in No. subscribing, 1912-19	+36%	+777%
Increase in No. of shares taken, 1912-19	+144%	+510%
Percentage of total subscribing employees, 1919	78%	22%
Percentage of total subscribing employees, 1912	98%	2%

The unskilled and semi-skilled who make the majority of the employees and were the vast majority of the strikers, therefore, have benefited less from the plan than other employees, in proportion to their numbers.

Eight years' operation of the plans cost the Corporation in the neighborhood of $9,000,000. This in turn must be converted into terms of the amount of money accruing to workers as individuals for any estimate of workers' views of the plan. The Corporation submitted the following table in the Senate inquiry:

SUBSCRIPTIONS TO COMMON STOCK

Employees receiving annual salaries of—	May subscribe for a maximum number of Shares	Employees receiving annual salaries of—	May subscribe for a maximum number of Shares
$690 or less	1	$8,740.01 to $9,660	10
$690.01 to $1,533.33	2	$9,660.01 to $13,225	11
$1,533.34 to $2,146.66	3	$13,225.01 to $14,375	12
$2,146.67 to $3,450	4	$14,375.01 to $15,525	13
$3,450.01 to $4,216.66	5	$15,525.01 to $16,675	14
$4,216.67 to $4,983.33	6	$16,675.01 to $17,825	15
$4,983.34 to $6,900	7	$17,825.01 to $18,975	16
$6,900.01 to $7,820	8	$18,975.01 to $32,200	17
$7,820.01 to $8,740	9		

Low-skilled workmen, therefore, limited to three or four shares, would receive dividends, etc., amounting to a few dollars a month. As an increase to wages, of course, it would not compare favorably with what have been standard wage increases in the industry.

The next thing in the workmen's view of the plan concerns its administration. We quote from " New Ideals in Business " by Ida Tarbell, page 237 (Macmillan, 1917) : " There is the sense of having a share, however small, in the undertaking with which you are connected, the sense of dignity that comes from the consciousness that you are accumulating. They see, too, that bulked this stock becomes a power. A remarkable incident at the 1914 stockholders' meeting of the Steel Corporation shows this. There appeared at that meeting employees of several of the Corporation's subsidiary companies. They had been elected by their fellows, and their expenses paid to go to this meeting and to vote their combined stock. After the regular proceedings the meeting was open for discussion. Judge Gary finally called upon one after another of these workingmen to speak. Their remarks may have been slightly moderated by the unaccustomed company in which they found themselves, but not sufficiently to spoil their flavor of sincerity and of thoughtfulness. They talked of many things. They made some suggestions which the Corporation ought to consider. They all approved the stock-holding plan." Yet the plan is guarded against any real invasion of control by the workmen-subscribers. The aggregate allotted for subscriptions is limited so that employees could never obtain a dominant voting power.

All questions arising about such subscriptions are subject to the " final and conclusive " decision of the Finance Committee of the Corporation. The number of shares for which each employee may subscribe is limited according to his annual income. Subscriptions must be canceled—with a refund of instalments paid—if the employee resigns, is discharged, or fails to " resume employment when requested." Shares are not transferable.

A special feature of the plan is that stockholders who have been in the employ of the Corporation for five years and who have " shown a proper interest in its welfare and progress " will receive a bonus of $5.00 on each share for each such period of five years, over and above the regular dividend. There is no definition of the term " proper interest in its welfare and progress." The question naturally arises, Would an employee who had become active in a union, or in an independent political movement, be held to have shown such an interest?

Another feature of the plan is that the special bonuses which would normally accrue but are forfeited because the stockholder resigns or is discharged, are paid into a special fund, which draws five per cent. interest per annum for a five-year period. " The Corporation will then by its own final determination on its discretion award to each subscriber whom it shall find deserving thereof as many parts of such accumulated funds as he shall be entitled to on basis of the number of shares then held by him under this plan." It would seem then that the older employees whom the Corporation regards as faithful and deserving are rewarded at the expense of the others.

The plan certainly puts a premium on whatever the Corporation considers loyal service, among the class of employees who are the most necessary to it. It adds to the control wielded by the Corporation and it is not a simple business proposition but part of a labor policy.

B—*Pensions and Accident Compensation*

The United States Steel and Carnegie pension fund was established in 1910 by the combination of a fund of $4,000,-000 previously given by Andrew Carnegie and another of $8,000,000 contributed by the United States Steel Corporation. It is administered by a board of directors through a manager appointed by the Board of Directors of the Steel Corporation. All men who have remained in the service of the Corporation or one of its subsidiaries twenty-five years must be retired and pensioned at the age of seventy. The retirement age for women is sixty. Men may be retired at sixty-five, and women at fifty-five, at their request or at the request of their employing officer. " Any employee who has been fifteen years or longer in the service and has become permanently totally incapacitated through no fault of his own as a result of sickness or injuries may be pensioned at the direction of the Board of Directors."

The pensions are calculated at the rate of one per cent. for each year of service, of the average monthly pay received during the last ten years of service. Thus, a man who had been in the service for twenty-five years and had received an average monthly pay of $60 for ten years, would receive a pension of twenty-five per cent. of $60, or $15 a month. No pension can be more than $100 or less than $12 a month.

The employees contribute nothing, and have no sort of representation in the management of the fund. A pension may be discontinued at any time on account of " misconduct," or " for other cause sufficient in the judgment of the Board of Directors." The following are extracts from the rules:

This Pension Plan is a purely voluntary provision for the benefit of employees superannuated or totally incapacitated after long and faithful service, and constitutes no contract and confers no legal rights upon any employee.

Neither the creation of this fund nor any other action at any time taken by the Board of Directors shall give to any employee a right to be retained in the service, and all employees remain subject to discharge to the same extent as if this Pension Fund had never been created.

Whenever it may be found that the basis named for pensions shall create total demands in excess of the annual income increased by any surplus deemed applicable by the Board of Directors, a new basis may be adopted reducing the pensions theretofore or thereafter granted so as to bring the total expenditures within the limitations fixed by the Board of Directors.

These Pension Rules may be changed by the Board of Directors at its discretion.

The number of persons benefited by this pension plan are naturally limited by its provisions. On December 31, 1918, there were 2,861 pensions being paid, only a small number of them being accident cases. In any industry the men who remain in the continuous service of one company for twenty-five years, and retire at sixty-five or seventy, are not numerous. In the steel industry particularly the plan tends to benefit chiefly the management and highly skilled groups, who are in the minority. At the beginning of 1918, 17 per cent. of the beneficiaries were from the management group, 62 per cent. from the skilled men, and 21 per cent. from the unskilled.

The total pension payment to employees during 1918 was $709,059.82, making an average of about $248 yearly per pensioner.

The Corporation spends a large amount every year for

relief of injured men and the families of men killed. The administration of this kind of compensation is regulated largely by the state compensation law, but the Corporation in many cases does more than the law requires. In 1918, $3,336,559.38 was distributed in this relief. In 1917, the total was $3,171,994.88. During the same year, the rate of accidents per 1,000 workers in the iron and steel industry was approximately 103.4, or over 10 per cent.

As the amounts of compensation vary widely according to the nature of the injury and the length of incapacitation, averages would be meaningless.

If, as compensation experts frequently insist, the rates of payment to the injured are too low, it should be borne in mind that the responsibility for low standards rests more with the community as expressed in legislation than with any one corporation.

C—Company Housing

The same observation applies to housing; single corporations cannot be held solely responsible for the wretchedly inadequate housing characteristic of many steel centers, notably Pittsburgh. The house shortage there is a community problem, to be worked out by municipal governments and the steel companies jointly. So far neither side has moved.

There is in the Pittsburgh district an absolute shortage of housing which could be recommended for the common laborers and their families. Any addition to the labor force will intensify the need. This lack of housing has come about through natural causes; the long, narrow valleys in which the rivers run limit the development of land; and much of the land is itself valued highly on account of sub-surface coal, oil and gas. The Steel Corporation has put up some housing here especially for the better paid employees.

In parts of the Pittsburgh district and much more in the south and in the west the Corporation has built whole towns. A report of the Bureau of Safety Sanitation and Welfare runs:

. . . Where great plants have been built at some distance from any city, as in the cases of Gary and Duluth, and in many isolated mining locations, the Corporation has been obliged to provide for such large numbers of its employees that it has built industrial villages adjoining the properties.

In the planning of towns or large dwelling communities the following objects have been kept in mind:

1. Comfortable housing of employees.
2. Healthful surroundings.
3. Education and religious opportunities.
4. Recreation facilities.
5. Civics—to give employees the benefits and opportunities of a small city.

Such housing represents a business necessity, intelligently carried out. In all, up to 1919, the Corporation had spent for housing $32,000,000, with millions more appropriated. Of the 25,965 houses built, less than 10,000 were for steel workers, the rest being for the company's miners, coke workers, shipbuilders, etc. Company houses thus were available for about one in twenty of the Corporation's steel workers. The houses are either rented at a low return on the capital invested, or are sold to the workmen on a partial payment plan.

In some cases, as in Donora, Pa., the houses are expressly built " for the use of the skilled and semi-skilled workman "; in others, it naturally results that the unskilled are not taken care of, since the better paid and more favored classes of workmen have the preference and common labor is in considerable part " floating."

One effect of company housing, whether the employer

intends it so or not, is to make the employee more dependent upon the favor and will of the boss. In the case of rentals, the dependence is direct, as the employee may be evicted during a strike. Many strikers were evicted in October and November, 1919. In the case of outright purchases, the dependence is indirect, but no less potent. We interviewed, for instance, a striker in Homestead, who happened to have valuable testimony to offer to the Senate Committee, but who at the last minute refused to testify when he thought he saw " company spotters " in the room. He explained that he had a family and owned a house, and was afraid he would be blacklisted, would have to go elsewhere for employment, and would lose his investment in his house. This man had kept a memorandum book to check up his time, and it showed that he worked 2,930 hours in eight months and twenty days—an average of over twelve hours a day, including eighteen twenty-four-hour turns; he had had only seventeen days off, including those he took on his own responsibility. Because he owned a house, he was afraid to complain in public, even to United States Senators.

It would be unfair to blame the Corporation's housing policy for this man's fear, but the case does indicate that without some safeguards in the matter of employee representation, even so beneficent a policy of welfare work as the housing plan may be dangerous to the independence of the individual.

D—*Safety and Sanitation*

On account of the danger in many operations in the steel industry, accidents have been numerous. Accidents are not only likely to be disastrous to the workman, but costly to the employer because of their frequent damage to equipment. The Steel Corporation has been energetic in its introduction of safeguards and discipline for the reduction of accidents, and is justly proud of its record in this regard. Writes Miss

Ida Tarbell in "New Ideals in Business" (Macmillan, 1917):

One of the finest points about the work is the fact that almost nobody devising protective devices has consented to have them patented. Not long ago I went through a big manufacturing plant in Wisconsin. There were a number of ingenious safety devices in use, all new to me, the inventions of the safety expert of the plant. "Why do you not have these patented?" I asked. It was the same answer that I had received again and again: "I couldn't do it. It's to save life. If anybody can get any help from them he is welcome to it."

The Steel Corporation opens its Museum of Safety in New York to everybody. It freely gives to all inquirers drawings of the various apparatus it has devised. It also distributes on request copies of its "Standard Requirements of Safety," a volume embodying the experience of its subsidiaries in preventing injuries. "This isn't the kind of thing to make money from!" they'll tell you.

The Bureau of Safety, Sanitation and Welfare has inspired the invention of many mechanical devices which have reduced danger and of many means to inform employees and to enforce the rules by safety police. The inauguration of the safety campaign in 1906 achieved the following results:

Note.—Frequency rates mean number of accidents per 1000 300-day workers; severity rates mean days lost per 1000 300-day workers.

	1906	1907	1908	1909	1910	1911	1912	1913
Frequency Rates	214	189	150	174	134	112	153	115
Severity Rates	54.3	38.1	29.1	23.7	19.9	18.6	14.3	21.3

During the war accident rates went up, but the average for the period from 1914 to 1919 was still held to the average for 1911. Taking 1906 as a standard from which to measure, the Corporation estimates that 25,853 workmen have been saved from serious injury in thirteen years.

It is noteworthy that in this successful portion of the Corporation's labor policy *it has consciously enlisted the cooperation of its employees as a group.* Committees of workmen have been appointed to advise in the development of safety work and help in carrying it out. The committees are not elected, but at least some attempt has been made to tap the resources of practical knowledge and power in the forces of labor. Over five thousand employees are serving on safety committees, and about eighteen thousand have been trained in first-aid and rescue work.

In spite of the improvements made, the danger in the steel industry is still high. No recent adequate government surveys have been made. It is a legitimate question whether it might be further reduced if the fatigue incident to the twelve-hour day were eliminated. No adequate study has ever been made of this phase of the problem. A report published in 1910 by the United States Commissioner of Labor states: " The Sunday rate is markedly higher than for other days. The possibility of the disturbing influence of mass accidents must be considered. The records show that none of the mass accidents occurred on Sunday and therefore its high rate cannot be explained on that basis. A rather strong tendency to frequency of ordinary accidents seems here to be evident in connection with the long turn." The same report finds that for the six years, 1905-1910, the night rate of accidents was 11.6 per cent. in excess of the day rate. In 1919 complaints of undue hazards in the mills were very general among the Corporation's workmen.

In sanitation the Corporation has also been progressive. It has installed in its plants many wash rooms, sanitary clothes lockers, showers, sanitary drinking fountains, etc. (See previous tables.) Certain of these provisions, such as the hospitals, nurses and surgeons, are necessary to any complete safety policy. Others, such as the playgrounds, tennis courts, bands and clubs, excellent in themselves, can of course be of little use to laborers who work twelve hours. They are, of course, extremely beneficial to the skilled and management forces.

Summary of Welfare Policy

The best summary of the United States Steel Corporation's welfare policy is contained in the words of Judge Gary himself in his address (January 21, 1919) to the presidents of the subsidiary companies. This quotation is used as a preface to the reports of the Bureau of Safety, Sanitation and Welfare.

" . . . Make the Steel Corporation a good place for them to work and live. Don't let the families go hungry or cold; give them playgrounds and parks and schools and churches, pure water to drink, every opportunity to keep clean, places of enjoyment, rest and recreation; treating the whole thing as a business proposition, drawing the line so that you are just and generous and yet at the same time keeping your position and permitting others to keep theirs, retaining the control and management of your affairs, keeping the whole thing in your own hands, but, nevertheless, with due consideration to the rights and interests of all others who may be affected by your management."

This indicates at once the strength and weakness of the Corporation's welfare policy. For the large amounts of money spent, for the care and attention devoted to the work, and for the results, particularly in the direction of safety, the Corporation claims and deserves great credit.

At the same time, however, the Corporation does not claim, and should not receive, praise for this work as if it were either a philanthropy or a concession to the rights of the workmen. It is a " business proposition," an attempt to make the Corporation plants attractive, safe and healthy for labor, particularly for the highly skilled and management forces which have been in the past the most necessary and the most difficult to secure in sufficient numbers.

This part of the Corporation's policy, like all other parts, has been imposed from above, and involves no recognition of the stake in the industry held by the minority of the employees. From this fact arises its defects. The majority, for instance, receive only a minor benefit from the stock subscription plan. They do not participate in the pension plan, and only an insignificant minority ever receive pensions. The unskilled have received little relief from the housing developments, and even in the case of the skilled, these developments incidentally furnish dangerous limits to the worker's freedom because of the lack of any safeguards such as would be furnished by collective bargaining. The safety work benefits all alike, and has been the most successful of all because it has enlisted the active cooperation of the men themselves. But even here the Corporation has failed to make any adequate investigation of the relation between the twelve-hour day, the twenty-four-hour turn, and safety. As for the libraries, the gymnasiums, the swimming pools and so on—they seem curiously insulated from the facts of the industry when we remember that most of the foreign-born workmen have never even had the time to learn English after their long hours, and that men working twelve hours a day, seven days a week, have little opportunity for culture and recreation.

In conclusion, we may say that while the Corporation deserves ample recognition of its efforts in welfare work, such efforts cannot be regarded as a substitute for those elements of an intelligent labor policy which would recognize the workers' rights in industry.

VI

THE PULPIT AND THE STRIKE

By M. K. Wisehart

Foreword, by Bishop Francis J. McConnell.—Introduction.—I. The Pittsburgh Council of the Churches of Christ.—II. Did the Laboring Man Distrust the Church and if He Did Who Was Responsible?—III. The Relation of Employers and the Church.—IV. Outstanding Instances of Independence.—V. The Questionnaire.—VI. Opinions of Clergymen on the Church and Industrial Unrest.—Addenda.

FOREWORD

IF any justification is needed for considering the relation of the pulpit to the strike, it will be found in the fact that no individual or institution can possess the spirit of Christ and not be concerned with the conditions under which people live and work. Ignorance of, or indifference to, these conditions is a surrender of the Gospel of Him who was the champion of human well-being and human welfare, who defined His religion in terms of love to God and love to man.

The difficulties in the way of the Church in dealing with a situation like the steel strike are well illustrated by the experiences of the Pittsburgh Council of Churches during the strike.

This council is a federation of the churches of Pittsburgh through the city organization of the various denominations,— that is, the membership is composed of representatives appointed by the Presbytery of Pittsburgh, the Methodist Episcopal Church Union of Pittsburgh, the Pittsburgh Baptist Association, etc., etc. The council is supported by the various city societies on the basis of each denomination's numerical strength in Allegheny County.

The first difficulty arose out of the fact that in such federative schemes the more conservative church groups and individual churchmen look a little askance at federative councils. Federation itself is to many churchmen a questionable, radical idea, and the Pittsburgh Council was in some quarters looked upon as too progressive from the beginning. As a matter of fact the council did undertake on its own account an investigation of the strike within three days after the beginning of the strike. Meetings were held every day for five or six days, and information of value was secured: for example, the letter of W. Z. Foster to Dr. Daniel L. Marsh, in answer to a request for facts. Before the investigation was well under way, however, the plans of the Interchurch investigation were announced. In view of the larger facilities of the Commission it seemed wise to the Pittsburgh group to await the Interchurch investigation.

When the investigators came to Pittsburgh the officers of the Pittsburgh Council provided a place for their meetings, opened channels for interviews with steel manufacturers and labor leaders, and otherwise aided the investigation. In 1917, under the supervision of the council, Dr. Marsh had published "The Challenge of Pittsburgh," a book which expressed dissatisfaction with industrial conditions in Pittsburgh and made constructive suggestions which were, in a sense, looked upon as the program of the council. In harmony with the general point of view of "The Challenge of Pittsburgh" the council issued during the steel strike the "Appeal to Americans" (Chap. II, p. 144), and after the strike protested against the continuance of the suppression of the right of free assemblage in the industrial section of the Pittsburgh district.

Considerable criticism has reached the Commission concerning the council,—some of it from individual pastors in the council itself, some of it from the Commission's inves-.

tigators,—almost all of it directed against the failure of the council to continue its own investigation. It seems to us that the criticism can better be leveled at the general church situation throughout the country. Just from the standpoint of expense, it is clear that the Pittsburgh Council could only with the gravest difficulty have financed an adequate investigation of its own. Moreover, the Pittsburgh district was merely the focus on which converged forces which started far away from Pittsburgh. An adequate investigation had necessarily to consider the entire field of the steel industry.

A final difficulty lay in the fact that investigations of industrial situations by local societies are not likely to be satisfactory. Local sentiment plays too large a part on one side or the other. The only satisfactory agency if a strike of nation-wide significance is under consideration, is an organization which in some sense represents the united forces of all the churches of the nation. Before we can have such an organization working on a permanent basis the doctrine of the responsibility of the churches for social conditions must be pushed farther than we have yet succeeded in doing.

This responsibility will have to express itself in some organ or organs or at least some methods of procedure which will have an influence on the general course of public opinion. It makes very little difference to the present argument whether the press in large industrial districts is dirctly controlled by industrial interests or whether it is merely anxious not to offend those interests. The fact is that the publication of news articles constantly favoring one side begets an atmosphere around the public mind which only the strongest individuals can withstand. It is said that a well-known publisher conducts his newspapers on the assumption that the public does not remember details longer than a week, and that no harm will be done to a newspaper, as a newspaper, by reprinting practically the same set of statements week after week as if they were brand new. During the steel strike the newspapers of the steel centers repeated practically the same statements not week after week, or day after day, but every morning and every afternoon. Because of the sheer force of the repetition a character almost of inevitability was given to the claims of the steel employers. The labor leaders themselves at times despaired [1] before the steadiness and vastness of the newspaper output of statements against them. It is impossible to overtake false statements when they are uttered on such scale. Even if the papers originally making a misstatement subsequently retract, the papers that have copied the statement seldom feel under obligation to retract.

It was in such an atmosphere that the Pittsburgh churches sat stifled during the steel strike. Of course, we must remember that there are in the Pittsburgh churches large bodies of members whose sympathies were openly and professedly with the steel employers. Such members were, in considerable part, against even the mildest expression by ministers of interest in the strikers. And there are churches in Pittsburgh and elsewhere whose ministers unconsciously reflect the feeling of their congregations. It is a well-known principle of homiletics that the most successful pulpit ministry is often that which interprets the best side of the hearers to themselves. But this power of interpreting an audience to itself becomes deadly when the minister has become so steeped in the spirit of the employing class that he speaks merely as the voice of that class. All this to one side, however, the constant iteration of one set of statements begot in the minds of thousands of church members whose sympathies would naturally rather tend toward the strikers a sort of half-conviction that, after all, the justice in the controversy was largely on the side of the employers. This came about in

[1] Cf. Letter of Fitzpatrick and Foster, asking Commission to attempt mediation, p. 334.

view of the psychologic principle that a mind which will reject on a single statement an alleged fact as obviously false, will on the fiftieth statement of the same alleged fact admit that there must be " something in it."

It was in this atmosphere that the Pittsburgh Council of Churches made its effort to get at the facts.   The leaders seem to us to deserve great credit for their attitude.   To have raised any question about the strike in Pittsburgh showed more social spirit and courage than more radical action at the distance of San Francisco or Boston.   But the course of events shows that little can be accomplished by a local organization in dealing with a widespread strike.   To be concrete, the final responsibility here comes back to organizations like the Interchurch Movement and the Federal Council of the Churches of Christ in America.

FRANCIS J. McCONNELL.

THE PITTSBURGH CHURCHES AND THE STRIKE[1]

An inquiry into the relation of the churches to the strike was deemed necessary on the following grounds:

1. The church as a social institution of persistent influence could not help having a relation, positive, negative or neutral, to so wide-spread a social episode as a large strike.
2. Churches in certain localities in the past had been described as having definite relations to the labor policies of steel companies.
3. Individual preachers during the strike publicity took the side of the companies or of the strikers.

The method followed by the investigator for the Commission was to take the inquiry to the clergymen themselves, partly by personal interviews, mainly by using a questionnaire propounding ten specific inquiries. The investigation was limited to the churches of Allegheny County (the heart of the Pittsburgh District) and mainly to the Protestant churches.

Organized religion is unusually strong in Allegheny County. There are 745 Protestant churches in the county with a membership of 235,182. Of these approximately 400 churches are in the city of Pittsburgh. The Pittsburgh Council of the Churches of Christ is an agency of fourteen denominations, including most of the Protestant churches of the county, with a membership of 200,000. The council is charged chiefly with responsibility for looking after " community matters." It is an agency through which the churches should have cognizance of, and are supposed to take action on,

[1] Certain sections were omitted from the report as here printed because the topics are treated in the *Foreword*, by the Chairman who had before him this report, along with later data.—H. B.

social conditions. It is an official body with compact organization.

The churches themselves vary from the very wealthy to the very humble; from churches that pride themselves both on the beauty of their houses of worship and the affluence of their individual members to churches in humble localities with members whose livelihood is derived from manual toil. There are congregations whose influential members are officials or stockholders in the steel industry and in banking institutions. There are congregations whose membership is made up almost entirely of wage-workers in the steel industry.

The clergymen vary in type from men who are themselves wealthy and who come from a social level on a par with that of their wealthy parishioners to the men who subsist on the most inadequate salaries. Among the latter are men who have come to the pulpit from workingmen's walks of life, including the carpenter's trade. Among the Catholic clergy there are men who minister to congregations largely made up of the foreign-born, themselves born in foreign lands and who must speak to their parishioners in their native language. In many cases such men are the most direct and effective means available for the " Americanization " of those who make up their congregations.

The relation between the churches of the city of Pittsburgh and the county as a whole is given in the following passage from " The Challenge of Pittsburgh," issued under the auspices of the Pittsburgh Council of Churches:

Allegheny County is industrially, economically and politically one. While some sections are purely rural and there are independent boroughs like Sewickley and Wilkinsburg, and little cities like McKeesport, yet to all intents and purposes Pittsburgh is the whole of Allegheny County. Especially is this true of the working church. For the missionary strategy of today views the total religious prospects of the county as a single problem. Our city missionary organization must include all the congregations in the county. That people out from the city have no responsibility toward the city is a fiction that misleads not even themselves. The detachment of local churches from the city society will not help them or the city. If parochial selfishness is persisted in, progress can only be downward.

With regard to the responsibility of "people out from the city" toward the "city," it is not out of place to note that the enormous wealth of Allegheny County as a whole is substantially if not almost exclusively represented in twelve congregations which are in the city of Pittsburgh proper or its closely related fashionable suburbs.

I—*The Pittsburgh Council of the Churches of Christ*

The severest criticism of the Pittsburgh Council which came to the attention of the Commission and its investigators was from pastors included in its membership. In general, this criticism was that the churches of Pittsburgh are "weak in social service," and that the responsibility for this rests largely with the council.

At the regular autumn meeting of the Pittsburgh Council on September 25, 1919, a special committee was appointed to study the strike situation and to report from time to time to the executive committee or to the council such courses of action as the committee might advise the churches and Christian people to take in reference to the strike, which had begun three days before.

The committee appointed met and made inquiries as to conditions leading up to the strike from one or two men representing the strikers and the employers. These preliminary activities prompted an informal request by the council's secretary to pastors not to comment on the strike.

On November 28 the council's committee reported formally to the council that a Commission of the Interchurch World

Movement was investigating the steel strike and that the council's committee had decided to cooperate rather than to conduct a separate investigation.

The council's committee did not proceed with the duties originally contemplated in its creation. It did cooperate with the Commission and handed on the results of its brief inquiry.[1]

II—Did the Laboring Man Distrust the Church and, if He Did, Who Was Responsible?

In spite of its large membership and latent power, the Church admittedly had not been a preeminently important factor in remedying social and economic conditions in Pittsburgh. Clergymen of various denominations in the Pittsburgh district have spoken with regret of their belief, and their personal experiences tending to show, that distrust of the Church was increasing among workingmen. Expressions of labor resentment were so common as to turn the attention of a few of the clergymen in the city of Pittsburgh and elsewhere in Allegheny County to the fact that real religion has its social as well as its individual obligations.

The attitude of the churches during the strike had a notably adverse influence upon the relation between labor and the churches in the community. This inquiry did not attempt to go thoroughly into the viewpoint of the Catholic clergy, but the steel workers of Pittsburgh drew no distinction as between Catholic and Protestant in commenting on the lack of any stand taken by "the Church." It has been noted elsewhere that comment both from the Protestant and Catholic clergy which urged the employers' viewpoint was not lacking for the purpose of newspaper display. If what appeared in the Pittsburgh press concerning the remarks and attitude of the clergy on the steel strike had actually

[1] See addenda to this report.

represented the clergy as a whole, the distrust of labor toward the Church would seem to be justified. The fact that the press gave publicity to the remarks and speeches and written opinions of clergymen who supported the employers' viewpoint while it was disinclined to give space to views on the other side, undoubtedly misled the public to some extent as to the attitude of the churches.

Pastors who were most pronounced in their hostility toward the strikers declared when interviewed by members of this Commission or its investigators that they had relied chiefly upon the Pittsburgh newspapers and steel mill officials as sources of information. Especially had they been greatly influenced by the publicity given the testimony of Mr. Gary before the Senate Committee on Education and Labor and by the whole campaign against the strike based on the syndicalist record of W. Z. Foster. A few examples of these interviews may be cited.

A member of the Commission visited a clergyman of Homestead whose pronounced views on the strike had been expressed through the press.

This clergyman talked freely. He expressed the belief that the strike was one of foreigners and entirely unwarranted. During the strike period he had not visited the foreign quarter nor conversed with immigrant workers, but through a young woman doing social work there he had learned that they were not satisfied with the strike. He put the " blame " for the strike on " outside agitators." At the same time he expressed the belief that the demand for collective bargaining was not justified. The leading officials of the steel company at Homestead were members of this clergyman's church and he had learned a good deal of inside strike history from them, especially details as to how the company had " padded " its reports concerning the number of men working the first few weeks of the strike, and of measures taken to discipline men who had gone on strike by demoting them to common labor jobs. It was apparent that this clergyman was thoroughly in accord and highly pleased with the various measures, such as demotion and discharge, taken by the company to discipline " disloyal " men. This clergyman, with prominent laymen, had been sworn in as a deputy. They had been prepared with arms to suppress trouble which had not materialized.

A member of the Commission interviewed a clergyman of one of the wealthiest churches in Braddock. Besides expressing the fear that the immigrant workers were being misled by Foster, this pastor expressed the belief that a twelve-hour working day was not altogether bad, that it was impossible to reduce it and that as a whole the men were working under good conditions. This clergyman's opinions had been formed largely by reading the Pittsburgh newspapers and he had scarcely any information whatever of the strike from first-hand investigation, though a large part of the population in his own town was concerned in it.

Interviews with other clergymen disclosed the fact that the same lack of information, or information derived from one side only, had influenced them. A clergyman of Tarentum, for instance, explained to one of the investigators that there was no excuse for the strike, since the local steel company officials were good men and had the interests of their workers at heart. The clergyman knew this because he was acquainted with the officials personally. He had not tried to seek any other means of information except the Pittsburgh newspapers, though if chance threw him in the way of one of his few parishioners who were on strike he would enter into conversation on the subject. He declared that none of the steel workers was justified in complaining about wages, not even the lowest paid among them. Ministers, too, he observed, are poorly paid, but don't complain. He held that twelve hours was too long for any man to work and that a seven-day week was not in accord with the Scriptures, but against these things he believed the workers ought not to strike because the company officials were good men and would undoubtedly rectify such grievances in the course of time. He understood that the suppression of strikers' meetings was not pleasing to the immigrant workers, but agreed with the officials who had ordered such meetings suppressed that it was necessary to prevent violence, although the immigrant workers had conducted themselves peacefully and in a law-abiding manner.

III—*The Relation of Employers and the Church*

If it appeared that pastors were inclined to take the side of employers on industrial question in general or in particular disputes, without an adequate investigation of the laboring man's point of view on such questions as hours and wages and the right to organize and bargain collectively, it would undoubtedly encourage such a distrust of the churches on the part of labor as some pastors of the Pittsburgh district have frankly admitted exists.

In view of the bias of the Pittsburgh press and other conditions in the district, it would not be strange if clergymen were better informed upon one side than the other, and it is possibly this fact that has made it appear that a considerable proportion of the clergy extended sympathy to the employers without adequate and tolerant consideration of the interests of labor.

Not only are some clergymen by virtue of the location of their churches brought in contact almost solely with employers, but the investigation undertaken by this Commission brought out the fact that Pittsburgh employers resent an independent effort on the part of the churches to inform themselves as to the facts involved in current labor troubles. Instances could be multiplied. An investigator for this Commission in the course of an interview with the president of an independent steel and iron company was given this warning and advised to notify those whom it might concern:

"I am a Presbyterian. If I thought the Presbyterian church was spending any money on this investigation, I'd never contribute another dollar to the Presbyterian church." [1]

IV—Outstanding Instances of Independence Among the Clergy

In the Pittsburgh district there were instances where the employers or mill officials had given to the clergy information of the strike issues from their point of view and had asked clergymen to so speak from the pulpit. Concerning one such instance and the independent position asserted by the Rev. Robert Kirk, pastor of the Central Presbyterian Church of McKeesport, the following details were obtained from three persons who were present:

On September 16 or 17, McKeesport clergymen received letters from Mr. Davidson, secretary of the McKeesport Chamber of Commerce, asking them to be present at a con-

[1] A year and a half after the strike Pittsburgh employers, as individuals and in associations, were openly acting on this belief. Citing the Interchurch Steel Report as the horrible example, the Employers Association of Pittsburgh, through its Vice-President William Frew Long, sent out on Jan. 12, 1921, a bulletin advising non-support of the local Y. W. C. A. because of the endorsement of collective bargaining in the National Y. W. C. A. program. On March 2, 1921, the Employers Association sent out a second letter referring to the first and adding: "The local Y. W. C. A. had just begun a campaign for $200,000, when our bulletin was issued. As a result of the information given to our members, the Y. W. C. A. raised only $90,000 of its $200,000. The ladies of the Y. W. were very 'wrothy' over our action." The letter concluded with an attack on the Federal Council of Churches of Christ in America as the agency continuing the work of the Interchurch Movement: "The radical and Bolshevik elements in the churches seem to be cooperating through the Federal Council and many of our members are expressing themselves as determined *to discontinue financial support of their respective churches* unless they withdraw all moral and financial support of the Federal Council."
In June, 1921, the Pittsburg Ministerial Union (interdenominational) by resolution denounced this attempted "dictation" by the employers. —H. B.

ference with the Mayor, in which the Mayor would state his position in regard to the coming strike.

On September 20, at ten o'clock, between twenty and twenty-three members of the Ministerial Association of McKeesport gathered in the Chamber of Commerce rooms. Besides the Protestant clergymen there were present two Catholic priests and a Jewish Rabbi. The Mayor, Sheriff William S. Haddock and a lieutenant of the State Constabulary were also present.

Mayor George A. Lysle gave his reasons for refusing to allow strikers' meetings in McKeesport. He said he would allow no meetings to be held without permits, as an old city ordinance required the issuance of permits for all meetings. He said further, " I intend to keep peace in this town at any cost, no matter what the personal cost to myself may be. I received threatening letters, but that will not change me for a minute." He urged the pastors to tell the workingmen of their congregations that they would be protected if they wanted to go to work.

Sheriff Haddock said he would maintain order in the county and to do so was prepared to use all the powers of his office.

Mr. Cornelius, superintendent of the National Tube Mills, called the ministers' attention to W. Z. Foster as the " leader of this crowd." He drew attention to Foster's booklet on " Syndicalism " and asked if that sort of a leader was not a dangerous character. He asked the pastors to read the " Red Book," some copies of which he had with him and which he said he would be glad to give out.[1] Several pastors availed themselves of this opportunity. Mr. Cornelius added that the question of the closed shop was uppermost in the strike situation and that the United States Steel Corporation was prepared to fight the closed shop to the bitter end.

[1] This was the " new edition," reprinted for the steel companies.

Mr. Fowles, one of the clergymen present, said that he did not know the purpose of the meeting, but that if it was for the purpose of opposing organization, he wanted to record the fact that he was in favor of the right of labor to organize.

Mr. Kirk then asked why the United States Steel Corporation did not eliminate the chief bone of contention in McKeesport, which was the seven-day week. It would be perfectly possible, he said, to avoid Sunday work in the mills by proper organization. At this point Mr. Cornelius interrupted to say that he did not allow any man to work seven days a week in the mills of the National Tube Company and that they could take a holiday on one of the days of the week. At the close of the meeting Mr. Kirk spoke further with Mr. Cornelius on this subject, reasserting that men were forced to work on Sunday and mentioned the names of several of his congregation who had been unable to attend church the previous Sunday because required to work in the mill.

Before the meeting closed Mr. Fowles suggested that as most of those present were members of the Ministerial Association some action might be taken by that body to deal with the strike problem. Mr. Stewart of the First Presbyterian Church objected to any such action being taken. Mr. Rutt also objected to action being taken, as the meeting was not a regular session of the ministerial body.

Basing his opinion on his knowledge of the clergymen present and on their comments after the meeting, one of the clergymen expressed the belief that fully three-fourths of the ministers in attendance were not in sympathy with the way the conference was called, nor with the Mayor's attitude.

On the first Sunday after the meeting Mr. Kirk preached on the subject, " Disturbers of the Peace." In this address he argued that the fact ought to be taken into consideration that the foreign workmen were brought to this country by the United States Steel Corporation. He urged that employers and the public must consider the position of the immigrant workers and their demand for better conditions and for the right to organize. He urged that capital should recognize the right of labor to organize. Mayor Lysle was in the congregation that heard this sermon. At the close of the sermon the Mayor remarked to Mr. Kirk that he had stolen a march on the authorities and had held a public meeting.

At the beginning and during the strike the Rev. Father Adelbert Kazinci, pastor of St. Michael's Catholic Church in Braddock, preached to his congregation the idea of loyalty to their union and urged them to stay on strike until the issue was decided in their favor. He was unqualifiedly in favor of the strikers' cause.

The members of his church are Slovaks. Father Kazinci himself is a Slovak, a naturalized American citizen. There are 450 families and about 1,890 members in his parish, only 23 to 30 per cent. of whom are American citizens. Before the Senate Committee on Education and Labor he testified as follows:

The Chairman. You say that over 50 per cent. of your church are not American citizens?

Father Kazinci. No.

The Chairman. Are you doing anything in the church, carrying on any work, to Americanize these men?

Father Kazinci. Yes, I certainly am. I insist upon them taking out their citizens' papers, first of all, to pay their dues regularly and get the papers and get instructed in American ways and other things that they should do. We have an Americanization course in project taking place, and they have been instructed to go and attend those night schools, but they are not a very great success, for the simple reason that the men are overworked, working from 10 to 13 hours a day; and they do not feel like going to the schools and depriving their families of their own company and society even after those long hours. Sundays, they have none, for most of them go off to work.

The Chairman. Have you noticed, in coming into contact with these men, any hostility upon their part toward the institutions of this country?

Father Kazinci. Absolutely none. They have been branded as anarchists and Bolshevists, and they resent it. . . .

The Chairman. You started to tell us about the conditions there.

Father Kazinci. The men are worked from 10 to 13 hours a day. The conditions under which they are living are bad for America. The housing conditions are terrible. The work conditions, the hours of work, are absolutely impossible, and I think that it tends to make the men become disgusted with the country, and they will say, " Well, let us go back to the old country; perhaps it is going to be better than it is for us here." There is no hope of them bettering their condition, for they work from the time the whistle begins to blow in the morning until they are whistled out at 6 o'clock in the evening; they must be at the gates there, and they have to work all the time.

Senator Sterling. Now, about the housing conditions, will you describe those?

Father Kazinci. Well, two rooms, as a rule, are the headquarters of the workers. The lower part is a kitchen and upstairs is the living room, if you can call it such, and the sleeping room for the family, and they have to sleep there. Sometimes they have boarders and sometimes there are four or five sleeping in a room.

Senator Sterling. As a matter of fact, do many of them have less than four rooms?

Father Kazinci. Yes; most of them have only two rooms.

There is no doubt but that for Father Kazinci the issues involved in the steel strike were peculiarly simplified. He saw the strikers' cause as a protest against oppression, oppression represented by conditions in the steel mills, by the activities of the State Constabulary and the county authorities as well as the authorities of Braddock. He testified before the Senate Committee of the interference by the State Constabulary with his parishioners as they were leaving St. Michael's Church after a mission on September 21. He wired an account of the circumstances to the Governor of

Pennsylvania, but so far as could be learned this telegram was without result. His church was attended by strikers who came from miles around Braddock. Sometimes they could not all be accommodated in the auditorium of the church and a special sermon was preached for a sort of overflow meeting in the basement of the church.

In direct contrast to the position taken by Father Kazinci was that of the Rev. P. Molyneux, pastor of St. Brendan's Roman Catholic Church of Braddock, Pa., as shown by the sermon preached by him on September 21, the day before the strike began. This sermon was afterward printed in a pamphlet, from which the following quotations are taken:

I wish to call your attention to a matter of vital concern and importance to this community, namely, this threatened steel strike that outsiders are coming in here to bring about. This strike is not being brought about by intelligent or English-speaking workmen, but by men who have not interest in the community, are not an element of our community, and who do not have the welfare of our men at heart.

Within the last two weeks I have talked to at least two hundred men with regard to this threatened strike—all intelligent, English-speaking workmen, some from my own parish, and some outside, and I could not find one instance among these two hundred men where the men wanted to go on strike. . . .

There is one thing I have noticed about these strike leaders, as I suppose most of you have, and that is—with very few exceptions, if any at all—that never a one of them ever had on a workman's blouse in his life—never went into a mill in a pair of overalls— these men were never seen with the honest sweat of toil on their brows. . . .

William Z. Foster, the transplanted strike leader and fomentor of trouble among the steel workers, is a rank, blood-thirsty, socialist. His philosophy is that of a mad-house. He calls himself a syndicalist; I consider him both a fool positive and an ass superlative. The wonder is that so many apparently sensible people stand to listen to the braying of this donkey, but, of course, those that do listen to him are of that class who think with their mouths open. . . .

I have gone through these mills around here occasionally. If, after one of these visits, I were asked who was the hardest working man I saw in that mill, I should say, if I told the truth, that the manager or general superintendent was the hardest working man on the plant. He has to look after all the details of every department—look after everything, with one man always asking him questions on one side and another on the other. . . .

Another thing I have observed with pleasure is that no man could be more solicitous for those under him than the leaders of these mills are. They have left nothing undone to provide for the welfare of their men that could be done. *I think they have reached perfection in this way.*

And sometimes, when I have been talking with them, I have been surprised to find how much they know about each man who works under them. They seem to care for their men with a tenderness equal to that which a mother has for her child. . . .

Another thing I want to tell you, that you may not have thought of, is this: you own these mills, these factories. They are yours inasmuch as they give you employment and a means of earning a livelihood. They are yours, inasmuch as these mills pay most of the taxes in this community which provide the fund to pay for highways, schools and institutions that shelter the aged, the poor, the insane, the needy, that pay for the hospitals for sick and afflicted. All this is done, in large part, by the mills and factories. Hence, you own them, in a way, and when you go to New York, Philadelphia, Cleveland, or Chicago, and naturally speak of " our " homes, " our " schools, " our " institutions, you are speaking the truth when you also say " our " mills and " our " factories. You own them, they are yours as a member of society.

I have talked to a lot of people to find out what this strike was about, what complaint they had to make.

But—you can't reason with these people. Don't reason with them. You can't, any more than you can reason with a cow or a horse. They remind me of a Hollander who became angry at an Irishman and gave him an awful tongue lashing. Pat took it all very meekly, and when it was all over they said to him, " Pat, why didn't you tell that fellow what you thought of him? " " Oh," said Pat, " the only way I could have made any impression on that fellow was to knock him down! " And that's the only way you can reason with these people; knock them down!

We dare those outsiders to start a little gun music on our streets, and they will quickly see how long we will stand it. . . .

What we must make these fellows understand is that we are not going to let them violate the rights of any individual in this community—that whatever they do elsewhere, our men will protect their homes and institutions. If it comes to a test, we will drive out these fellows—the whole lot of them—and never stop driving till we get them the other side of the River Styx, to the land from which no traveler returns.

What if they start to pillage or destroy? If you see a man take from a store or house something that is not his, do not reason with him, knock him down! If you have a revolver, shoot him right down then and there. Don't hesitate, for that is your duty as a citizen. They talk about sympathy for the workman, and no one has more human sympathy than myself—when there is an occasion and a just cause for sympathy. But here the facts are too plain, and we are face to face with facts.

In case this strike should take place, and there is a riot, I want to give you people a solemn warning; smother your curiosity. Let the women keep off the streets with their children, and give the men a clear field, and we will show these hoodlums what we are. I want all these men that have been abroad to put themselves at once under the direction of the men in authority who can use them. Show them that you fought for liberty abroad, and will maintain liberty at home!

The *News-Herald* of Braddock of October 23 printed a letter from Governor Sproul to Father Molyneux which, the local paper declared, " speaks for itself."

My dear Father Molyneux:—

Through the generosity of some unknown friend, I have received a booklet containing a copy of the sermon preached by you, on September 21st last, and I wish to compliment you for the very good judgment expressed therein, and for your more than generous contribution to our efforts to maintain order and enforce laws.

I heartily agree with your analysis of the present situation. The danger comes not from the English-speaking workmen, but from the foreigners of the community, who have neither sympathy

for our policies nor interest in our institutions. Tradition means
nothing to them, and lawlessness and disorder are " music " to their
" ears," and a realization of their fanciful dreams.

I wish that there were more clergymen in our Commonwealth
who, not only thought, but expressed their thoughts as you do. I
wish to thank you sincerely for your efforts of the past and have
the courage to express the hope that they will be continued in the
future.

> Very respectfully yours,
>
> (Signed) Wm. C. Sproul, (Governor).

To the newspapers of Pittsburgh Father Molyneux's views
during the strike were " good news," obtaining space, but
Father Kazinci's views were " crowded out." A little weekly
called the *Inner Mission Worker,* issued by the Lutheran
Inner Mission Society, the Rev. Ambrose Hering, superintendent, contained the following (issue of November, 1919)
expression of independence which was not welcomed by Pittsburgh newspapers:

THE STEEL STRIKE

The steel strike cannot be considered alone. It is but the
symptom of a wide-spread social and economic unrest. The poor
misguided officials who think they can end the strike by suppressing
free speech and the right of assembly will have a wide awakening
not far hence. And the Corporation which insists in getting its
claws upon the machinery of government by handling mayors,
sheriffs, and state constabularies will also have a premature awakening. It is significant that the present steel strike has been called
" a strike for freedom."

The report comes now that the Winnipeg strike had features
which the newspapers dared not tell, and Mayor Hanson, of Seattle,
after all was not the hero the press claimed. We talk about
Americanization. Will the repression of speech, the deportation of
aliens without public hearing, the imprisonment of labor leaders
without bail and the injustice of the minor courts make for law
and order? One of the Homestead strikers said: " The government stood for these things during the war, Mr. Wilson has written

them in the international labor treaty; the government has invited other nations to endorse them. Why does Congress not stand by us? Our boys helped to make the world safe for democracy; have we lost it for ourselves?"

"A good deal is being said about the 'foreign element.' Who brought this foreign element to America? Did not the Corporations comb Europe for cheap labor? Capital advertised. 'Men wanted—foreigners only need apply.' Foreign labor was cheap. Racial and religious differences kept them from uniting and organizing. Now when this 'foreign element' insists on organizing it is called, I. W. W., Bolshevists, Reds, etc. One of these days we shall have to face the real facts. All of us know that at present it is impossible to get the real facts. Why do the newspapers deliberately withhold the truth? Why is even the religious press colored?"

V—*The Questionnaire*

To all the pastors on the mailing list of the Pittsburgh Council of the Churches of Christ, approximately six hundred in number, a questionnaire with regard to the steel strike and the industrial situation was sent on November 19 by this Commission. Eighty-eight answers were received.

The questionnaire was designed to give results that might be of interest and instruction to all the congregations reached by the Interchurch World Movement, and particularly to bring out the fact whether or not the pastors believed existing facilities were sufficient to give them and their congregations adequate information regarding not only the steel strike, but the industrial situation as a whole.

The answers received are obviously the result of serious reflection upon such information as is available to pastors. Many indicate that pastors have felt it their duty to make personal inquiry and investigation of points at issue and many also indicate a dissatisfaction with existing facilities for getting at the facts involved, especially with the public press.

The questionnaire was as follows:

1. Do you think you are getting the facts in the present local industrial situation?

2. Do you think the laboring man has any grounds for saying that the newspapers are unfair to him?

3. Do you think that any efforts are being made, for example by the press, to have native Americans suppress strike meetings and meetings in favor of the strikers?

4. Do you feel that there is a need for a newspaper to be founded, owned and controlled by all the cooperating churches of the Pittsburgh district for the purpose of furnishing full, unbiased news reports on local, state and national questions including that of industrial relations?

5. Could such a newspaper be made self-supporting by clean and honest methods of advertising?

6. Why do you think the native American workmen are on the job while the foreigner-workmen are on strike?

7. Do you believe that labor has any just grievance against capital today?

8. The Federal Council of Churches and most of the individual denominations in the United States have adopted the "Social Creed of the Churches," one statement of which is that the churches must stand "for the most equitable division of the product of industry that can ultimately be devised." Do you feel that labor is getting its just share of the product of labor today?

9. Another statement from the Social Creed of the Churches is that the churches must stand for the "right of employees and employers alike to organize." Does this in your judgment mean that the churches must stand for collective bargaining? Do you agree with the statement in principle?

10. Would you be in favor of establishing Industrial Study Groups in every congregation, the purpose of the groups to be as follows: To study both local and general industrial problems; to hold weekly group discussions or bi-weekly public forums or monthly public forums in conjunction with the groups in the various churches of the community; to study working conditions and industrial crises such as strikes and conditions threatening strikes?

In classifying the answers to the above questions answers such as "Emphatically" or "Not at all" and other answers carrying merely the import of " Yes " or " No " are included in the " Yes " and " No " results. Otherwise the comment given in answering the various questions is noted. In some cases answers were omitted.

Question 1, *Do you think you are getting the facts in the present industrial situation?* was answered in the negative by thirty-six and in the affirmative by fifteen, two of the fifteen indicating that they were getting the facts by personal investigation.

There were thirty-five answers that could not be classified as simply " yes " or " no." Eleven correspondents indicated that they were getting only a partial view of the facts, and among the other answers were the following : " Not altogether sure," " No, nor in other distressing situations either," " Pretty fully, but not through the press," " Biased, naturally," " The real facts on the laborer's side are not printed," " My experience has been that capital cites best cases as typical and labor the poorest. By taking the two and striking an average, one could probably come near the truth," " Not both sides," " Not from daily press, but from certain weeklies, yes," " So far as newspapers are concerned, no," " Only one side," " Not from daily press," " Not enough in local press," " Not impartially," " As well as we get any facts through the press," " Yes, through Pittsburgh press and other papers representing the other side. Pittsburgh papers too frequently represent the side of capital."

Question 2, *Do you think the laboring man has any grounds for saying that the newspapers are unfair to him?* was answered in the affirmative by forty-four and in the negative by twelve.

There were twenty-five exceptions to the " yes " and " no " classification and these mainly called attention to the fact that in some cases the newspapers were fair and in other cases unfair. Among the other exceptions were these, " The followers of Gompers and Foster have no just grievance," " Labor, too, is unfair. He's getting his own medicine," " The newspapers pretend the men are returning to work when they are not doing so," " There may be a bias, but not to the limit of being unfair," " This claim has more basis locally than nationally," " Public also has larger reasons for complaint against both laboring man and newspapers," " The newspapers covered up many things," " Not more than any other class."

Question 3, *Do you think that any efforts are being made, for example by the press, to have native Americans suppress strike meetings in favor of the strikers?* was answered in the affirmative by thirty-four and in the negative by fifteen.

The exceptions were all of the following nature, " In Pittsburgh through the proclamation of city and borough officials," " See no evidence of it, but they should in many cases," " Not except where radicals are wild," " The press of the country, I think, has been truly American in urging American workmen to break up un-American meetings," " Only where such meetings ought not to be held because detrimental to the public good," " If these meetings were held in the spirit of Americanism they would be O K," " I think efforts are made through political and other machinery to suppress meetings that are harmless," " Yes, most labor activities are now characterized as ' Red ' affairs. The workers have been denied their constitutional and God-given rights in many cases. The right of free speech has been almost entirely taken from them in public. These restrictions are not in line with true democracy," " In the steel strike public sentiment has influenced Americans more than the newspapers," " Think strikes at present are uncalled for," " Most of the meetings in question should be suppressed," " If the question means do the newspapers encourage lawlessness on the part of the State Constabulary and the American Legion, yes," "Not unjustly," "Why should not every red-blooded American who loves his motherland be against strikes called by a Foster and such ilk to raise the hell of Bolshevism and stir up lawlessness," "I believe there is an effort to suppress meetings. Personally I am convinced that meetings should be permitted, even of a radical nature. Every effort to suppress adds fuel to the flames. A vocal expression often causes the blowing off of steam which proves to be harmless. But fire under a boiler and not letting out any steam produces a pressure so great that there will be an explosion. I do not believe that labor in America is permitted anything like the freedom that is permitted in labor discussion in England. There is an effort to make war conditions apply to present-day conditions. Even during the war there was much more freedom in discussion than in America, especially criticism of the Government."

Question 4, *Do you feel that there is a need for a newspaper to be founded, owned and controlled by all the cooperating churches of the Pittsburgh district for the purpose of furnishing full, unbiased news reports on local, state and national questions including that of industrial relations?* was answered in the affirmative by fifty-seven and in the negative by fifteen.

There were seven exceptions to the " yes " and " no " classification. They were as follows: "I think the need is rather for Christian direction of the existing newspapers," " Yes, because our journals are all politically owned or controlled and are horribly partisan. Almost every one represents either one man or one machine. Few represent Christ or the Church and much that should get to men's eyes is suppressed," " Would prefer to see an interdenominational paper achieved by uniting some of the denominational papers," " No, because such a paper would be used for union labor and not for free labor," " Wouldn't be satisfactory to churches three months," " Might be a good move if impartially edited, but if put under the direction of men inclined to either side better not try it," " Yes, provided that they publish the facts concerning the unfair and un-American treatment of negroes in public places and demand a Federal law against lynching, Jim Crowism, etc."

Among the direct affirmative " yes " and " no " opinions some based their affirmative answers on the belief that such a newspaper could be impartially edited and some based their negative answers on the belief that it could not be impartially edited.

Question 5, *Could such a newspaper be made self-support- ing by clean and honest methods of advertising?* was an- swered in the affirmative by twenty-five and in the negative by 23. A number of correspondents who answered affirma- tively to the question concerning the need for such a paper answered this question in the negative. Many felt unquali- fied to answer the question owing to lack of experience.

Among the various comments in answer to this question were the following: " Not at first," " I should think so if the people of the churches have the courage of their convictions," " It might not until its reputation was demonstrated," " Not unless sufficient money were invested to make a first-class paper," " I should hope so, but doubt it without a large sum back of the enterprise for a long time," " The Detroit *Times* has shown that this can be done," " If unpartisan com- manding a large circulation, advertisers would seek its col- umns," " If Christian people were not afraid it could." The Rev. W. P. Vasner of the Noblestown Methodist Episcopal Church, after citing a case of such a newspaper in his ex- perience, said, " This plan with organized church leadership would produce clean moral results and financial success. I believe there is a possibility of starting such an enterprise with 50,000 stockholders."

Question 6, *Why do you think the native American work-*

men are on the job while the foreigner-workmen are on strike? was answered by statements that can be classified as follows with the figure after each statement representing the number who expressed the same view:

Because a larger percentage of the American workmen are the skilled and receive higher wages, 13.

Because the Americans were influenced by the charge of radicalism, 11.

Because the foreign workmen are more easily influenced, 22.

Because the foreign workmen are not sufficiently Americanized, 1.

Because of German and Bolshevik propaganda among the foreign-born, 3.

Because of union leadership which appealed chiefly to foreign workmen, 1.

The foreign workmen are the dupes of agitators, 1.

Foreign workmen can live cheaply and move easily, 1.

Because the Americans distrusted Foster, 2.

Because the aliens are badly treated, 1.

Eleven correspondents questioned the hypothesis on which the question was based and properly called attention to the fact, which was true of many communities, that the American workmen were out solidly with the foreign workmen. Thus it is clear that at least eleven of the correspondents were informed of a fact which the newspapers generally were inclined to suppress. The Rev. Carroll C. Byler of Pittsburgh made the following observation: " I know personally to the contrary. Wherever the unions are organized the great majority are close together, American and foreigner. In the steel situation the Americans who are on the job are the ones who have union agreements with their employers. The foreigners likewise will be found working side by side with them."

Question 7, *Do you believe that labor has any just grievance against capital today?* was answered in the affirmative by
thirty-five and in the negative by six. In addition eight
others answered the question in this form: " Yes, but Capital,
too, has a just grievance against Labor." Three correspondents put their answer in substantially this form: " Not the
present wage scale, but the attitude of Capital toward Labor is the basis for Labor's grievance against Capital." Two
correspondents offered the comment that the grievance of
labor is really based on a demand for a more equitable division of the product of industry. Five correspondents made
the observation that in some industries labor has a just grievance and in other cases none. Three correspondents said that
though labor had some just grievance, it was not as great as
some labor leaders would imply.

The following comments were also offered:

" Labor's grievances not sufficient to justify its demands," " Capital thinks of itself first and labor as it must in most instances,"
" Labor has a just grievance against Capital and the public against
both," " The wage system fails to afford the worker a personal interest in the success of industry." " Labor has a just grievance in
the arbitrary stand of executives like Gary," " Labor has a grievance and against the Steel Corporation, but the organizers did
not inspire confidence. Many concerns are fair, others are not,"
" Labor has a just grievance in two ways only, regarding the eight-
hour day and Sunday for all who desire it, not as regards more
pay and collective bargaining in the mills," " Labor has a grievance against Capital as part of the general public," " Labor has
some grievances against capital, but it is fair to say that the employer is making a sincere effort to better working conditions and
home surroundings of employees," " We need a new order, a new
relationship. The wage system is outgrown. Labor should share
in profits and management."

More extended comments were as follows:

" I think the basic principle in all relationships of Capital and
Labor is wrong at the present time and results in injustices both
ways. The present basis is ' competition for gain,' which is the
industrial term for ' the struggle for existence,' whereas the basis

should be the truly scientific one, ' Cooperation for mutual service.' "

" Labor has always had a just grievance. Capital, through oppression, exploitation and high cost of living, is pressing harder than ever upon the rights of men. There is a solution that is never touched by our industrial leaders. The real question will be properly and justly solved when excess and other profits are reduced or divided with the worker. Capital has shown labor that whatever betterment in conditions are had, Labor must fight to the bitter end to that attainment. . . . Labor makes her many mistakes, true, and is justly condemned, but she is the oppressed, the exploited, and her mistakes are made in her sincere efforts to uplift humanity, to aid the poor whom Jesus Christ came to as a special friend and saviour."

" Labor's grievance of today is based upon the treatment which it received from capital in the past. True, as capital says, labor never received so much as in the present time. But capital forgets the days when it paid the minimum for existence, made people work under dangerous conditions, the lack of safety devices, the following deaths and the generally brutal treatment of widows and orphans, the loss of time during accidents. All these are back sins that capital has against it and for which it is now indicted. So far capital does not admit any past sin. It has yielded through pressure. And labor is driving its bargain just as hard as it can."

Question 8, *The Federal Council of Churches and most of the individual denominations in the United States have adopted the " Social Creed of the Churches," one statement of which is that the churches must stand " for the most equitable division of the product of industry that can ultimately be devised." Do you feel that labor is getting its just share of the product of labor today?* was answered in the negative by thirty-seven and in the affirmative by twelve. Seventeen correspondents made the comment that in some cases labor is receiving its just share in the product of industry, while in other cases it is not. Four correspondents offered comment to the effect that labor is not yet receiving its just share, but is doing so in increasing measure.

Other comments offered were as follows: " Some labor is receiving its just share, but there is too much centralization of wealth," " Union labor is getting more than its just share," " Salaried men and mental workers are not getting a just share," " Capital and labor are dominated by insatiable greed for which the public pays."

Question 9 was as follows: *Another statement from the Social Creed of the Churches is that the churches must stand for the " right of employees and employers alike to organize."* (a) *Does this statement in your judgment mean that the churches must stand for collective bargaining?* (b) *Do you agree with the statement in principle?* Division (a) of this question was answered by forty-three in the affirmative and eleven in the negative. Division (b) was answered by fifty-two in the affirmative and nine in the negative.

Such comment as did not give direct answers to the points raised were to the effect that the proper form of organization would be cooperation, or that while collective bargaining may be right in principle it is subject to abuse in practice.

Question 10 was as follows: *Would you be in favor of establishing Industrial Study Groups in every congregation, the purpose of the groups to be as follows: To study both local and general industrial problems; to hold weekly group discussions or bi-weekly public forums or monthly public forums in conjunction with the groups in the various churches of the community; to study working conditions and industrial crises such as strikes and conditions threatening strikes?* The question was answered in the affirmative by forty-two and in the negative by twenty-seven.

Some of those answering in the negative gave comment explaining that they were opposed because such a plan was foredoomed to failure because of insufficient interest in the community. Some of the objections were based on the claim that such study groups would be taking the activities of the Church out of their proper sphere. In a few cases comment raised the question as to whether competent leadership representing both sides of industrial questions could be found for such study groups.

*VI—Opinions of Individual Clergymen on the Church
and Industrial Unrest*

Little comment is necessary in presenting the material included in this sub-division of the report on the relation of the pulpit to the strike. The views expressed are those of clergymen of the Pittsburgh district. With the exception of the first two statements and other exceptions which will be noted, an expression of their views was asked for from men who had been more or less active in seeking information as to the strike and as to the relation of the Church to the industrial problem as a whole.

The first statement is from the Rev. William M. Woodfin, pastor of the First Presbyterian Church of Homestead, Pa., who has been mentioned elsewhere in this report. His statement came in the form of a supplement to his answers to the above "questionnaire," his answers being for the most part "*yes and no.*" The position taken in the following letter is substantially the same as that taken in his article against the strikers and their grievances in the New York *Tribune,* his information and views being based largely upon the testimony of Mr. Gary before the Senate Committee and upon an investigation of working conditions through the accommodation of employers or mill officials. His letter follows:

"I do not think that a paper owned and run by the church movement would be a success for the simple reason it would have no more influence than the other papers. Who would edit it? If you got an editor who is like some of your representatives then the conservative employers would not support it, and if you got a conservative editor then the radicals would not support it. I had rather trust the present newspapers to handle this matter than a lot of church people. It would harm the church more than it would help the cause. The laboring man gets a square deal from the press when he gives the public a square deal in service to the country and he gets what he deserves when he tries to put over things that are wrong. When the church cannot speak with one voice upon religious matters, how do you expect her to speak with one voice in matters of industry, in which she has limited knowledge and diversified interests.

"Labor always has just grievances against capital from the standpoint of the laboring man who believes that capital should be eliminated. The place where labor and capital clash is not over present conditions, but over the fundamental principles of the rights of private ownership of property. Labor, led by certain radicals, will have just grievances until the public works are bought or seized and turned over to them, as Foster and his associates promised to the men here in Homestead in order to induce them to strike. The laboring man is getting a good wage—lots better wage than the school teachers and preachers who are trying to right his wrongs. The alien in the mill, with no asset but brawn, is making twice the wage that the college-bred teacher is making in our public schools. It is time for the Interchurch Movement were turning its attention to a propaganda to these people who are responsible for the ideals of the country rather than the men who lift and handle steel.

"We recognize the right of capital to organize, and if so then labor has the same rights. But that does not deny the employer the right to say who shall work in his mill or shop. The whole controversy is open and closed shop. If labor would accept and stand by certain obligations I would be favorable to recognizing her unions, but when she gets a bit of power she proceeds to exploit it and violate her obligations. The steel mills here had the union, and the union, when it got into power, proceeded to dominate the management, with the result that production was reduced and efficiency was decreased. This led to the death of the union and the open shop policy of the company.

"I do not consider that any creed adopted by the Federal Council of Churches has any binding force upon the churches of the country on the labor question. The men who wrote the creed may be good men and they may be experts on the question, but I resent the attitude of any group of men solving at long range the labor problems of the local communities which they know little or nothing about. And further there are some of us that resent the advise of the Interchurch World Movement sending out appeals to ministers and churches to keep quiet and say nothing on this strike situation until they could go to the bottom of the matter and make a decision for them to give to their people. Such a policy on their part has tended to destroy local leadership at a time when leadership was vital to the life of the community and the stability of the country. After you investigate matters the questions are all settled and any man can speak. The Interchurch World Movement ought not to put itself up as the final voice of authority of the church on the labor question when there are thousands of men who are just as competent to pass on the rightness and wrongness of a strike as the splendid men who constitute your committee.

"The Roman Catholic Church did not wait until they heard from their hierarchy before telling the people what they should do. They studied the question for themselves and hit straight out from the shoulder and the people respect them for it. It was the Roman Catholic ministers who spoke out in this strike and told their people what they should do while we, the Protestants, were exhorted from your headquarters[1] to keep quiet on the question until a commission could pass on it.

"The solution of the labor question is not one that can be solved by increasing the wages of the men. Wages have increased here for more than 100 per cent. It is not a question that can be solved by better living conditions, for there are many of the people who live well. It can be solved by the Gospel of Christ, the gospel of unselfishness, the gospel of a square deal on the part of both labor and capital, the gospel of a full day's work for a full pay envelope, the gospel that recognizes property rights, human rights and personal rights, and this is only possible by the church preaching and living the Gospel of Christ."

The following letter is from the Rev. E. J. Headley of Castle Shannon, Pa., in reply to the questionnaire:

"I always have felt that labor does not get a square deal from capital, speaking generally. There doubtless are exceptions. Labor does not get a just share of what it produces. If capital has a

[1] No such appeal or advice was sent out by the Interchurch World Movement nor did the Interchurch Movement have any knowledge of an appeal for silence sent out by the Pittsburgh Council.

right to combine for the development of industry; labor without doubt has a right to unite for self-protection and betterment of their conditions. But I further believe that labor has no moral right to strike and cause a whole nation to suffer as is being done now, any more than capital has a right to 'profiteer' and rob the country.

"I fear we are not getting all the facts in regard to the present labor troubles. I believe the publication of an independent unbiased newspaper would fill a great need. But it must demonstrate that it was not influenced in the least by capital on the one hand or labor agitators on the other. It should speak the truth fearlessly notwithstanding the rich in the churches. It must be established on an ample independent financial basis, so as not to be dependent on advertising from the monied interests.

"I feel the opportunity of centuries is before the church now. And if the church wishes to propagate herself and carry out the Master's Program she dare not let this opportunity pass. This is no ordinary time. I feel we must make a strong bid for the laboring man. I have had them tell me that the church does not care for the laborer. We must, in some way, prove that we do. We must not only Americanize the foreigner, but Christianize the American."

In reply to a request for a statement of his views on the relation of the Church to the steel strike and to the industrial problem, the Rev. Ambrose Hering, superintendent of the Lutheran Inner Mission Society, presented the following statement:

"As a matter of general principle, let me quote the opinions of men whose ideas are worth a good deal more than my own. Years ago before the days of corporations, Dr. C. F. W. Walther said, 'We know that the sufferings of the laboring class are mainly due to the blood-sucking tyranny of the rich. We are not the friends of the heartless employer who lives in splendor while his laborers suffer want, but we are in principle his enemies. O, brethren, what would we be if we did not sponsor the cause of the oppressed masses, but the cause of the bloodsuckers? We should then be the scurviest and most infamous hypocrites on the face of the globe if, in that case, we still pretended to accept the Bible as our guide in religion.'

"Four hundred years ago Luther advocated arbitration as a means of settling differences between the employing nobility and the laboring peasants. Let representatives be appointed from both groups, 'who shall in an amicable manner discuss and adjust the matter; that you lords lower your stiff-necked pride, as you must do, willy-nilly, in the end, and that you cease from your tyranny and oppression, so that the poor man also may have room to breathe and live; that the peasants also come to their senses and give up those articles of theirs that go too far.'

"We can all agree that the fundamental duty of the Church is to proclaim the truth. The true Church stands for liberty and it is not afraid to turn on the light. It is becoming increasingly clear that the newspapers, at the bidding of the steel trust, have conspired to keep the facts from the public. They have become the most formidable agents of a power which hates the light. When it comes to the facts which the average Pittsburgher has of the steel strike his mind is rather darkness. He does not know. It looks as though the employers feared the light. Also it is becoming increasingly evident that from the state 'Cossacks' down there is a peculiar bond between the public authorities and the steel corporations. The lid has been down absolutely tight on meetings and free speech. In the midst of such darkness liberty becomes a mockery and ignorance makes slaves of us. The public, the third party in this crisis, is denied the real facts, and in the long run the public becomes the jury which decides the merits of the case. The fundamental things for which the Church is in the world are being trampled under foot. For my part, I say, let the Church accept the challenge of this darkness loving agent. We welcome this inquiry into the present situation.

"The local churches should have done something long ago. Here and there pastors promptly rose to the occasion but the press faithfully ignored them."

The following statement on " What Should Be the Attitude of the Church in the Industrial Situation? " is from the Rev. Daniel L. Marsh, superintendent of the Methodist Episcopal Church Union of Pittsburgh and pastor of the Smithfield Street Church:

" Neutrality in the Kingdom of Christ is impossible. True religion touches all of life. The Church must proclaim the whole Gospel for the whole man.

" Jesus not only forgave the individual sinner who came to Him; He also interested Himself in the physical well-being of children and the amelioration of the hard conditions of the poor. He declared that He came not to destroy the Law and the Prophets, but to fulfill them. And He did fulfill them, as the oak fulfills the acorn, as the noon fulfills the dawn. By His life, His death, and His teaching, He fulfilled the Law and the Prophets.

" Read the Old Testament Prophets, such as Amos, Hosea, Isaiah, and see if they remained neutral on social, political and economic questions. Christ's sermon on the Mount is a thunder-crash of condemnation against unrighteousness, and a lightning-flash of truth that illumines the whole landscape of personal and social righteousness.

" Therefore, the Church dare not seek to remain neutral in the industrial struggle. It can't be done. In my book, ' The Challenge of Pittsburgh,' after having described Pittsburgh as the industrial metropolis of the United States, I go on to speak of the message of the Church for this industrial age, as follows:

" ' What about the responsibilities of the captains of industry who have achieved success in Pittsburgh? And what about the great army of men and women whose toil gives to Pittsburgh this industrial supremacy? Has the church any message for an industrial age? The stress and strife and struggle of our time are industrial and economic for commercial advantage. Our sins are industrial; our injustices are industrial; even vice has been commercialized; political scandals, due to commercial corruption, come and go.'

" But, indeed, the Church does not seek to remain neutral. It has a message, both for capital and labor. Witness, for example, the ' Social Creed of the Churches' and the more recent pronouncements of the leaders of the most of the denominations.

" The Church should never apologize for making an honest investigation of particular industrial disputes in order to determine the side of justice.

" But the Church must never become the champion of one ' class ' against another. The Church must know nothing about ' classes.' It must insist upon justice and righteousness being done by all and to all. It must do this without fear or favor. It must so conduct itself as to merit the common opinion held of our Lord in the days of His flesh, viz.: ' Teacher, we know you are sincere and fearless; you do not court human favor. You teach the way of God honestly.' "

The following statement is from the Rev. Charles Reed Zahniser, executive secretary of the Pittsburgh Council of Churches:

" The Pittsburgh Council of Churches has been going on the principle that the church should be to the state and to all other institutions of organized society, as ' an enlightened pedagogue, ever nudging on toward better things.' We have assumed that the preacher should be to the people as the prophet of God who stands on the wall and cries aloud to warn the people or to call them forward. It is ours to bring the facts in any given matter before the people, measuring the facts up against the principles of Jesus, and keeping them there till the people change them. This sometimes means to be very explicit, even personal, and say ' Thou art the man ' responsible for a certain unwholesome situation. But it is not the normal function of the religious institution to become the executive, either in social control or social service.

" Applied to industrial relations and progress, this means that the church should be forward in insisting that they be brought into conformity to the principles of Jesus, but it is not hers to work out detailed programs of industrial reconstruction or to sit as judge in industrial disputes. Jesus was fearless and explicit in attacking men in high positions of economic power because they devoured widows' houses and left undone the weightier matters of the law, justice, mercy and truth, but he absolutely refused to be an arbiter in a given dispute, saying, ' Who made me a judge or divider over you? '

" This does not mean, however, that the churches should limit themselves to innocuous generalities in times of tense industrial strain or in a situation like the steel strike. I think it is ours first of all, to help the people get the actual facts and that without bias. In many cases this will be sufficient. It will show some Christian principle or human interest so involved as to make clear where the wrong lies. The fact that labor particularly, often complains that it does not get a fair chance through the daily press and other agencies of publicity to get its side before the people, makes this all the more important.

"Frequently there is involved in an industrial dispute some principle for which the church stands and which is so clearly in evidence that the church should speak out plainly, at least on that issue of the controversy. Such is the sanctity of contract which involves personal integrity. Such is the right of free speech and free assembly. Such also, I believe, is the right of labor, by collective bargaining or some equally effective measure, to have an actual part in control of the terms and conditions of industry, and such also is the eight-hour day in necessarily continuous industries where the alternative is an inhuman twelve-hour day through a seven-day week. Other examples are unsanitary or dangerous conditions of industry, child labor and wages so low as to force overcrowded housing, under-feeding or the supplementing of family income by outside labor of the mother or others who should not be so employed. On issues such as these the churches should speak plainly and demand that any necessary readjustments be made to right them."

I. The following letters were the records transmitted to the Commission by the Committee of the Pittsburgh Federal Council of Churches as obtained in their investigation:

Pittsburgh, Pa., October 1, 1919.

Mr. W. Z. Foster,
Magee Building,
Pittsburgh, Pa.

Dear Sir:

Pursuant to your conversation with the committee of this organization yesterday, I am instructed to ask you the following questions and respectfully request that you answer them in writing for the information of the people we represent:

1. We understand that you acknowledge the authorship of the book entitled "Syndicalism" which bears your name and is now in circulation here, but say that it does not in all regards set forth your present views. Do you today advocate the theory of social organization there set forth, namely: the substitution for the present political and social order, of one constructed on an industrial instead of a territorial unit, and in which the entire social control shall be exercised by workers as such?

2. If so, do you today advocate and believe in undertaking to secure these ends by methods of violence in which the workers proceed by violent seizure of property?

3. Do you believe in and advocate personal violence on the part of workers as a means of securing their ends?

4. Do you believe in and advocate sabotage, in the sense of deliberate crippling of machinery and destruction of other property as a means of accomplishing the above ends?

5. Do you believe in and advocate the taking of property without compensation to the present owners as a means or method of arriving at the above ends; by this is meant property in

general, not only such as may appear to have been secured by flagrantly unscrupulous methods?

6. Do you believe and advocate that "No considerations of 'legality,' religion, patriotism, 'honor,' 'duty,' etc." should stand in the way of "the workingman accomplishing the above ends," by this we mean those fundamental virtues as such, not their occasional perversion by interested parties for their own advantage?

7. Has the above named book been circulated or issued in any way by the Committee for Organizing the Steel Industry or by you as their agent in the present campaign?

8. Are the theories or principles of this book the real purpose of the present strike, and was it started principally or in any part as a means to that end?

Thanking you for your courtesy when with our committee and in readily agreeing to set forth the matters then discussed, in writing as we are now requesting, I am

Respectfully yours for the Committee

(Signed) C. R. Zahniser,

Secretary.

P. S. Kindly address your answer to the Chairman of the committee, Rev. Daniel L. Marsh, Smithfield Street & Seventh Avenue, City. On account of his having been called from the city today, I am writing for him.

CRZ

NATIONAL COMMITTEE FOR ORGANIZING IRON & STEEL WORKERS.

October 8th, 1919.

Rev. Daniel L. Marsh,
Smithfield Street & Seventh Avenue,
Pittsburgh, Penna.

Dear Sir:

A few days ago I received a letter from Rev. Zahniser asking me to state my position upon a number of points suggested by the present steel strike and requesting me to direct my reply to you. If you failed to get my answer sooner it has been because I have been out of town and consequently unable to send it to you. Rev. Zahniser asks me a series of questions, numbered from 1 to 8. I shall reply to them in the same order, taking up each one separately:

1. Yes, I am one of the authors of the pamphlet "Syndicalism." But since writing it a number of years ago my ideas have changed so radically that it no longer represents my trend of thot. Whether or not our future government will be based upon territorial or industrial lines is a question that I concern myself very little about nowadays. My plan is to improve conditions as I find them and to not waste my time speculating about ideal systems of government.

2. I believe that the best way for the workers to secure their ends is to proceed in a way that will retain for themselves the support of public opinion. This of course would exclude all sorts of violence, except possibly under such extreme circumstances as existed in Colorado, where the workers were literally hunted like beasts.

3. Same answer as to No. 2.

4. No, for reasons outlined in No. 2.

5. This question is too general for a specific answer. I will say tho that what any man has honestly earned I consider to be his and will do what I can to help him retain it. But what a man has stolen I favor making him give up. I will say frankly that I consider many of the fortunes of today in the latter class. I don't think their present holders have any better title to them than the southern planters had to their black slaves.

6. By the terms "Legality," "Religion," "Patriotism," "Honor," "Duty," is meant the use of them by those selfish interests who find nothing too sacred to use in covering their schemes of self aggrandisement. For example, I have nothing but contempt for that conception of duty which holds that for an American to be true to himself and his country he must take work in the steel mills and become a strike-breaker. Of course, I have nothing but respect for the fundamental virtues, as such. It is perversion of them to selfish ends that I condemn.

7. The pamphlet has been out of print for a number of years so far as I am concerned. We have not circulated it in this campaign. But we have very good reason to believe that the steel corporations have sent it out in thousands. This should be looked into by the Department of Justice. I have no doubt but that if

any but powerful interests were circulating this book now they would be brot up with a round turn.

8. The present strike is one of the most important moves for liberty ever undertaken by workingmen in this country. It is aimed to secure fundamental justice from one of the most heartless and unscrupulous aggregations of predatory wealth upon the face of the globe. The strike is being conducted upon 100 per cent. trade union principles and for trade union ends. That is all there is to it. The effort being made to distort it from these principles and ends is merely part of the general campaign of the United States Steel Corporation to defeat the legitimate hopes and aspirations of its down-trodden workers.

I trust that I have fully answered the questions posed in Rev. Zahniser's letter. If I have not done so to your satisfaction I'll assure you that it is not from any desire to dodge the issue.

With very best wishes, I remain,

Fraternally yours,

(Signed) Wm. Z. Foster,

Secretary-Treasurer.

II.   Letter of John Fitzpatrick to the Commission of Inquiry. At the outset of the investigation the Commission explained its purpose in identical letters to the leaders of both sides of the strike, requesting their cooperation in securing the necessary data. This reply is here quoted for its evidence, contained in the fifth paragraph, on the attitude of local organized religion at the beginning of the strike.

Nov. 3, 1919.

Rev. Dr. Francis J. McConnell,
   Rev. Dr. Daniel A. Poling,
      Interchurch World Movement,
         111 Fifth Avenue, New York City.
Reverend Gentlemen:

Your letter of October 28th, informing us of the intention of the Interchurch World Movement to request an independent commission of representative clergymen to investigate the steel strike, and inviting our cooperation, has been received.

We welcome the interest of any fair-minded investigators and appreciate the spirit of your approach which you state to be the desire "for information, the fullest and most reliable possible, on which Christians can base some understanding of this strike and current industrial unrest."

We assure you and your representatives the fullest possible co-operation in any and all ways that you may request it of us. Any body will perform a real and needed service which will assist in fairly informing the public of the facts of the steel strike—the methods which have been used by the steel companies and sub-servient officials, courts, newspapers and even clergymen to break it; to confuse the issues; to discredit both leaders and strikers; to distort "Americanism" to the ends of corporate greed; in brief, to prostitute every possible person, instrumentality and ideal to the relentless purpose of profits.

Our cooperation will be given gladly whatever the direction and scope of your investigation; but, if a suggestion may properly be offered, ours would be that your study should reach into the homes and lives of the steel workers for, behind any strike of great num-bers of workers thus voluntarily acting together, must be great human issues, the evaluation of which seems to us the most im-portant part of the whole problem.

With a few isolated exceptions, those who speak for organized religion have thus far ignored or opposed the strike. This will in no wise lessen the completeness and cordiality of our coopera-tion; neither will our desire to assist you be reduced by the diffi-culty which we have to conceive it possible that those who furnish financial resources to the churches will, if they can prevent it, permit the application of Christian principles to a specific in-dustrial issue, any more than they will allow American ideals to be preached or applied. These things must sometime change, of course, for the might of right cannot permanently be defeated. It may well be that your great organization will materially further honest use in industrial conflicts of the principles taught by the Carpenter of Nazareth.

We are at your service at any time and place possible. Details will be arranged in accord with your desires if you will com-municate with the secretary of the National Committee, William Z. Foster, at the above address.

Very truly yours,

(signed) John Fitzpatrick,
Chairman.

III.   Father Ryan of the Catholic University of Washington addressed a public meeting in Johnstown, Pa., during the strike.   He said that Judge Gary's rejection of a meeting with representatives of employees was a rejection not of radicalism but of the first step to a sound system of cooperative economic life.   He said further that collective bargaining was only the beginning, and that the future of the world was a choice between Socialism, Guild Socialism, and Cooperative Production, in which the wage-earners would be advanced to the standing of owners.

THE STEEL REPORT AND PUBLIC OPINION [1]

CONTENTS

SWEEPING statements printed recently, such as "the Interchurch steel report at one stroke reversed the public opinion
of a nation," are more apt to provoke questions than to prove
facts. What is public opinion? Is there such a thing?
How measure it and its reversals?

For conducting an inquiry into "public opinion" and the
Steel Report's effects the Interchurch Commission of Inquiry
would be the last agency to qualify; it might be the first,
however, to apply to for data. These pages note some of
the facts for the future analyst of public opinion, particularly such facts as appear in the records of the Commission
after the publication of the report. The activities took the
forms chiefly of speeches, "open letters" and a Memorial
to Congress.[2] Without being over-solemn about the importance of its own activities, the Commission herewith attempts
a matter of fact record of what happens, or fails to happen,
when a body of citizens investigates a great industry.

The report received the widest publicity, when handed,
complete, to the newspapers on July 28, 1920. Three circumstances contributed to this: first, the report's findings

---

[1] By the Secretary of the Commission.

[2] Unquestionably the Steel Report's whole relation to the public has
afforded sufficient data for a more or less scientific inquiry into "public-
opinion": including such topics as the report's distribution, its effects
or lack of effect on newspapers, public institutions. the government, the
steel industry. Its effect on the organization which made it and on the
relations of church and labor would be especially interesting.

were completely counter to popular estimates of the strike published during its progress; second, the Interchurch Movement's size and nation-wide organization had established noteworthy prestige for its pronouncements; third, charges of suppression had been published, due to the long consideration of the Report by the Interchurch and to the existence of efforts to block publication of the inquiry.[1] Most newspapers in the country, and many abroad, all large news agencies and many periodicals " carried the story," certainly in greater length and prominence than was customary in the case of church reports.

After forty-eight hours, most newspapers' news columns dropped the report. There were exceptions to this; notably the *Christian Science Monitor* subjected the report to many tests by submitting its sections to all sorts of authorities and in eight weeks published seventeen stories or editorials on the report. Labor papers, however, kept publishing the report serially for months; the railroad workers' weekly, *Labor,* reproducing about one hundred and fifty pages of the text for its 200,000 readers, which were in turn copied by the *Journal* of the Amalgamated Iron, Steel and Tin Workers and by numerous other union organs.

The gist of the report thus became sufficiently well known for public men to refer to it in addresses in every part of the country, without explanation, as a matter of national public knowledge. Such references were made for many months; the following from the Syracuse (September 6, 1920) speech of William G. McAdoo, ex-Secretary of the Treasury, being typical:

Suppose that in the recent steel strike, a United States Commission, armed with full authority, had investigated every phase of the steel industry, its books and accounts, its methods and

[1] Some of these efforts are detailed in the Steel Report (pp. 7, 233-34) and in the present volume (Chapter VI, " Under-Cover Men ").

practices and the general conditions surrounding its employes, who can believe that the management would have had the sympathy of the public. On the contrary, the findings of such a Commission, as indicated by the recent illuminating report of the Interchurch World Movement, would inevitably have turned public sympathy in favor of the just demands of the men!

And let me say here, that the recent report of the Interchurch World Movement on the conditions in the steel industry must shock the conscience of America. The truly patriotic and Christian men, who interested themselves in this investigation and brought to light such convicting facts, deserve the praise and support of every good citizen. Men must not be permitted to work 12 hours per day and 7 days a week in this country. Such conditions will not be tolerated by an enlightened public opinion.

The great bulk of editorial comment on the report expressed approval; this meant generally a reversal of the editorial opinion during the strike. At the same time a militant minority, led by trade journals, financial organs and spokesmen of great corporations, assailed the report not on points of fact, but for the character, or alleged character, of its authors. The minority made little headway openly chiefly for one reason: the silence of the steel companies in the face of many demands for a reply.

After one month the status of the report's relation to public opinion was summarized by the Commission's officers in the following, dated August 31:

Open Letter to the " Iron Age "

In the month since the publication of its report on the steel strike the Commission of Inquiry of the Interchurch World Movement has waited patiently for the public reply of the steel companies.

It is astonishing, though understandable, that not one statistical or analytical reply from the criticized managers of the industry has been put forth to challenge the report. The report's fundamentals, viz.,

—the 41 pages on the twelve-hour day and seven-day week and the causes of the companies' failure to reform;

—the 39 pages of wage and living-standard analyses and the resultant living conditions;

—the 45 pages of evidence on effects of arbitrary control in the plants, grievances, welfare work, etc.;

—the 40 pages of evidence, largely documentary, on the social results of a "no-conference" industry;

—the 62 pages of analyzed data on the organization and conduct of the strike, its aims, leaders and failure;

—the 18 conclusions, carefully formulated, and the findings:—

these remain unattacked on points of fact. The report stands.

Mr. Gary unfortunately sailed for Europe within a few days of the report; his secretary, when asked for the Steel Corporation's reply, handed out for publication a letter from a clergyman praising the Corporation's welfare work.

The Corporation's position has been quoted to the Com‧ mission as follows: "The *Iron Age* is talking for us. It tells what we found out long ago, that a lot of Reds made that report." Various letters received by us, moreover, refer to your columns as containing the industry's answer.

Therefore, in this letter, which we ask you in courtesy and fairness to print,[1] we shall: (a) correct certain misstatements made by you, (b) ask questions, (c) make a final effort through your editors to bring the industry's managers to a detailed discussion of the serious facts disclosed.

First permit us to point out that your articles give some justification for the above quoted steel man's characterization of your reply. You have printed four articles;—the first a fair, succinct and almost adequate summary of the contents of the report. This was accompanied by a lengthy editorial, which, aside from one paragraph of seven lines on the industrial facts set forth in the report, is devoted to asserting that

[1] The *Iron Age* declined to print.—H. B.

the report is really the work of investigators "known to entertain radical opinions," that the report was "not a judicial investigation," that "the importance of the red book of syndicalism is belittled," that "the report minimizes the revolutionary sentiments," and calls statements in the report "false and reckless" and "envenomed." (Issue of July 29.)

Your third article (editorial, issue of August 5) condemns the report without reservation, referring to "its obvious bias against the iron and steel industry," asserts "that the Interchurch World Movement has been repudiated by many who at first were disposed to give it support," declares that the Commission was "without adequate knowledge of industrial and labor conditions," but nowhere cites sections of the report which would bear out such charges of ignorance.

Now comes a fourth article, reprinted in the *Wall Street Journal* and elsewhere, by one of your editors, who went to Pittsburgh " to find out if possible how it is feeling in regard to the labor problem and especially the two recent attacks on the steel companies," one of which is asserted to be the report of the Interchurch World Movement, "which made a monumental blunder in meddling in a labor controversy and has published a report which shows how far well-meaning men can be misled." Asserting that Pittsburgh is "too busy and prosperous to be disturbed," this article under the subhead "Fake Pictures Used" asserts that "inquiry as to the methods adopted by Foster and also by the Interchurch Movement has developed some interesting facts." Then follows a column or so charging that photographers faked pictures of the strike and implies that fake methods were characteristic of the Interchurch Movement; "as to the methods of the Interchurch Movement much might be said in the way of unfavorable criticism. Evidence is not lacking that socialistically inclined employees of the Movement were very closely connected with Foster, if indeed he did not direct their movements." [1]

Your article fails to cite the "evidence alleged"; and as to detailed discussion of the Commission or its report, it has one paragraph and this is characterized by such preposterous remarks as, "the twelve-hour day and the seven-day week which *still prevail to some extent.*"

Gentlemen, this is not the reply from the industry which public opinion seems to expect as far as public opinion can be judged by newspaper comment on this report. Classification of the first 111 newspaper clippings received (disregarding labor papers, trade journals and denominational and weekly periodicals), discloses the following: News columns (judged by headlines and general treatment) favorable to the report—49; unfavorable—10; neutral—14; editorials, favorable—26; neutral—4; unfavorable—8 (largely financial journals). Examination of hundreds of later clippings apparently increases heavily the proportion of favorable comment. The following are samples from different parts of the country:

"The steel trust may make a pretense of indifference to all appeals, but it cannot fail to note how steadily the weight of opinion is increasing against it. Industry, the government and organized churches, acting as separate units, are of one mind. The ranks are closing around the steel trust in a way to cause it grave concern." (New York *World,* July 29th.)

"The report of the Interchurch Commission, composed of men whose good faith will not be questioned, concerning conditions in the steel trust industry, is such as to require the Steel Corporation either to refute the charges or to change its policies." (New York *Tribune,* July 29th.)

[1] Recently some interest has been mailing, in plain envelopes, to newspapers throughout the country a circular reprinting an article from a manufacturer's organ attacking the Interchurch Movement as radical. The article, which may be the "evidence" referred to, follows the line of the old material furnished by spies, as recorded in the Steel Report, and adds another document from a spy. The "events" revealed in the new document, however, never took place.

"The report is a challenging document not to be set aside by any suspicion of radical prejudice on the part of the Commission or its agents or by any theory respecting the proper sphere of Christian church activity. Are the facts as stated and are the conclusions warranted? The whole question of industrial relationships is raised by these queries and needs to be raised." (Springfield *Republican,* July 28th.)

"Whether or not the survey and report of the conditions in the steel industry in the United States, planned and carried out by a Commission of the Industrial Relations Department of the Interchurch World Movement, have turned against the Movement certain great business interests in the country that were formerly supporting it, the survey and report have a deep significance." (*Monitor,* Boston, August 2d.)

"The report of the Interchurch World Movement on the steel strike contains a lesson for both the Steel Corporation and its employees. . . . Public opinion does not approve of shifts eleven to fourteen hours long, nor of arbitrary power of bosses, nor of absolute denial of the right to organize." (*Oregonian,* Portland, Oregon, July 31st.)

European comment is not lacking. The Manchester *Guardian* under the caption "A Fearless Strike Inquiry" has this:

"The struggle to establish collective bargaining in the steel industry is by far the greatest industrial conflict of this generation in America. The policy of Judge Gary is reactionary beyond the understanding of British manufacturers. All students of American labor conditions would agree that what is known as Garyism is the greatest breeder of disorder in American life to-day. This report of the churchmen sustains the belief with overwhelming detail."

In the face of such demands do you really consider that suggestions about "Reds" and "bias" constitute an adequate answer to the steel report? Is it being "socialistically inclined" to analyze statistics from steel companies and collect data from hundreds of steel workers? Can the report be painted red because it dissects the records of the strike committee? Do you agree with the New York *Times* which (July 31) declared, as did your latest article, that "the workers were happy and contented" and assailed the report and which has now gone a step farther in a column editorial (August 22)? It concedes that "it is doubtless true that something over one-third of the steel workers are subject to the twelve-hour day, and that a similar number are subject to the seven-day week. It is doubtless true that the Steel Corporation made a highly questionable use of spies and detectives to gather evidence against employees with a tendency to unionism. On the face of the facts produced, moreover, Judge Gary was sadly ignorant of conditions in the works or he willfully misrepresented them in his testimony before the Senate Committee." Then, like your editor, it finds the report "radical," as follows:

"Among the remedies proposed at the conclusion is 'a substitution of industrial democracy for industrial autocracy.' In modern radical parlance 'industrial democracy' is only a politer phrasing for the idea which is basic in Guild Socialism and in the theory of Bolshevism. Doubtless the nine clergymen, including three bishops, comprising the committee are not to be described as bloody revolutionists, nor even as 'Reds.' Yet one cannot escape sympathy with a certain 'under-cover man' who, in a contretemps worthy of crook melodrama, shadowed the clerical party and reported his opinion of them—an opinion which the report quotes in pious horror: 'These are the worst kind of Reds to be connected with, as they are to a certain extent high up in circles that are hard to reach, and they can spread propaganda that hurts.'"

Is it also *your* conception that "industrial democracy" is socialism or Bolshevism? Is it the conception of the steel industry that the system of control called "arbitrary" by Mr. Gary is the only possible kind not liable to charges of "redness"? . . .

You refer (August 5) to the report's " obvious bias against the steel industry."

The steel industry consists of over 400,000 workmen and one huge and many smaller companies whose officials manage the plants in behalf of thousands of stockholders. The Commission had no bias against the workman nor the stockholders nor the machinery and it had for the company heads only a determination to find out the facts about their management of the industry; on the facts the report emphatically condemns the chief policies of the chief managers. Frankly, is not this talk of " bias " principally the reaction of officials in an industry which has fallen so far behind the times in the matter of industrial relations that the directly worded criticism of the ordinary progressive citizen sounds to them like sacrilege?

You assert (July 28) that " the Commission had little active participation in the investigation apart from some open hearings at Pittsburgh, etc."; and " the real work was done by a number of employees of the Commission . . . several of them known to entertain radical opinions on the existing industrial order."

This has been considerably reprinted. It is echoed in the *Wall Street Journal* (July 29). " Interchurch World Movement Commission seems to have an unworldly faith in its Bolshevist employees; " and more recently (August 23), " Subscribers to the Interchurch World Movement have perhaps analyzed its foolish, provocative and biased report of the steel strike. They may have realized how the investigation for that report was made by agents in sympathy with the principles and aims of Bolshevism, and signed by self-deceived altruists devoid of mental grasp or reasoned conviction."

In behalf of the other members of the Commission permit us to say that they include men who have long filled responsible positions with their denominations and a woman noted for philanthropy, some of them active students or mediators in industrial conditions for twenty years, men whom presidents have consulted on public problems, and men who served in public positions or in France during the war. And every one of the seven members of the active Commission took part in the field investigation for this report and spent long days in the consideration of the evidence. Different members can speak for themselves, and the inquiry's files contain the records of their activities; here may be cited the itinerary and calendar of the vice-chairman of the Commission as an example:

Active and daily relation to all phases of the report for eight months.

Personal conversation with the leaders of all groups in all areas investigated, including interviews at length with Judge Gary, President Williams, Mr. Fitzpatrick, officers of independent companies and with the municipal authorities.

Aside from conferences, nine days spent in the field in the Pittsburgh territory, three in Youngstown and Canton, three in Cleveland, two in Chicago.

Homes of scores of strikers visited. Men not on strike and opposed to it conversed with. Cases of alleged attacks by the Pennsylvania State Constabulary looked up. Members of the constabulary interviewed on duty and in living quarters.

Particular attention given to interviews with Catholic and Protestant clergymen, and with representative unrelated citizens.

Mills were watched during changes of shifts and inspected while in operation.

Strikers' homes visited; newspaper reporters conversed with.

Relation of "Reds" to strike leaders was closely studied and an effort made to follow specific clues indicated in conferences with steel officials.

Strike meetings were attended.

Of more than one hundred interviews with individuals interested in leadership activities, more than seventy were with men opposed to the strike.

Followed through the charges furnished by "under-cover"

methods against the Investigating Commission until these attacks were withdrawn and apologized for.

The testimony of a single open hearing conducted by the full Commission constitutes a volume of 248 typewritten pages. Finally our report was unanimous and after months of examination was unanimously adopted by the Interchurch Executive Committee.

Gentlemen of the steel industry, can you answer the nation with anything less than detailed reasoned discussion of the facts disclosed and with action thereon? We found among you, especially among the "independents," not a few men who professed repugnance to "no-conference control" and the means used to maintain the corporation's system. For reasons concerning the corporation, they professed themselves unable to speak out. Are cold facts on an actually existent autocracy to be met forever by trite fears of another, non-existent autocracy, or by talk of "wonderful progress" when the hours in the industry are longer now than ten years ago? Are blacklists and spy-systems the industry's pride? Face the facts.

The above letter, which was fairly widely published in summary, represented the first active effort of the Commission to drive home its report. Simultaneously it published the following:

Open Letter to the Public

The Commission of Inquiry of the Interchurch World Movement appeals to the public to consider one phase of the Commission's report on the steel strike in the light of significant developments since the publication of the report.

Our report set forth the fundamental causes of the strike, pointed out that strike-causing grievances persist so that the industry is drifting toward unrestricted warfare, recommended primarily that the Federal Government set up a Commission which should initiate free open conference between employee and employer and in conclusion phrased in these words a question which the Commission's activities had raised:

Is the nation helpless before conditions in a basic industry which promise a future crisis? Can our democratic society be moved to do industrial justice without the pressure of crisis itself?

Three developments have occurred since the report was published on July 28:

1. The President of the United States has referred the report to the Secretary of Labor, who has taken up the matter with the Commission.

2. On August 3 the American Federation of Labor announced that it would make a " new drive " to organize the industry.

3. On August 17 a new association of steel manufacturers was formed with the announced purpose of meeting the " attack of the unions."

Our report was formulated last winter. Its six-months-old predictions are not denied by the march of events. We hold that the events punctuate the report's question—cannot a democracy govern itself; must the public, forewarned, rest inert while a basic industry prepares trouble for all? Just because the strike is some way off, or because the national campaigns to allocate our political governance are on, is the great democracy to let economic governance go by sheer default?

. . . Meanwhile we call upon the public, under whatever forms of organization it merits the term public-spirited, to offer service of cooperation to the Federal Government, to initiate or extend independent investigations into conditions in the steel industry, to meet the challenge to orderly progress which is implicit in the present preparations by unions and owners for a new conflict. The alternative possibility is e nployee-employer conference, under Federal auspices, begun now. Let the public press for this first step.

The twelve-hour day involving hundreds of thousands, the seven-day week, wages that make for unhealthy communities and an underbred race, arbitrary management which penalizes the American spirit and corrupts its institutions— is the reform of all this to be left simply to the hazard of a strike?

Individually members of the Commission were making addresses on the report at the invitation of forums, city clubs, churches, universities, etc. So many demands were made on some Commissioners that they could have done nothing else for months if they had desired to forget their regular official duties.

The distribution of the full text of the report in book form was brought about through the regular book trade. In February, 1921, the book had gone into its fifth large printing. During the winter of 1920-21 labor unions in several steel centers began buying the report in quantity for distribution among the clergymen of their localities. The report was being used as a text in colleges and in men's Bible classes; it became the subject of comment by scientific publications, here and in Europe.

Reasoned opposition to the report disappeared from newspapers. The following typifies the character both of opposition and support. On February 24, 1921, in Buffalo, N. Y., the report was brought before the Council of Cities of the Methodist Church, debated in the morning session, referred to a committee which reported in the afternoon, and the report was unreservedly recommended " to the ministers and laymen " for study.[1] Following are the reports in two newspapers:

[1] For resolutions, see following pages.

Buffalo *Evening News*
Feb. 24, front page

Pittsburgh *Chronicle-Telegraph*
Feb. 25, front page

METHODISTS ENDORSE STEEL STRIKE REPORT

STEEL STRIKE REPORT REJECTED BY CHURCH

The Church has the right to concern itself with any industrial situation in which moral issues are involved, according to resolutions adopted at the closing sessions this afternoon at the Lafayette Hotel of the M. E. Council of the Cities.

Endorsement was given to the report of the Interchurch World Movement on the steel strike of 1919, in which the steel trust was flayed.

[*Resolutions and debate follow*]

The report on conditions in the steel industry, upon which the Commission acted, was one of the most startling acts performed by the Interchurch World Movement. Following the steel strike a Commission, headed by Bishop F. J. McConnell, of Pittsburgh, conducted a wide investigation into conditions, summoning numerous witnesses and examining many reports. The report presented to the Interchurch World Movement and adopted by that body vigorously flayed the magnates of the steel industry.

Buffalo, February 25.—The report made by the Interchurch World Movement on the steel strike of 1919 provoked a spirited debate at the closing session here of the Council of Cities of the Methodist Episcopal Church. An attempt to place the council on record as fully approving the report failed and a committee was appointed to consider the Commission's findings and other industrial questions.

(*The Gazette-Times and the Dispatch also carried items indicating that the Report had been repudiated by an overwhelming majority. Later one paper printed a letter of correction.*)

As public opposition dwindled secret opposition greatly intensified, taking the form of systematic distribution of pamphlets against the report's authors rather than its facts. This opposition extended beyond the report and fought against the right of churches to investigate or speak upon any industrial conditions whatsoever. A pamphlet was distributed by the United States Steel Corporation [1] throughout steel plants, through banks, through commercial clubs, through manufacturers' associations covering every part of the nation, even through lists obtained from some church organizations and, in a Pittsburgh Unitarian church, to the congregation after the service. Commercial organizations also distributed the spy reports devised to discredit the Commission.[2]

The situation at the end of 1920 was described by the vice-chairman of the Commission,[3] as follows:

Let us take stock of the force commonly called public opinion by measuring it against the persistence of the twelve-hour day in the steel industry. It is over four months now since the publica-

[1] The address of a New England clergyman, 1,200,000 copies of which the Corporation distributed. The following excerpt from its treatment of the twelve-hour day is typical:

"Somebody is responsible for an industrial heresy about hours of work that may have poisoned the judgment of our Interchurch Commission. It is the first principle of their industrial creed and it advocates gradually and reasonably reducing 'the hours of labor to the lowest practicable point.' This is the hobo's doctrine. It glorifies leisure and denounces toil. How could it ever be advocated by a confessed follower of the ceaseless Toiler of Galilee who said in reply to his critics that objected to his Sunday work, 'My Father worketh hitherto and I work!' The extent to which this heresy has spread amazes us. It was adopted by our last Congregational Council in its industrial platform and is published by our social service department throughout the country. It ought to bring the blush of shame to every one of us that believes in work as the greatest means of character building and as the demonstrator of the highest manhood. How can we advocate reducing work to its lowest practicable point if we have left in us any of the spirit of him who said, 'I must work the works of him that sent me while it is day; for the night cometh when no man can work.'"

[2] See concluding Chapter, "Under-Cover Men."

[3] "Still Silent on the Twelve-Hour Day," by Daniel A. Poling. Reprinted from the *New Republic*, December 29, 1920.

tion of the Interchurch Report on the steel strike with its condemnation of the autocratically enforced two-shift system in steel
plants. Recently other waves of public criticism have broken
against the twelve-hour day, one started by societies of engineers,
the other by the Lockwood Committee's investigation. Results to
date: silence from the owners of the industry; in the steel plants
the now generally admitted inhuman schedule of hours for half
the workers of an entire industry. . . .

The uncontroverted report really made public opinion; we are
asking how much that opinion is worth.

It has not forced any public reasoned statistical formal answer
from the steel companies. It has not drawn any reply from the
accepted spokesmen of the United States Steel Corporation except
one which I shall cite. It has not disturbed the twelve-hour day.

Following the Interchurch Report the engineers spoke, basing
their conclusions on an investigation made this fall. On December 3d, at a joint meeting of the Taylor Society, sections of the
American Society of Mechanical Engineers and of the American
Institute of Electrical Engineers, Horace B. Drury, economist,
presented to an approving audience a detailed comparison of the
twelve-hour vs. the eight-hour day. Insofar as the two reports
cover the same ground, the engineers' report strikingly supplements that of the Interchurch World Movement. They, too, find
the twelve-hour day still the habit of the industry, apparently related to the lack of labor unions, characterized by waste, demoralizing to the worker, generally hated by him, an anachronism which
has passed from European plants. Going further, into twenty
plants which adopted the eight-hour day (mainly right after the
1919 strike), the engineers find that "taking it all in all, the
manufacturers now operating on the shorter day are practically
a unit in saying that it means more satisfactory operations and
is better business. The experience of these twenty plants has
revealed no real obstacles to putting the steel industry on a three-
shift day." They find that "if all the departments were to be
changed from two to three shifts the increase in total cost for the
finished rail, bar or sheet, could not on the average be more than
3 per cent. But the increase need not be nearly so great. Some
manufacturers going on eight hours have been able to reduce their
force of men 10 per cent., some more. . . . Others have found their
rolling mill output going up 20 to 25 per cent. . . . The men have

been so glad to get the shorter hours that they have been willing to make substantial concessions in daily wages."

And finally the engineers point out that this is a fine time for the Steel Corporation to do the inevitable because now there is so much unemployment!

Reaching the same conclusions, the engineers' tone, it will be observed, is very, very different from the churches'. We call for the abolition of the long day because it is inhuman and makes un-American citizens; we call for the maintenance of wages. The engineers urge that the shorter day is better business. Our report points out to Casabianca standing stiffly on the deck of the autocratic twelve-hour day that the deck is burning; the engineers sampling the rising flood of the eight-hour day call "Come on in; the water's fine; analysis indicates there is money in it." The two reports show the steel corporations not only reactionary but rather absurd.

No more than our report has the engineers' pronouncement broken the silence of the industry unless a certain pamphlet is intended to be the answer. Following our 275 pages of statistical analysis the Steel Corporation circulated a letter from a minister praising the Corporation's welfare work. Following the engineers the Corporation has made a booklet of another minister's address before a Boston association. . . .

Such an "answer" has significance only for this reason: it bears the endorsement of the chairman of the United States Steel Corporation. Public opinion has brought forth this.

Finally the public has been stirred by the Lockwood investigation in New York. The admissions of the head of the Bethlehem Company, the testimony of the head of the spy system for the National Erectors' Association, the revelations of an interlocking drive against labor centering in the Steel Corporation, the meaning of these things is recognized widely; for example, editorially,[1] as follows:

The attitude of the steel makers confirms everything charged against them last year at the time of the strike and since sub- stantiated by the report of the Interchurch committee.

Thus the existence of an industrial autocracy which defies Congresses and snubs Presidents easily becomes a menace to great populations far removed from its thundering mills and

[1] The New York *World*, Dec. 15, 1920.

squalid camps of imported labor. At great cost it suppressed the effort of its employees to better working conditions. We have yet to learn whether its power is to remain unbroken.

It is ten years since " public opinion " began to break against the twelve-hour day. With the recent history these questions are raised: How much are certain social forces really worth? Church and press are speaking more or less persistently; scientific business as represented by the engineers is speaking. If the industry holds silently to the twelve-hour day are we to infer that only labor unions in the steel industry can bring a change? Are we to infer that a main reason for not granting the change is the fear that it may redound to the furtherance of the unions?

The article points a change in the Commission's interpretation of public opinion on their report. They considered that the report stood and they turned their attention almost wholly to what had become their main interest—public action on the recommendations for the steel industry. The Commission stuck to this during the next episode of the report's history—the hearing held in the Capitol by the Senate Committee on Labor and Education (January 27, 1921), on the motion of Senator Walsh of Montana (Senate, December 7, 1920) to make the report a public document. The Commissioners in testifying refused to urge this resolution, leaving it to the judgment of the senators, but they took occasion to demand action on the report's recommendations, in the shape of a memorial to Congress.

Previously the Commission had done all it could to obtain action from the Federal Administration. President Wilson had referred the report to the Secretary of Labor, who declared the administration unable to move; the final interchange of telegrams reading as follows:

Washington, D. C., Aug. 28, 1920.

In response your telegram, relative to appointment by President of a special Federal agency to initiate free, open conference between employers and employees in steel industry and further recommending that the Federal Government inaugurate full inquiry into the past and present state of civil liberties in Western Pennsylvania, Congress has made no appropriation available for the purpose set forth in report and unless and until it makes such appropriation it will not be possible for the President to appoint an agency as suggested. Further without authority of Congress such commission would have no authority to send for persons and papers.

W. B. Wilson, Secretary of Labor.

New York City, August 30, 1920.

Secretary of Labor, W. B. Wilson,
Washington, D. C.

The Commission of Inquiry appointed by the Interchurch World Movement to investigate the steel strike appreciates the consideration given its report, but is unable to determine from your reply whether the Administration is considering any definite move toward furthering the recommendation with which you seem to agree in principle, but to which you indicate technical objections. We are under the impression that the presidential commissions for anthracite and bituminous coal disputes, appointed by the President and cited by us as precedents, required no special Congressional authority. If Congressional authority is necessary will your Department recommend that the President ask for such authority? The Commission has reason to believe that the public would give strong support.

F. J. McConnell, Chairman.
D. A. Poling, Vice-Chairman.

Washington, September 1st, 1920.

Bituminous and Anthracite Coal Commissions were not appointed until both sides had agreed to submit dispute to Commission and abide by award. Authority of law already exists for appointment of Commission under such circumstances. Situation in the steel industry is different. What you suggest is that an investigation be made not only of the industrial conditions but of the status of civil and political liberty in certain steel producing centers. To make such an investigation successful the Commission that undertakes it should have authority to subpœna persons and papers and examine witnesses under oath. Such authority does not now exist and can only be granted by Congress. The difficulties in the way are not technical objections but practical obstacles: first the lack of sufficient authority to make a proper investigation and second, the lack of funds. I am not at present prepared to make any recommendations to the President on the subject matter.

W. B. Wilson, Secretary of Labor.

The Administration did not raise with the managers or the workers in the industry any preliminary inquiry as to attitudes to an investigation. The matter was left to Congress, without specific communication to Congress.

The memorial to Congress represented the last effort of the Commission in what it conceived to be its duty to its own report and to the Interchurch World Movement and to the public. The situation at the time (February, 1921) was as follows: Support of the report in meetings in many parts of the country was increasing. Organized direct support of it, either by churches or labor or any institutions molding public opinion, was occasional.[1] Organized opposition was increas-

[1] The action of the Methodist Council of Cities, referred to earlier, reads,—(Committee's resolution as adopted by the Buffalo Conference):

We, the members of the Council of Cities of the Methodist Episcopal Church, in annual session at Buffalo, N. Y., Feb. 24th, 1921, recommend to the ministers and laymen of our churches:

First—The conscientious reading of the report of the Interchurch World Movement Commission of Inquiry into the Steel Strike of 1919 as a definite and comprehensive moral utterance by a large part of the Christian Church of America in a particular industrial situation, and record our appreciation of the work done by this Commission.

Second—Because adequate knowledge is essential to correct judgment concerning great moral issues, we assert the right and consequent duty of the Church to acquaint itself with any industrial or social situation where moral issues are at stake in which labor or capital, either separately or together are involved.

Third—We assert the more fundamental right and duty of the Christian Church to preach and to teach those ideals of social and industrial justice which will prevent the misunderstandings and strike now so characteristic of our human relations.

Daniel L. Marsh
William S. Mitchell
James M. Beebe
George G. Vogel
E. C. Thorpe
William H. Wehrly
Committee.

ingly bitter, but not public. Results as regards governmental action were nil. In the industry it became known, though unannounced, that the Steel Corporation had appointed a committee to draft a plan and public statement dealing with the twelve-hour day. The highest officials in the industry were privately quoted as citing the Interchurch report as one of the causes of the appointment of the corporation's committee.

Public response from the industry even in the shape of words had been confined to but one occasion and that in Glasgow, Scotland. On July 29, 1920, a contract for 10,000 tons of steel rails let to the United States Steel Products Co. (the export selling organization of the United States Steel Corporation) was held up by the opposition of city officials based on a cabled press digest of the Interchurch report. Labor members of the city government forced reconsideration of the contract because it failed to contain the legally required guarantees of manufacture under " fair wages and conditions of labor." The controversy lasted a month. The president of the Steel Products Co. wrote the city authorities his " personal guarantee " that the rails were made under " fair conditions," with wages " based on an eight-hour day." The report was cited in the city council to prove that the Steel Products Co. letter " could not be a genuine guarantee." On September 1 the city council let the contract stand " because the rails were already on the way."

In the face of silent watchful waiting within the industry, inaction of the government and stagnation of labor, the Commission published the following (January 31) and distributed it to one hundred members of Congress and responsible government officials. Very few newspapers printed it in full or in part; the labor press carried it in full.

Memorial to Congress

The members of the Interchurch World Movement's Commission of Inquiry into the steel strike respectfully submit certain questions to the members of Congress based on facts developed at the hearing (held in the Capitol January 27, 1921, by the Senate Committee on Labor and Education) on the motion of Senator Walsh (Montana) to make the Commission's Report on the Steel Strike a public document. . . .

The report's opening words are:

The Steel Strike of September 22, 1919 to January 7, 1920 in one sense is not over. The main issues were not settled. The causes still remain.

The report continues:

After the strike no effort was being made to settle the issues raised in the steel industry through reasoned public discussion of the basic facts. Employers and employees began to wait for "the next strike"; they and the public wondered, careless rather than fearful, whether "the next strike" would come in months or years, and whether it would be "without violence" as in 1919 or with guns and flame as at Homestead in 1892. . . .

It was expected that the next outbreak would be precipitated as was the last by efforts for workmen's organization and collective bargaining.

The report gives as its principal recommendation:

That the Federal Government set up a Commission for the industry, in order to initiate free, open conference between those who must always be chiefly responsible for settlement of the industry's problems:—its owners and its workers.

The letter to the President transmitting the report says:

The Commission finds in the iron and steel industry conditions which it is forced to describe as not good for the nation. It fails to find any Federal agency which with promise of early result is directly grappling with these conditions.

The report's concluding pages raise the questions:

Is the nation helpless before conditions in a basic industry which promise a future crisis? Can our democratic society be moved to do industrial justice without the pressure of crisis itself?

The foregoing statements, the Commission now submits, are as true as they were when the Commission concluded its investigation a year ago. . . .

Concerning the most outstanding of the two chief evils in the industry the report noted:

If the twelve-hour day is bad for the country, the government is to blame and as long as it fails to tackle the twelve-hour day it imposes upon the trade unions alone the humane task of moving the Steel Corporation in the direction of reform.

Moreover, the conclusion is unescapable that a real cause of the persistence of the twelve-hour day and the seven-day week is the defenselessness of the unorganized immigrant worker. Again the government, as much as the Steel Corporation, is to blame and again the Corporation and the government have seen fit to leave the field of reform to the trade unions.

The press in January, 1921, contains new notices of attempts by trade unions to recommence organization and by steel companies to combat it.

In the seven months since their report was given to the nation, the members of the Commission, in pursuit of their customary official duties in every part of the country, north, east, south and west, have sensed a public opinion which quietly but strongly supports their report and its recommendations. Moreover, they have noted in recent pronouncements of church organizations an increasing insistence that industrial relations such as are typified in this industry be righted. Thus, though they speak as the humblest individuals, the Commissioners feel that they present the views of very many when they raise for the third time the questions:

Is the nation helpless before conditions in a basic industry which promise a future crisis? Can our democratic society be moved to do industrial justice without the pressure of crisis itself?

We ask, specifically, that Congress act along the line of the recommendations from the Steel Report; we are unwilling to believe that the Government does nothing and leaves the field to a contest of trade unions against manufacturing corporations.

Respectfully submitted to the President of the Senate, the Speaker of the House of Representatives, the Chairman of the Senate Committee on Labor and Education, and to individual members of Congress.

Two sorts of comment were observable in the succeeding fortnight. Paragraphs in trade journals remarked that " even if the Senate Committee on Labor did not pigeonhole the resolution " to make the report a public document, " it would still have to go to the Senate Committee on Printing " which was " unlikely to recommend increasing government expenditures in a time of retrenchment." Of comment by labor the following editorial (from *Labor* of February 19, 1921) was the most significant:

Clearing the Track

" We are unwilling to believe that the government leaves the field to a contest of trade-unions against manufacturing corporations."—*Interchurch Memorial to Congress.*

The government will do nothing to establish any kind of " conference between employes and employers " in the steel industry, nor even to abolish the notorious 12-hour day. That will be the answer to the Interchurch Commissioners' Memorial to Congress demanding a " conference " as recommended in their Steel Report.

The Interchurch, then, has put the government on record. And more: it puts in the record that such inaction leaves the field to trade-unions. Still more: it implies that when the trade-unions start to reform the Steel Corporation the place of the churches should be at the trade-unions' side.

We know the familiar outcry from government and newspapers as any great strike starts: "The public demands that this controversy cease so that the public can evolve a permanent solution. The strikers must go back to work so the public can act."

This time the churches have put it down in black and white, where it can be pointed to in future, that "the public" in the shape of the government has had its chance in the steel industry. Cleaning up steel is left to that part of the public which is in the labor movement.

ADDENDUM:

THE COMMISSION'S MEDIATION EFFORT

CONTENTS

A RECENT episode has clouded the facts of the effort at mediating in the strike made by the Commission of Inquiry. A pamphlet is being widely circulated by the United States Steel Corporation, written by a clergyman of New England and containing assertions as to how the Interchurch Commission " with the innocence of teasing childhood " asked Mr. Gary to " negotiate with the labor unions." The pamphlet goes on:

> I am not surprised that Mr. Gary, in his courteous way, diverted the conversation and almost humorously toyed with them—a man of less grace would have shown his annoyance, for this must have seemed to him a supremely stupid performance on the part of the Commission.[1]

These assertions acquire importance because they are endorsed by Mr. Gary. The pamphlet is prefaced by a letter to its author, dated December 1, 1920, signed by Mr. Gary and reading:

> We are surprised that you, an entire stranger, should have taken the trouble to present the Interchurch Report in its true light. We are very appreciative and grateful.

---

[1] The pamphlet adds: "The Interchurch Commission feeling itself snubbed by Mr. Gary's refusal to deal with the A. F. of L. through them, commenced its study of the steel business with a strong prejudice." The pamphlet has its dates mixed. The Commission " commenced its study " the first week in October and by Dec. 5, the date of its last interview with Mr. Gary, the Commission had put in seven weeks of hard work and had already gathered most of the facts presented in the report.—H. B.

Have you any objection to our having this address printed and widely circulated?

Because of the rather confidential character of the interview with Mr. Gary, the Interchurch report contains no account of the informal mediation approach. In order to clear the record, now that the question has been raised with Mr. Gary's approval, the following is transcribed from the record by the Commission's secretary, made in February, 1920, the original in the files being headed "Footnote to History."

The Commission of Inquiry undertook its mediation approach (November 27 to December 5, 1919) with great reluctance because it conceived its prime duty to be inquiry and publication of facts, rather than intervention (in a struggle begun before the Commission was created) or settlement (without the resources in personnel or finances requisite for such a task). That the Commission attempt mediation was the desire of the Industrial Conference, New York, October 2-3, 1919, which led to the creation of the Commission. The resolution of that conference was:

The Findings Committee recommends to the Industrial Relations Department of the Interchurch World Movement of North America that it make careful and thorough going investigation of the strikes in the steel industry, and that the Department make a report on the matter; likewise that the Department be requested by this board, in addition to making the investigation and getting the facts, to use their offices in trying to bring about a joint conference and a settlement of this dispute by mutual agreement.

Nevertheless, the Commission made no move toward mediation during its first interviews with Mr. Gary and its open hearings conducted in Pittsburgh in mid-November, but concentrated its activities solely on obtaining information.

In the interval after these hearings and before the session in Chicago, while the Commissioners had scattered to their homes in different states, a request was made to the Commission for mediation that could not be entirely disregarded. Mr. Fitzpatrick, chairman of the National Committee for Organizing Iron and Steel Workers, came to New York on November 27, asking that the Commission hear from him a plan of settlement. Calls for an emergency meeting of the Commisson were dispatched to all available members. In the meantime Mr. Fitzpatrick informally explained the ideas of the strike leaders and declared that they would accept any settlement, the terms of which were acceptable to the Commission. The next morning, Friday, November 28, Mr. Fitzpatrick formally made his proposal to the emergency meeting. He submitted a proposal in writing, signed by himself.

The upshot of the conference was that the Commission decided to formulate its own plan of mediation on the following bases rather than on Mr. Fitzpatrick's proposal alone:

1. To mediate in behalf of all the steel workers, both those still on strike and those who had gone back to work:

2. that the purpose of the mediation should be to establish a new deal in the steel industry rather than merely end the strike;

3. that the ending of the strike should be arranged solely with a view to giving the new deal the best possible chance.

All this in turn was conditioned on acceptance of the Commission's counterplan through formal ratification by the National Committee for Organizing Iron and Steel Workers. In brief, the proposal was that the Commission of Inquiry would become responsible for a settlement in the steel industry and that in case the Steel Corporation accepted the plan the strike leaders should step out of the situation after ordering the men back to work. Mr. Fitzpatrick went to Pittsburgh to call a meeting of his committee.

On December 2, the Commission in New York received the following communication:

The National Committee for Organizing Iron and Steel Workers met in Pittsburgh on last Monday, November 24th. Representatives of the twenty-four national unions, district and local secretaries, and local organizers, were present. The meeting was conducted for nearly twelve hours, in which every angle of the steel strike situation was gone over. Finally, by unanimous vote, the National Committee decided to re-affirm its former declarations and that the steel strike would be continued.

After the meeting adjourned, several responsible men in the situation got together and talked over the possibilities of settlement of the steel strike. We all agreed that, because of the tremendous power and influence of the Publicity Bureau of the United States Steel Corporation over the newspapers of the country, the men in active charge of the strike have been thoroughly discredited, and it is impossible for them to be of service in bringing a reasonable, fair and just termination of the controversy. Realizing this, they searched around for some neutral interest sufficiently interested who might be able to exert their influence that a reasonable and fair conclusion of the strike could be brought about and, inasmuch as the Commission representing the Interchurch World Movement had come into the situation for the purpose of investigation, etc., we decided to ask the Commission to use their good offices in bringing about an adjustment of this controversy.

We feel that the workers can look to the Commissioners representing the Interchurch World Movement that their interests will be properly safeguarded and protected. We also feel that in this situation there is no other institution that combines all of the elements necessary to go into this very difficult situation, but we do feel that the best interests of our Country and of our Movement and the cause of right and justice will be best served by placing this matter in their keeping for such action and consideration as they will be able to secure.

In the event of the Commissioners securing authorization to act as mediators for the adjustment of this controversy, we will induce the workers to return to work and to accept such program as the Commissioners may secure and recommend for their protection in the industry. The workers have absolute confidence in their present leaders and will not forego their present position except on our advice and we feel confident that they will take such action as we recommend if this plan is accepted by the Interchurch Movement.

We do not ask, nor expect, the Interchurch World Movement to use our old original demands as a basis of negotiation, but to start anew with whatever requirements they feel justice demands.
NATIONAL COMMITTEE FOR ORGANIZING IRON AND STEEL WORKERS,
CHAIRMAN (signed) John Fitzpatrick.
SEC'Y-TREASURER (signed) Wm. Z. Foster.

This represented formal action taken by the National Committee. The Commission reaffirming to the Executive Committee of the Interchurch Movement its conviction that mediation would be worth while if based on the hope of " a new deal in the steel industry," obtained an appointment with Mr. E. H. Gary, chairman of the Board of Directors of the United States Corporation, after consultation with and in the full knowledge of the Executive Officers of the Interchurch Movement, not to make a formal presentation, but to discuss informally the possibility of mediation.

On the morning of December 5, the Commission's representatives—Chairman McConnell, Vice-Chairman Poling and Dr. McDowell—had a two hours' interview with Mr. Gary in the offices of the Steel Corporation. After the episode relative to the " anonymous report "[1] the conference continued. The Commission did not present in detail its plan of mediation, inasmuch as Mr. Gary immediately and persistently refused to hear any such plan. He explained at length his general philosophy of the control of industry, and insisted that the aims of this strike were " the closed shop, Soviets and the forcible distribution of property." The following is from the report on the conference dictated by Bishop

[1] See record in the Steel Report, pp. 28-29 and last chapter on " Under-Cover Men," this volume.

McConnell with the assistance of Dr. Poling immediately after leaving Mr. Gary:

Mr. Gary insisted that the point at issue was not now unionism as such, but whether the American Government should be supported and Americans' institutions upheld. He insisted that the whole movement of the steel strike was a movement of red radicals. He repeatedly avowed his belief that the only outcome of a victory for unionism would be Sovietism in the United States "and forcible distribution of property." "And, therefore," he said, "my positive word is a declination to arbitrate."

In reply to that, the Chairman said that we had not used the word arbitrate, that, so far as we were concerned, the union leaders were out of it except in the sense that we had agreed to use the union machinery for the purpose of seeing that the men returned to work on terms satisfactory to the Interchurch Commission. The Chairman suggested that, if any word was to be used characterizing the proceeding, it would be the word mediation.

Judge Gary then reaffirmed his unwillingness to say anything that would even be reported to Mr. Fitzpatrick or Mr. Foster. As to the workers' desires, he was anxious to do everything possible for their welfare. If an eight-hour day could be adjusted in any way, he most earnestly desired it, he said.

The Chairman then said, "Judge Gary, you are on record in your own testimony as being in favor of collective bargaining. Would you look with favor upon an organization in your shops in which the workers should choose their own representatives to state any grievances to the authorities that they might have?"

Judge Gary replied that he was heartily in favor of such an organization, "provided it be the right kind of organization." He went on to express his great disappointment that the Colorado Fuel and Iron Company, which on his statement had been out since the 22nd of September, had not been sucessful with its plan for a company union because the men insisted they would not go back with the Rockefeller Plan still in force.

The Chairman then called attention to the fact that the testimony gathered by our investigators and by the members of the Commission themselves showed that, while Mr. Gary's statement might favor collective bargaining, as a matter of fact the men could not get their grievances beyond the foremen.

Mr. Gary then rather closely cross-questioned the Chairman and Mr. Poling on the type of men whom the Commission had interviewed, insisting that it could only have been men to whom we were directed by red radicals.

At this point, Mr. Poling told of a visit he had made to an Ohio steel city and stated that six thousand men had, in the steel group in that city, gone out and had then gone back, but had gone back with hate in their hearts.

Mr. Poling laid stress on the underlying issue that the Commission had before it in coming to Mr. Gary, namely the Christianization of the Industrial situation, regard for the welfare of humanity involved, and regard for the ultimate effects on Americanization. To all of Mr. Poling's positions, Mr. Gary gave his enthusiastic approval. Mr. Poling then asked Mr. Gary, or rather tried to—it was rather difficult to ask questions—whether, on the basis of humanity, we would not be able to get to some agreement with reference to the plan of mediation. Then, for the first time, Mr. Gary retorted with the statement, which he used several times afterwards, that nobody represented by Foster and Fitzpatrick would be allowed to go back into the mills anyway, that they were radicals, and that all men being taken back into the mills now were being asked about their political beliefs as part of the examination.

The Chairman then asked Judge Gary this question: " Supposing all the men have gone back and the strike has failed in the sense that the men have returned to work, returned to work with a consciousness of failure, with the feeling that they have been beaten, what kind of a situation is produced by the presence of men in such a temper in the mills? "

Mr. Gary replied that this statement was not adequate to the real situation, that the men were contented and had been intimidated into going out and as soon as adequate police force and United States soldiers arrived on the scene they voluntarily returned and they returned all the more willingly because Mr. Gary himself had stated to his officials that the strike was not voluntary and that they must see that the families even of the strikers suffered no lack of food or other necessities while they were out. Mr. Gary stated positively, " We fed the families of strikers."

In reply to repeated insistence by Mr. Gary that he was willing to receive shop committees, the Chairman said to Mr. Gary that he violated no confidence in saying that Mr. Foster had testified that in case there had been such committees the strike movement never could have been started. Mr. Gary met this by saying that we "must remember that Mr. Foster was a very slick one."

Mr. Gary was asked to drop for a moment all thought of union leaders and to consider the fact that we were speaking in behalf of men, women and children who, on the simple basis of humanity, needed some consideration. He said, "Then whom do you represent? If you represent the men who have not gone back to work, they are nothing but a group of red radicals whom we don't want anyway."

This led up to a further statement of the tests to be applied to the workers in the steel mills on their patriotism. Mr. Gary insisted that the issue was not unionism but fundamental devotion to American institutions. He spoke quite strongly that "there had been red organizations in Pittsburgh known to the officers of the government which the government had not broken up."

Mr. Gary said that of course this Commission could make any public statement that it pleased, but he warned us "to bear in mind that the very foundations of the American government were involved in the matter."

When asked whether rebellious men would not hurt production, Mr. Gary said that it made no difference, that if production remained such that the Steel Corporation did not make one cent all the rest of the year, it made no difference because of the great principles involved.

Mr. Gary said that he was just as much opposed to the concentration of money power involved in one big union of all the steel companies as he was to one big union of all steel labor.

Dr. McDowell then asked, "In your mind, then, Judge Gary, you consider that for you and the Steel Corporation there is no issue to be discussed?"

Judge Gary's last word, apart from bidding us goodbye, was, "There is absolutely no issue."

The Interchurch officials after learning the result decided to issue no public statement. The Commission dispatched to the strike leadership the following communication signed by the secretary.

The independent Commission of Inquiry, instituted by the Interchurch World Movement to investigate the steel strike, received on December 2 a communication, marked confidential, dealing with an official action taken by the National Committee for Organizing Iron and Steel Workers, signed by Mr. Fitzpatrick and Mr. Foster.

On December 5th, members of the Commission informally conversed with Mr. Gary for two hours, proposing to plan a new basis of relations in the steel industry, with an ending of the strike best calculated to further better relations. They offered to act as mediators both in behalf of the men still on strike, whose leaders were to order them back and then step out of the situation, and on behalf of still dissatisfied men who had nevertheless returned to work.

Mr. Gary refused to confer with these representatives of the churches as mediators in behalf of any interests represented by you in the strike, on the ground that the men still out were bolshevist radicals who were not wanted in the mills and who would not be taken back.

As to mediating in behalf of any other interests, Mr. Gary said that the men were contented and that " there is no issue."

I am requested to communicate the above information to you by the Chairman of the Commission of Inquiry.

In accord with a request by the Interchurch Executive Committee, the Commission refrained from issuing any statement to the press during the investigations or making public utterances on the inquiry. In every way the Commission tried to bring about the rendering of a full and carefully considered report whose public reception should not be hindered by accusations of " interference."

For further information on points suggested by Mr. Gary the following letter was sent by messenger on December 9 to Mr. Gary, signed by the Vice-Chairman:

Dear Mr. Gary:

The Commissioners of the Interchurch World Movement are very grateful for the courtesy accorded them by you in the interview last Friday.

Several points were brought up by you in the conference with members of the Commissioin of Inquiry that greatly interested us—points that we are sure you would wish to have brought formally to our attention so that they may be included in the report that we make to the Executive Committee.

The statement was made that in your conception the steel strike was a " movement of radicals;" that the men in charge, and that the men still out, were extreme radicals or " Reds." We are having difficulty in securing from company officials in local areas, evidence on the above points. This matter is most vital. Will you please indicate to us what steel company officials have this evidence and how and where it can be put before us?

You also made the very interesting statement that families of strikers had been fed in accordance with your orders during the strike. Will you please indicate to us to whom we should apply in order to get details of such feeding of strikers' families and its effect?

On Friday last you questioned us as to whom the Commissioners and investigators had seen in the securing of their data and we replied somewhat in detail. Thus far all efforts to obtain from Mr. Williams and Mr. Burnett, of the Carnegie Steel Company, statistics and documents which they offered to place at our disposal when the Commissioners met with them personally, have failed. Since November 20th representatives of the Commission have been met by the statements that either Mr. Williams and Mr. Burnett were " out " or that " all of the information must be obtained from the New York office."

For example, Mr. Burnett promised evidence of intimidations in specified cases. He has since refused to see investigators asking for this evidence.

If objection is made to those who may have approached Mr. Burnett or Mr. Williams, we will be very glad to follow any suggestions that you may have as to how the approach should be made.

There are several other questions raised which can be answered by officials in your service. Would you be willing to designate who should be seen by a member of our Commission or by Mr. Blankenhorn, in order that the information the steel corporation wishes to convey may be secured?

Our only desire is to be sure that the Commission has before it every scrap of evidence which the United States Steel Corporation feels should be considered in this inquiry, in order that a comprehensive, unprejudiced and a complete report may be brought to the Executive Committee of the Interchurch World Movement.

Very sincerely yours,

P.S. Our telephone number is Stuyvesant 6330. If your secretary could communicate with us during the day we would be indeed grateful.

This letter was not answered by Mr. Gary nor by any one representing the Steel Corporation; later letters on other subjects were answered.

On the two specific questions the Commission pressed its inquiries in the steel regions. As to "radicalism" in the strike the Commission's findings are detailed in full in its report.[1]

[1] See "The Steel Strike of 1919," first 38 pp. and pp. 144-188

INDEX